THE ENGLISH IN LOVE

THE ENGLISH IN LOVE

THE INTIMATE STORY OF AN EMOTIONAL REVOLUTION

Claire Langhamer

OXFORD
UNIVERSITY PRESS

OXFORD
UNIVERSITY PRESS

Great Clarendon Street, Oxford, OX2 6DP,
United Kingdom

Oxford University Press is a department of the University of Oxford.
It furthers the University's objective of excellence in research, scholarship,
and education by publishing worldwide. Oxford is a registered trade mark of
Oxford University Press in the UK and in certain other countries

First Edition published in 2013

Impression: 1

British Library Cataloguing in Publication Data
Data available

ISBN 978–0–19–959443–6

Printed in Great Britain by
Clays Ltd, St Ives plc

For Izzy Langhamer

Acknowledgements

This book would not have been completed without the help and support of numerous family members, friends, and colleagues over the last ten years. At the University of Sussex I would particularly like to thank Hester Barron, Vinita Damodaran, Carol Dyhouse, Ian Gazeley, Lucy Robinson, Chris Warne, and Clive Webb, whose distinctive ways of writing history have strongly influenced my own approach. Their good humour and collegiality has been invaluable in more trying times. Former colleagues Saul Dubow, Alun Howkins, Ben Jones, Rebecca Searle, Alex Shepard, and Selina Todd offered help at different stages of the project and friendship throughout. I have learned a great deal about the mid-century from my doctoral, masters, and undergraduate students. In particular I would like to thank students on my history special subject course 'Domesticity and Its Discontents: Women in Postwar Britain', not least for humouring my tendency to relate most things back to love. Teaching and research are always entwined and some of the student dissertations I have supervised in recent years have had a profound impact on my own thinking.

I owe all those connected with the Mass-Observation Archive, Sussex Special Collections, and the University Library a massive debt of thanks. Particular gratitude is due to Fiona Courage, Jessica Scantlebury, Karen Watson, Rose Lock, and Kirsty Pattrick who make working and teaching in the archive such a pleasure. The Mass-Observers themselves deserve a special mention as so many of their words fill the pages that follow. I never fail to be impressed by their good-will and commitment to the Mass-Observation project and the smartness with which they theorize everyday life. Dorothy Sheridan's role in the history of Mass-Observation is well known but I would like to thank her here as a friend, colleague and—at the risk of embarrassing her—inspiration.

Beyond Sussex, a number of networks and seminars have proved invaluable in helping me develop my ideas about love. Those who participated in the ESRC funded 'Women in the Fifties' seminar series between 2009 and 2011 merit particular thanks alongside my fellow organizers Penny Tinkler and Stephanie Spencer with whom it was a pleasure to work. The 20s30s Network organized by Matt Houlbrook, Elizabeth Darling, and Richard Hornsey offers ongoing intellectual delight as well as quality accommodation and very nice cakes. Two events in 2012 were particularly timely in contributing to my thinking in drafting this book. Tehila Sasson and Radhika Natarajan were kind enough to invite me to commentate at the 'Burdens: Writing British History after 1945' postgraduate conference at Berkeley in April 2012. The proceedings helped clarify my thoughts on periodization, as well as allowing me the privilege of hearing some excellent new work. The 'New Histories of Love and Romance, c.1880–1960' Cardiff conference organized by Tim Jones and Alana Harris a month later was such a lovely event that I returned to the book afterwards with renewed enthusiasm.

There are a number of people without whom I would not have completed this project. My family have been a huge support, helping with childcare, a rather fraught house move, and much more besides. Chapter Three of this book reflects the complexity of mid-century love in my own family within which relationships across class, religious, ethnic, and national boundaries abound. I am particularly grateful to Don McKay for talking to me about his parents' wartime experience. Carol Dyhouse helped me think things through right from the start. I have benefited hugely from her ferocious intellectual generosity at every stage of the project—not least in the final revision stages when her kindness, patience, and intellectual sharpness made completion possible. My editor Luciana O'Flaherty helped turn a rather dry academic book proposal into something that is hopefully more readable. Her comments on the draft were consistently incisive and I owe her and her OUP colleagues Matthew Cotton, Sophie Basilevitch, and Emma Barber a particular debt of thanks. I would also like to thank Tom Chandler and Andrew Hawkey for their work on the text. Stephen Brooke read the whole thing with characteristic kindness and good judgement. Lucy Robinson has long watched my back, made me laugh and encouraged me to think more creatively as a historian. Andy Wood made me see that the project was realizable when I was tempted to give it up. Without his insightful criticism, active encouragement and unfailing support the book would still consist of huge piles of paper randomly distributed around my house. That he was able, and willing, to do this whilst completing his own monograph says a lot about the burdens and rewards of love. My 11-year-old daughter, Izzy, is as old as this project. In recent times she has developed a passion for history that surprises and delights me. She has offered to finish this book for me on a number of occasions—she may even have made a better job of it—and will be pleased to see the project concluded. *The English in Love* is, of course, dedicated to her.

Earlier versions of some of the ideas presented here have been published as 'Love and Courtship in Mid-Twentieth-Century England' in *The Historical Journal*, 50:1 (2007), 173–96 and 'Love, Selfhood and Authenticity in Post War Britain' in *Cultural and Social History*, 9:2 (2012), 277–97.

CL

Contents

List of Illustrations xiii
A Note on Sources xv

Introduction 1

Part I: Love

1. An Emotional Revolution 23
2. Love, Passion, and Pragmatism 41
3. Suitability 61

Part II: Courtship

4. Meetings 91
5. Private Spaces 109
6. Exchange and Negotiation 125

Part III: Commitment

7. Making Commitment 149
8. Happy Ever After? 177

Epilogue 207

Endnotes 213
Bibliography 252
Picture Acknowledgements 273
Index 275

List of Illustrations

1 Pencil drawing from a Mass-Observation report, Worktown Collection 1937–40 xix

2 Leonora Eyles problem page, *Woman's Own*, 9 May 1936 16

3 Front cover, *Modern Marriage*, April 1931 26

4 Advert for Fortune chocolates, back cover of *Bandwagon*, April 1950 27

5 'Love at first sight', R. Edynbry, *Real Life Problems and Their Solution*, 1938 31

6 Embrace image from *Every Woman's Book of Love and Marriage and Family Life*, 1937 43

7 *'I know where I'm going!'*, *Picture Show and Film Pictorial*, 12 January 1946 53

8 Advert for Pears Nutriline, *Men Only*, October 1950 65

9 Courtship image from *Every Woman's Book of Love and Marriage and Family Life*, 1937 112

10 'Don't rustle your chocolates', cartoon, *Woman's Own*, 2 May 1936 114

11 Front cover of *Picture Post*, 23 May 1942 133

12 'Café Congo', *Boyfriend*, 16 May 1959 150

13 'It is one of life's great moments . . .', R. Edynbry, *Real Life Problems and Their Solution*, 1938 153

14 'I am unhappy because my fiancé is sometimes the worse for drink', *Every Woman's Book of Love and Marriage and Family Life* 1937 157

15 'Small advertisements department', *Blighty*, 13 January 1951 162

16 'Oh please propose', advert for milk, *Woman*, 1 June 1963 173

17 'A kiss is a two-way activity', Barbara Cartland, *Etiquette Handbook*, 1962 182

A Note on Sources

In writing this book I have drawn on a diverse range of source material, some aspects of which may be more familiar to the reader than others. Political interventions, feature films and teenage comics all find a place. A whole raft of social studies emanating not just from the universities but from politics, the law, medicine, and the churches provide a body of detailed survey evidence.[1] Readers will also encounter the prescriptions of numerous 'everyday experts'. We will hear what the Marriage Guidance Council—founded in 1938—had to say about love, and will ponder the wisdom of the most widely-read agony aunts. At the heart of this book, however, lies the everyday experience of ordinary men and women. In order to get at this I have made substantial use of evidence held in the Mass-Observation Archive and a brief explanation of this material may prove helpful.

Mass-Observation was established in 1937 by a group of left-leaning intellectuals keen to create 'anthropology of ourselves'.[2] 'Mass-Observation intends to work with a new method,' they confidently asserted, 'it intends to make use not only of the trained scientific observer, but of the untrained observer, the man in the street. Ideally, it is the observation by everyone of everyone, including themselves.'[3] A fascination with the minutiae of daily life was a defining feature: it emerged out of the broader documentary impulse of the 1930s and took it in new directions.[4] Its birth was announced in the *New Statesman* along with a diverse, surrealist influenced, list of possible interests:

Behaviour of people at war memorials.
Shouts and gestures of motorists.
The aspidistra cult.
Anthropology of football pools.
Bathroom behaviour.
Beards, armpits, eyebrows.
Anti-Semitism.
Distribution, diffusion and significance of the dirty joke.
Funerals and undertakers.
Female taboos about eating
The private lives of midwives.[5]

Mass-Observation's approach was eclectic but included social investigation, often based in particular localities, the accumulation of diaries, and the collection of responses to a monthly questionnaire called a 'directive'. Following the establishment of the Mass-Observation Archive at Sussex University in the 1970s, a new Mass-Observation Project emerged which continues to generate life histories up to the present. Taken as a whole this material offers access to the ways in which individual men and women experienced, perceived, and remember the profound social cultural, political and economic shifts of the twentieth century. It also provides routes into people's affective worlds, operating as an archive of feeling. The navigation of emotion was, and remains, central to the self-fashioning of its writers and Mass-Observation has frequently asked them to write about love, desire and intimacy.

Describing Mass-Observers as 'ordinary' is not unproblematic. Those who volunteered to write in diary or directive form were, and remain, a distinctive group of people, not least because they believed their own thoughts to be worth recording. Other motivations for participation over the years have included a sense of citizenship, a commitment to self-improvement, and the wish to be creative. Emotional disturbance could also drive participation. 'I frequently write to release pent-up emotion of a turbulent sort', confessed a Cricklewood housewife in 1937.

> Happiness I can express through normal channels—the children can cook sweets in the kitchen, I can buy 1lb of fresh herrings for supper etc.—but depression and disappointment make me mute with misery. Instead of giving the children a good whack when they annoy me, I repress my anger and remonstrate with them, afterwards perhaps pouring out my passions on paper.[6]

Those who wrote undoubtedly self-censored and self-fashioned. They composed and re-composed their lives and viewpoints allowing access to forms of everyday philosophy forged in the midst of massive social and economic change. They were explicitly encouraged to navigate the boundaries of public and private, feeling and argument in their writing. With a predominance of lower middle-class and upper working-class participants, Mass-Observation's panel was not representative in the way we understand the term today, but Mass-Observation understood its volunteers to be 'ordinary, hardworking folk', who were 'intelligent and interesting enough to want to help us'.[7] Their writings do not provide access to a 'typical' experience—if such a thing exists—nor are their accounts unmediated. Rather, they offer what Dorothy Sheridan has described as 'collective documentary'.[8] 'The observers are cameras with which we are trying to photograph contemporary life', the organization explained, '... *subjective* cameras, each with his or her own individual distortion. They tell us not what society is like, but what it looks like to them.'[9]

Mass Observation's interest in what it identified as 'ordinary' British people led it to supplement self-observation with social observation. Running alongside the diary and directive output of its volunteer panel was research activity which spanned all areas of mid-century life; from the public house to people's homes, from capital punishment to dogs in war. Love and commitment attracted their sustained attention. When a team of investigators set up camp in Bolton, Lancashire—or 'Worktown' as they named it—courtship was an area marked out for participant observation. When they investigated the public house, sexual banter was included amongst the recorded conversation. When they followed Bolton holiday-makers to Blackpool they, perhaps voyeuristically, 'combed the sands at all hours, crawled around under the piers and hulkings, pretended to be drunk and fell in heaps on couples to feel what they were doing exactly, while others hung over the sea-wall and railings watching couples in hollowed-out sandpits below'.[10] A pencil drawing of a couple's embrace illustrated a report on a pre-war dance where 'the people danced very close: with the bent arm—which meant that the hands were near the heads of couples...And because there was not much room it meant a good deal of shuffling'.[11] In 1949, a street survey of 2,052 people, a postal survey of 1,000 each of clergy, teachers and doctors and directive responses from its panel of volunteer writers formed the basis for Mass-Observation's 'Little Kinsey'; a comprehensive study of sexual attitudes.[12]

Mass-Observation provides a wealth of survey-style information on attitudes and practice and has often been used alongside other social investigations to map social change. It is at its richest, however, when providing a window on intimate worlds and subjective feelings. Those who have read the published diaries of Nella Last would probably agree.[13] Throughout this book we will encounter numerous individuals—some only once, some a number of times—who have deposited traces of their emotional lives within the archive boxes. Some of these accounts were created in the last decades of the twentieth century and the early years of the twenty-first. Participants in the Mass Observation Project write about their life experiences and emotional journeys from the vantage point of these more recent times. Past and present collide in the telling as the personal past becomes bound into the personal present. Each account is richly imbued with popular as well as individual memories.[14] Other accounts were generated contemporaneously by Mass-Observation in its original guise. We will meet, for example, Olivia Crockett, a mid-century woman unable to marry the man she loved because divorce was so difficult to come

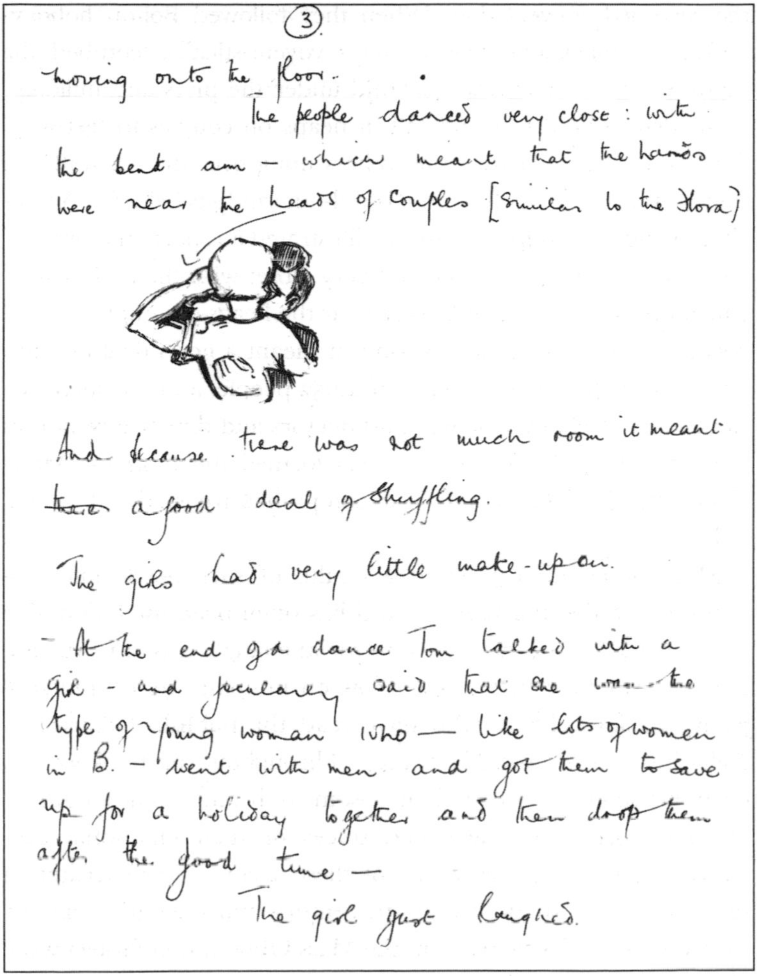

(3)

moving onto the floor.

The people danced very close: with the bent arm — which meant that the hands were near the heads of couples [similar to the Hora]

And because there was not much room it meant ~~there~~ a good deal of shuffling.

The girls had very little make-up on.

– At the end of a dance Tom talked with a girl – and jocularly said that she was the type of young woman who — like lots of women in B. – went with men and got them to save up for a holiday together and then drop them after the good time —

The girl just laughed.

FIGURE 1 This pencil drawing was included in a Mass-Observation report on Bolton dance culture.

by. We will encounter the impressions of a young woman serving in the Women's Auxiliary Air Force who filed regular reports on courtship culture. And we will share the feelings of diarist number 5165 as he lived through the early years of war as a newly married man. The distinctive value of Mass-Observation material to a history of love can perhaps best be illustrated with an extract from his 1940 diary.

> Wednesday, 25.12.40
> We had a quiet, happy Xmas. I came over at about 8 o'clock, bathed, and clean from head to foot. We prepared our Xmas dinner, the chicken and vegetables, and I cleaned the room out thoroughly. Then we had our meal and ate some pudding prepared with a special brandy sauce. It was really nice to be just two, and happy without any cares or thoughts except of ourselves. When I came this morning I spent some thrilling minutes searching for presents hidden all over the room. They were little things my darling had thought of for me, and I was so happy that I cried. Some gloves, and slippers, and handkerchiefs, two little Faber books, Modern poetry and Huxley's essay on Vulgarity in Literature, and even some razor blades; all wrapped up in special paper, with red father Christmasses all over it, and silver string. I gave my darling her breakfast in bed and I sat beside her, opening my parcels and kissing her, because we were so happy and in love. We had a little walk in the afternoon but the weather turned nasty, and we came back quickly and sat by the fire in each other's arms and reading little poems out or laughing at what Huxley said about vulgarity. It is so much what we think and so little what all others think, that it was to [sic] laugh as we read it. When we had had tea, and eaten more cakes than we should, we went to bed and spent two hours, very close in each other's arms and very warm. We got up at half-past eight and washed. I shaved, cleaned my buttons, and caught the last bus to the Depot...when I kissed my darling good night I felt I had never spent a happier Christmas.[15]

This extract describes a familiar festival in extraordinary times. The combination of precise everyday detail—the chicken, the razor blades, the silver string—and self-consciously profound feeling—'I felt I had never spent a happier Christmas'—tells of much more than the events of a single day. The life writing of diarist number 5165 occupies a space between private confession and public assertion: it is in fact a public assertion of privacy. In the pages that follow it will sit alongside the words of many other 'ordinary' mid-century people who wrote at length about their everyday lives and loves and in so doing illuminate 'the live dynamic whole of feeling and behaviour'.[16]

Introduction

In October 1955, Margaret Rose Windsor announced the end of her relationship with a divorced father of two:

> I would like it to be known that I have decided not to marry Group Captain Peter Townsend. I have been aware that, subject to my renouncing my rights of succession, it might have been possible for me to contract a civil marriage. But, mindful of the Church's teaching that Christian marriage is indissoluble, and conscious of my duty to the Commonwealth, I have resolved to put these considerations before any others. I have reached this decision entirely alone, and in doing so I have been strengthened by the unfailing support and devotion of Group Captain Townsend. I am deeply grateful for the concern of all those who have constantly prayed for my happiness.[1]

Princess Margaret's apparent willingness to place 'duty before love', as the *Daily Mirror* newspaper put it, met with the approval of a Church and state anxious to avert another royal marriage crisis so soon after the abdication. In 1936 Edward VIII had made a different decision, declaring it impossible to continue as King 'without the help and support of the woman I love'. The Queen's sister, by way of contrast, seemed to choose service over self-fulfilment.

Ostensibly the totemic events of 1955 support a well-worn view of post-war Britain as stable, conservative, and emotionally controlled. And yet reaction to the Margaret–Townsend affair was mixed, revealing a nation at a point of emotional transition. The

Daily Express used its editorial column to castigate those religious and political leaders it held responsible for the princess's decision, asserting that 'the pity is, that she should give up so much when neither right nor morality demands it of her'.[2] The William Hickey gossip column did not hesitate in framing the affair as one of history's great love stories:

> You will be telling the story of Princess Margaret and Peter Townsend not just this year, not just next year: You will tell it to your children as they grow up. You will, some of you, tell it to grandchildren when the new century comes in. And when you tell it...tell it with compassion: tell it with love. For this is one of the great romances of history: a tale of a beautiful Princess and a brave airman who fell in love—and whose love was star-crossed.[3]

Even an anarchist weekly felt obliged to comment:

> It may seem all wrong for anarchists to feel sorry for a princess, but isn't it pathetic that a young woman can be surrounded with unlimited wealth, privilege, pomp and circumstance, and yet be denied the very thing which every working-class girl takes for granted—and which in real human terms matters more than pomp and circumstance? Princess Margaret is a bird in a gilded cage—and truly a pitiful sight to see.[4]

The public response to the story was complex. National pollster, Gallup, found that 71 per cent of those asked believed Margaret should 'please herself' in the affair.[5] The *Daily Mirror* consistently found a majority in favour of the match.[6] A Mass-Observation inquiry found that levels of interest varied. A school teacher felt, 'indifferent: but my wife showed enough interest for two people'.[7] Some believed Margaret to have made the right choice. 'She realises that Great Privileges imply great responsibilities which the duke of Windsor was too selfish to do!' asserted a 65-year-old woman. In this reading Margaret's royal status and outward religiosity set her apart from the crowd. For others the royal drama raised questions with a wider applicability. Could married love flourish between partners of different generations and social backgrounds for example? According to a middle-aged housewife, 'a woman who marries out of her own circle is generally more lonely and unhappy than a man and therefore I do not think Princess Margaret would really be happy after the first glamorous excitement has passed off'.[8] A young woman pondered the relationship between self-fulfilment and self-control: 'Princess Margaret should not have put state and religious interests before her personal happiness,' she concluded.[9] In contrast, a practically minded 62-year-old woman contested the significance of love in constructing a path through life: 'At my age you know that the world is seldom worth losing for love and there were so many things about the marriage that were wrong.'[10]

The royal crisis occurred at a time when the emotional landscape was changing. Margaret's battle between love and duty was one manifestation of a wider conflict between self-discipline and self-expression. Speaking to the Mothers' Union in 1949, Princess Elizabeth had criticized what she saw as the growing self-indulgence, hardening materialism, and falling moral standards of the age.[11] In 1955 a retired civil servant detected a modern tendency to 'consider that "right" is what one desires—and that personal satisfaction should not be sacrificed to any ideal'.[12] Among the complex web of interacting variables out of which these changes occurred, particularly significant were the impact of war, secularization, and affluence—together with major demographic and representational shifts. Some, such as Lord Justice Denning, blamed women. 'It is not perhaps a mere coincidence that, with the emancipation of women, there has come a great rise in the divorce rate', he told a meeting of the National Marriage Guidance Council in 1950.[13] And yet emotional culture did not simply reflect and respond to wider structural shifts. Emotion was itself a causal factor, re-shaping the everyday experiences of millions of people. Romantic love, allied to sexual expression, became central to the making of subjectivities in this period. By the century's end, self-fulfilment appeared to have triumphed over self-restraint, leading some sociologists to diagnose 'radical transformations of the social order', and the 'democratization of love'.[14]

* * *

Love has a history. It has meant different things to different people at different moments and has served different purposes. This book presents a social history of heterosexual love and commitment—homosexual love lies beyond its remit—between the 1920s and the 1970s. This fifty-year period was a moment of overlap between older and newer senses of the self, the sexual, and the emotional. The years after the First World War were marked by a conscious and distinctively pervasive sense of public and private modernity. Love and marriage were remade within this context. The book ends as a different landscape for emotional intimacy began to emerge but argues that this apparently new world had its roots in the central years of the twentieth century.

In many ways this period looks like a golden age of marriage: 'the only age, of the near universal, stable, long-lasting marriage, often considered the normality from which we have since departed.'[15] More people were marrying than ever before in the demographic history of modern Britain. Those born in 1946 were less likely than *any* other cohort to remain single.[16] Marriage became increasingly more difficult to avoid and, alongside motherhood, continued to be conceptualized as a woman's primary 'career'. The persistence of formal bars to the employment of married women—abandoned at Barclays Bank as late as 1961 and not until the early 1970s in the Foreign Office—provide stark material evidence of this assumption. While part-time employment opportunities for married women expanded, the welfare state continued to define wives as dependants and banks demanded a male guarantor if a loan or mortgage was to be made.[17] Within this context staying single was widely viewed as a denial of woman's destiny: by 1970 only 8 per cent of women aged between 45 and 49 had never been married.[18] Marriages also lasted longer than they had in previous periods. Fewer marriages were disrupted by premature death and, crucially, divorce was still difficult to obtain.[19] The 1857 Matrimonial Causes Act had introduced a fault-based divorce process with a sexual double standard at its core. From the early twentieth century the 'poor person's procedure' provided a mechanism through which those with an annual income of less than £50 could receive legal advice. But additional costs were not covered and divorce remained beyond the reach of many unhappily married people. A cheaper way of breaking commitment was to obtain a summary separation order from a magistrate. Separation was not legal divorce, however, and did not allow for re-marriage.

Pressure to reform the divorce laws developed in parallel with the increasing emphasis upon emotional and sexual satisfaction within marriage. The Herbert Act of 1937 added new matrimonial faults; the desire for further reform was fuelled by wartime conditions. 1946 was a peak year for divorce petitions with two-thirds of these initiated by husbands: the number of divorces granted in 1947 was not surpassed until 1972.[20] The introduction of a comprehensive system of legal aid in 1949 provided for a peacetime opening up of the divorce process to those hitherto excluded on financial grounds. There was no easing of the legal criteria for attaining a decree absolute, however, until the Divorce Reform Act of 1969 became effective from 1 January 1971. While marriage became increasingly popular in the mid-twentieth century, it also remained difficult to escape.

Those entering marriage for the first time were doing so at increasingly younger ages, although those younger than 21 required parental permission to do so. In 1931 the mean age at first marriage for men was 27. By 1971, and notably after the last national servicemen had been discharged in 1963, it was a century low of 24. Amongst women the mean age dropped from 25 in 1931 to 22 in 1971.[21] Working-class people tended to marry younger than their middle-class counterparts, a phenomenon related to their more rapid progression through education and training to adult economic status.[22] There was an age differential of approximately three years between social class I (professional occupations) and social class V (unskilled occupations) across the twentieth century.[23] As sociologist Pearl Jephcott observed in 1942, 'Marriage is more imminent for the shop girl and factory girl than it is for girls of the professional classes, which explains why the working-class girl of nineteen might be really perturbed and harp on the fact that she has not yet got a boy!'[24] Professionally trained and graduate women were more unlikely to marry than their less formally educated married sisters: the ability to earn a decent wage into adulthood perhaps making marriage less essential.[25] Nonetheless passage through key demographic milestones—courtship, marriage, parenthood—became increasingly homogenous: 'any significant deviation from what could by the 1950s clearly be called a "normal" life course was likely to label the perpetrator as "odd", "unlucky" or worse.'[26]

The relationship between marriage and love was complex. Although often conflated in this period, the two were not necessarily coterminous. Clearly love could transcend the bounds of committed heterosexuality. Nonetheless, in the first half of the twentieth century love seemed to offer a way of mitigating the threat posed by uncontrolled desire in a Freudian age. Marriage reformers saw lovc as a mcchanism for containing, or perhaps more accurately taming, sex and preventing it from becoming an independent and unregulated source of everyday pleasure. Sex and love became tightly bound together within widely promoted notions of modern marriage. After the Second World War romantic love also offered a way of binding self-actualizing individuals to the social contract of marriage amidst concerns about family disintegration. Married love increasingly promised more than mere companionship: it offered a dynamic emotional connection where personal transformation was a shared project achieved through togetherness. Because of this, love came to be increasingly valued above all other factors in the making of legal commitment.

And yet, romantic love, particularly when tied to sexual satisfaction and emotional growth, was an unreliable foundation upon which to build life-long commitment. It made demands upon individuals which went well beyond the successful performance of established gender roles and generated expectations which proved hard to meet. Although it appeared to offer a way of revitalizing marriage for the modern age, love actually created more fundamental problems for matrimony. Crucially, love had the potential to evaporate over time and under pressure. If we scratch beneath the surface of the golden age, we uncover a mid-twentieth century of quiet emotional instability and gentle subversion of established norms: a story of discontinuity and relative speeds of change.

A number of unsettling questions about life and love emerged in this period. Ordinary people wondered, for example, just how important love should be when selecting a marriage partner and whether pragmatism also had a role. They debated the relationship between love and marriage and asked whether marriages could, or indeed, *should*, survive in the absence of love. Crucially, concerns emerged about how to balance desire, agency, and social obligation. If people were not responsible for falling in and out of love, as Mary Grant of the *Woman's Own* problem page suggested in 1950, what would happen to lifelong commitment?[27] Ultimately a matrimonial model based upon the transformative power of love carried within it the seeds of its own destruction. Extra-marital sexual desire had long been accommodated within certain types of British marriage; extra-marital love proved more of a challenge. The end of century decline of life-long marriage was rooted in the contradictions, tensions, and illogicalities that lay at the heart of mid-century intimacy.

* * *

In recent years historical research has taken an 'emotional turn', driven by an assertion that feeling is shaped by time and culture.[28] 'Emotions themselves are extremely plastic,' observes the medievalist Barbara Rosenwein, 'it is very hard to maintain, except at an abstract level that emotions are everywhere the same.'[29] A rich corpus of early research dwelt upon dominant emotional codes and standards, revealing how people were instructed to behave, if not what they actually did.[30] More recently historical interest has turned to the complex and contradictory ways people employ emotions, interact with dominant codes and navigate between 'emotional communities'.[31] The everyday experience and use of emotion is increasingly of interest to historians; so too are its political dimensions.[32] Fear, anxiety, and anger have emerged as particularly popular areas of research.[33] Love has also attracted attention.[34] Richly suggestive treatments are offered in the recent work of historians Stephen Brooke, Martin Francis, and Simon Szreter and Kate Fisher.[35] Studies by Luisa Passerini, Marcus Collins, Simon May, and Lisa Appignanesi have mapped dominant ideas and representations of love producing enlightening intellectual and cultural histories of the emotion.[36] Collins's *Modern Love*, for example, shows how 'mutualist' reformers tried—and ultimately failed—to redefine twentieth-century love as a relationship based on 'intimate equality' between women and men.[37]

A social history of love offers a different perspective to those of an intellectual or cultural nature. It directs attention to the changing ways in which love was understood, invoked, and deployed by what contemporaries regarded as 'ordinary' people.[38] This book therefore tells its story not through the cultural interventions of philosophers and artists but through a series of intimate stories located within everyday life. As we will see, ordinary people were surprisingly forthcoming on the subject of their intimate lives when asked directly about them. Their stories draw attention to the ways in which historical moment, gender, status, material circumstance, and generation shaped understandings of love. They also help us dissect the relationship between experience, subjectivity, and cultural representation in a rapidly changing world. The boundary between private and public was always gently shifting across these years and was sometimes directly challenged. The sources consulted here allow these fluctuations to be accessed at the micro-level.

The Tudor historian G. R. Elton once characterized social history as possessing 'a charming quality of timelessness', but the social history presented here emphasizes the dynamics of change.[39] Although this book explores love across the period 1920–1970—the mid-twentieth century—the 1940s and 1950s lie at its interpretative heart. These were decades when the emotional landscape changed dramatically for large numbers of ordinary people; a period that witnessed a revolution in the value attached to emotional intimacy within heterosexual encounters. In particular I see the Second World War as an emotional watershed; that is, as a period of rapid discontinuity out of which emerged a subtly different set of intimate relations embedded in, and expressive of, changed gender and social relations.[40] Richard Hoggart recalled the shift in his autobiography:

> By 1944 there was an unusual feeling in the air among servicemen, not often articulated cogently, but indicated by banal-sounding phrases: 'We don't mean to go back to what it was like before'; 'Things have got to change'; 'I'm not standing for that lot again'; 'We didn't go through all this just to settle back where we were'. There had been a sea-change among men who had been, most of them, ill-educated, not encouraged to have many expectations or to look to any change for the better, to progress, to movement.[41]

A 28-year-old looked forward to 'Day nurseries, all jobs open to married women and maternity grants on the Russian lines'.[42] The experience of war had a profound impact on individual world-views, as this young woman suggests:

> [T]he main change in personal outlook as far as I am concerned, since the war, has been the realisation of my responsibility as a citizen. Another change which has been brought home to me recently was the non-importance of material possessions in the face of one's life. My husband and I have always taken great pride in our home

> but since we have again been subjected to war conditions at home, and since we have lost our home during the flying-bomb attacks, we realised that life is the most important thing, and the lives of other people as well as the people all over the world, should be our main consideration after the war.[43]

Yet within post-war reconstruction narratives, the making and securing of British family life took centre stage. The physical and psychic space of home was where personal and family identities were to be developed and—according to some—defended. 'Britain has always been proud of her family life. It has been the backbone of her national greatness', observed the general secretary of what became a *National* Marriage Guidance Council in 1946.[44] He issued a stark warning: 'Today it is threatened as never before. We know we're up against it—just as we did when the Germans got to Calais. But we know too, as we knew then, that we've got to win. The only lasting foundation for a sound national life is sound family life.' If home and family life was the bulwark of the nation, so too, increasingly, was love. As the historian Martin Francis has argued, 'Love and marriage, as much as a new council house or free hospital care were the right and reward of the post-war citizen, provided they remained within the domains of sexual continence and heterosexuality.'[45]

This turn to love was framed on the one hand by rising expectations and national optimism and on the other by critical introspection and cold war anxiety. 'There's been a tendency to look on the fifties as simply a damp patch of ground between the battleground of the forties and the fairground of the sixties,' the journalist Katherine Whitehorn has written, 'yet it was anything but.'[46] Recent histories have characterized the post-war period as one of sexual and generational upheaval.[47] Media historian Adrian Bingham suggests that the boundaries between public and private in the popular press crumbled in these years.[48] The post-war world was a place of emotional fragility rather than conformist calm: Britain had, apparently, been 'stabbed awake'.[49] Complex shifts in emotional culture—perhaps even an emotional revolution—preceded the changes in sexual culture so characteristic of the latter years of the twentieth century. As we will see, change was not necessarily linear and certainly not straightforward. Nonetheless the ways in which love was fashioned in the 1940s and 1950s were central to the dramatic social and cultural changes that occurred in the decades that followed. And what came next was not necessarily a rejection of love. By the 1960s the primacy of love was striking: for many, the decade could more accurately be described as a golden age of romance, than an age of sexual permissiveness.

* * *

In this book I argue that there is something distinctive about the ways in which love, sex, and marriage were interwoven within mid-century England. This is not to suggest that love had no significance for ordinary people prior to the twentieth century or that there was somehow 'more' love in this period than ever before. While some historians have attempted to date the emergence of modern affective relations from around 1700, others point to essential continuities in emotional capacity across time.[50] Romantic love is hardly a modern invention, but the sources that allow us to access ordinary people's emotional lives are more prevalent for the last two hundred years. For example, stories of falling in love deeply or being head over heels in love frame the autobiographical accounts of some nineteenth-century working-class people.[51] Love at first sight was clearly not a twentieth-century invention, as the shoemaker William Smith's mid-nineteenth-century experience demonstrates:

> I was introduced to a young lady (as was the custom in those days) by an elderly lady when going into a class meeting at the chapel. She was dressed in black, having just lost and buried two brothers. She was very dark, with long black hair and dark eyes which she modestly fixed on the ground. But she gave me such a shake of the hand

that I have felt it hundreds of times since then and sometimes feel it now. I was smitten at once. It was love at first sight. But don't think I am going wrong in my head as I record this, for I am quite sane.[52]

Working men and women of earlier periods did not conduct their emotional lives in silence. In an autobiography written in 1849, the working-class radical, Samuel Bamford, recalled a time when 'the young germs of love [were] beginning to quicken in my heart' and wrote of abandoning himself 'to delicious heart-gushings of romantic feeling, bowed in silent and earnest regard to female loveliness...'[53] The Victorian maidservant Hannah Cullwick wrote extensively about her lover Arthur Munby addressing, for example, the relationship between love and marriage:

I car'd very *very* little for the licence or being married either. Indeed I've a certain dislike to either, they seem to have so little to do with our *love* & our union. *They* are things what every common sweethearts use whether they love really or not. And ours has bin for so long a *faithful, trustful* & pure love, without any outward bond, that I seem to *hate* the word marriage in *that* sense.[54]

Nor was romantic gift exchange something confined to twentieth-century people living in an age of mass consumption. Love tokens such as engraved coins, gloves, love spoons, and true-love hearts have long been exchanged by ordinary people. Indeed Bamford described receiving an early nineteenth-century Valentine that would put twenty-first century versions to shame. 'Cupids, and darts, and bars of love, and birds, and chains, and bleeding hearts, all cut out, and coloured, and set forth in most approved form.'[55]

Twentieth-century people were not innately more likely to fall in love than their predecessors, but this does not mean that the nature and meaning of love and marriage have remained historically static. In medieval and early modern England clandestine attachments based on the simple exchange of verbal vows were contracted in a variety of locations: a priest was not always in attendance. Hardwicke's Marriage Act of 1753 attempted to formalize and regulate marriage in England and Wales but lovers did not always see the need to involve the state in their intimate affairs. Amongst certain sections of the nineteenth-century working class legal forms of marriage apparently mattered little. 'Free unions are at least as old as marriage itself,' suggests the historian Ginger Frost, whose study of *Living in Sin* explores the nature of cohabitation in nineteenth-century England.[56]

For those who did wish to marry, emotional factors vied with material considerations. If we look back to 1500, we might presume that concern for the consolidation and transmission of property alongside dynastic and political allegiance, shaped marriage more than love. However an argument such as this is likely to relate to privileged sections of society: working people's concerns were undoubtedly different. A shifting constellation of factors framed the marriage choices of ordinary people and these included family and community influence, material consideration as well as sexual desire and love.[57] While it would be inaccurate to suggest that pre-twentieth-century marriages were characterized by lovelessness, love was not always deemed sufficient reason to marry. Indeed pragmatism could loom large long even before the wedding day. When Ellen Calvert became engaged to Arthur Gill in the early years of the twentieth century she rejected a ring in favour of a sewing machine.[58] Domestic skills and proven breadwinning ability were highly desirable spousal virtues: they could make the difference between getting by and floundering. Thomas Carter, a working man who married in 1819, 'learned to believe that my domestic happiness did not depend upon my having what is quaintly called a "bookish woman" for my wife, but that it would be greatly dependent upon my choosing one of plain good sense and of thoroughly domestic habits'.[59] In the early twentieth century such characteristics continued to be much prized. While poverty did not 'obliterate emotion', material circumstance tempered the willingness to act on emotion alone.[60] By the 1950s emotion alone was increasingly enough.

* * *

Ordinary people's experiences of love cannot be understood in a cultural vacuum. The dynamic relationship between prescription and practice, the expert and the everyday, lies at the heart of this book and is reflected in the sources consulted. *The English in Love* asks questions about the ways people adopted, adapted, subverted, or rejected the strictures of others—be they family, neighbours, churchmen, politicians, the police, social commentators, or film stars. It explores the ways in which mid-century people made sense of the world around them and their own experience of it. It examines what they did with the ideas they encountered and what happened when cultural expectations and experience collided. It assesses the extent to which experience itself operated as a source of knowledge and considers how much trust was put in feeling as a basis for action and understanding.

Emotional intimacy was certainly a topic upon which self-declared authorities were keen to pontificate. According to the National Marriage Guidance Council it was 'the expert's job to disentangle emotions which are not working normally; and it is foolish not to seek expert help in these matters'.[61] By 1949 the National Marriage Guidance Council had secured state funding for their efforts.[62] Emotional expertise was also available through the mass media. Newspapers and magazines regularly published syndicated columns on love, marriage, and domesticity apparently penned by the great and the good—stars of stage and screen in particular—whose claim to be taken seriously was founded upon their celebrity rather than training. In 1930, for example, the composer, actor, and playwright Ivor Novello offered Manchester his thoughts on matrimony.[63] As the appetite for advice apparently grew there was no shortage of people willing to cater to this market. Manners books, etiquette guides and popular psychology experienced a golden age in England and beyond.[64] Through the 1940s and '50s, expertise became more culturally formalized. The BBC radio and later television programme *The Brains Trust* provided a playful forum for experts to engage with public concerns and moral quandaries. 'What does The Brains Trust consider the basis of happy marriage?' asked Corporal Alice Kettering of the Women's Auxiliary Air Force in 1945.[65] When Mass-Observation surveyed Britain's sexual attitudes in 1949 it likewise assembled a board of expert assessors to offer general advice including Dr David Mace, 'a quite tireless worker in the cause of sexual enlightenment', and Dr Clifford Allen, 'psychiatrist to the ministry of pensions'.[66] A 1951 *Picture Post* series entitled 'Sex and the Citizen' detailed the discussions of a panel of experts from the fields of sociology, industrial psychology, family planning, gynaecology, and child psychology.[67] 'Why only one woman?' asked a reader, not unreasonably.[68] Radio, television, and the ever-expanding print media provided copious channels for expert views to be ventilated and also, but more occasionally, for the voices of ordinary people to be heard.

Within this context, the mid-century agony aunt, purveyor of everyday advice to a mass audience, merits particular attention. The problem page was not a twentieth-century innovation: it was invented in 1691 by a troubled adulterer, John Dunton. Nonetheless it was an established feature of women's magazines and popular newspapers by the mid-twentieth century.[69] Best-selling novelist, journalist, and socialist, Leonora Eyles was *Woman's Own*'s first agony aunt.[70]

Writing under the strapline 'Life and You', she self-advertised as 'the woman who understands'. Angela Willians—better known as 'Mary Grant'—succeeded her in the *Woman's Own* chair, while at *Woman* magazine Peggy Makins responded to reader's letters as agony aunt 'Evelyn Home'. On the whole personal problems were deemed to be best answered by women journalists, although the occasional man did contribute to the genre. Nigel Mansfield was *Glamour* magazine's resident 'Love Expert', whilst tireless marital campaigner David Mace ran his own advice column in the pages of *The Star* newspaper in the late 1940s.

The personal problems which fuelled magazine problem pages and some advice manuals reflect the limits of the possible within

188 WOMAN'S OWN May 9. 1936

If you would like her help over any private worry, write to Leonora Eyles. Enclose a stamped-addressed envelope if you require an answer by post—and remember that replies cannot appear on this page until several weeks after you have posted your query. Address your letter to Mrs. Eyles, c/o WOMAN'S OWN, 18 Henrietta Street, London, W.C.2. All correspondence is treated in confidence.

Life—and You

Escorts Other Girls Home

"I have recently had to take a job away from home. My boy, I hear, is taking other girls about, bringing them home from dances and parties. This has grieved me awfully. Is there not one faithful man in the world? And is it any use sticking to a man who is not faithful?"

My dear, you are making a very grave mistake. Your boy is not being unfaithful to you at all. Surely you don't expect him not to go out at all while you are away? Do you never go out with anyone because you are away from him? It does not matter in the least how many girls he takes out, as long as he makes no secret of his preference for you. You would have a right to resent it if he made love to other girls, but as for taking them home from a dance, any gentleman would do that rather than allow girls to go home alone late at night.

An Etiquette Problem

"I am hoping to have a few friends in to tea when I have my twenty-first birthday party. What is the correct form of inviting them? I am also wondering exactly what thin, one needs for one's bottom drawer."

The best way of inviting your friends is to tell them about your little tea-party, if you happen to meet them, or, if not, write them short informal notes. If you will write to me privately I will send you a rough list of what is needed for your bottom drawer. Nowadays, as you know, it is not such a hide-bound thing as it used to be.

Sick of Keeping House

"We married just over a year ago, and I love my husband, but I am just sick of housework and cooking. Whenever I think of the forty odd years in front of me, and the number of meals I have to prepare in them, and the beds to make, I think I will go insane. There is no prospect of any help yet, and now there is a baby coming it is farther away than ever. Is there anything I can do? It is impossible for me to go out to work. There is no one I can confide in, and I wouldn't hurt my husband for worlds."

We all get that feeling sometimes, my dear. Cheer up! You see, what has happened is this. To begin with everything was new and lovely, and then things began to lose their novelty. But very soon now your duties will get into a better routine, and you will do your housework in half the time. I've little doubt that when your baby comes you will feel far better about things. I tell you what I always did when I felt I could not wash another dish; I deliberately cleaned out a room, washed a carpet, or did something else out of the routine. Slacken off sometimes. It is better for you to be happy just now than for your floors to be fit to eat off!

Who is Responsible?

"Am I responsible for my maid's insurance stamps? I am afraid I have not bothered about them, and have just given her the money to buy them. Now I find she has not done so."

I am afraid you are responsible. Keep the card in your own possession and give her three weeks in which to buy those that are in arrears. In future, keep her share of the weekly stamp out of her wages and buy it yourself. You can be fined if you fail to do this.

Lost All Interest

"For the last year my husband seems to have lost all interest in me. He never makes love to me at all, and hardly ever even kisses me. He is quite contented reading a paper in the evenings, and just seems satisfied in knowing I am about. He is not interested in other women. Do you think it is my fault? I must admit that sometimes I used to be a bit cold towards him, and I wondered if this has anything to do with it."

I wish you would write to me privately, and give me your full address. There are several reasons which would possibly explain your husband's attitude. It might be, as you think, because you did not seem to like his love-making in the past. If I were you I would talk to him frankly and see if you can find out the reason for his indifference to you.

Her Only Complaint

"I am in love with a very nice boy; my only complaint is that if we come home late from a dance he is inclined to want to take liberties with me, although he stops when I tell him I don't like it. Ought I to give him up?"

No; he does not deserve that. Many boys lose their heads a little after dancing, and it is up to a girl to keep them sensible. Go home in a party of people; that is much the safer way, and will save awkward moments and quarrels.

"Reverend" or "Mr."

"Should I call a clergyman 'Reverend' when I speak to him, or only 'Mr.'?"

Never call him "Reverend." Only use that word in writing to him. Nonconformist and ordinary Anglican clergymen are called "Mr." Roman Catholic and very High Church priests are often called "Father."

Profitable Side-lines

"We live on a main road and are very hard up, as my husband is ill and cannot work much, but must live practically out of doors. We have a very nice fruit garden and we run a tea shop, but can you suggest any side-lines?"

There are several ideas that occur to me. You could make jam, pickles, chutney, cakes, and scones, serve them in the teashop and get custom for them locally; and you could keep bees and sell honey, and have a few fowls and sell eggs. Also, if you are in a district not served with a fiction library, you might get a hundred cheap books and start lending them at 2d. each, increasing your library if it goes well. I can give you information about this, as a member of my family is doing well with a 2d. library.

Wants Him Back

"Some time ago a man whom I liked and respected asked me to marry him. I could not then, but now circumstances have altered and I wish I had not refused him so very decidedly. Is there any way I could find out, without showing or hurting my own feelings, if he has changed his mind?"

It is very difficult. The only thing you can do is to go on being friendly with him, seeing as much of him as you can, and trying to show him that the things which prevented you from marrying when you were first asked no longer matter.

Where Should They Live?

"We are moving up to London very shortly. My husband has been transferred to the City branch of his office. I was wondering if you had any suggestion about the best place to live in London. We have two children."

It is very difficult for me to advise you about this, as I know nothing about your income or personal taste. As your husband will be working in the City, you can live practically anywhere in London, because trains are so good. As you have children, you should see that you are fairly near a good school and, if possible, that your house has a garden for them to play in.

Sunny side up! Isn't it nice to meet a really cheerful sunny-natured soul—it brightens up the whole day for me! Have you ever thought what you could do to bring a little gaiety and happiness into the lives of those around you? There's always scope for being cheerful you know, so next time you've got the "hump" remember that—

"Every time we sing a song,
It helps the world to jog along."

Leonora Eyles

FIGURE 2 Leonora Eyles was *Woman's Own*'s first agony aunt. During the Second World War she also penned a short-lived advice column in the socialist weekly *The Tribune*.

any given moment, both in word and deed, even when massaged or, less frequently, fabricated.[71] The agony aunt herself inhabited a complex position: her advice reflected dominant codes but had to be palatable if her readership was to be maintained. In effect she mediated between the prescriptive and the subjective, operating in the blurred space where norms are rendered practicable. Advice givers had to negotiate, rather than impose, if they wished to be commercially successful. Some were explicit about the interactivity between their words and lived experience. Sex manual author 'Rennie Macandrew' told readers of his 1939 book, *Friendship, Love Affairs and Marriage* that,

> I don't want you to study this book as you would a school text-book or a cut-and-dried work of reference. By all means let its contents sink into your mind, but after you have done so allow the PRECISE expressions and methods to recede from memory. From the knowledge gained you should be able to invent Your Own New ideas and methods and produce them indefinitely.[72]

This position of negotiation encouraged the dispensers of advice to adopt a self-consciously down-to-earth conciliatory identity which could set up tensions between the advice giver and other authority figures. 'I think your mother is being just a little bit old-fashioned' was an often repeated assertion.[73]

The status of expert advice within the realm of emotional intimacy was nonetheless ambiguous; not least because of changing modes of selfhood which privileged personality and interiority. As we will see, the emotional revolution brought with it growing confidence in self-diagnosis based on the primacy of experience over the wisdom of trained experts. As Mass-Observation put it in 1949,

> Perhaps what stands out most clearly is the fact that in the field of sex, as in many others, modern man is confused...the 'leaders' are talking one language, the 'led' another. Is the 'common man' to believe the law which tells him that homosexuality is a punishable offence, or the two Lesbians next door who harm nobody, and are,

> in other respects, apparently 'moral'. Is he to believe the church which preaches that all fornication is sin, or his own life in which he had intercourse before marriage without apparently suffering. Is he to believe pamphlets that tell him that masturbation will do him incalculable physical harm, or to trust his own experience?[74]

As this book will make clear, neither sex nor love were subjects on which the experts had all the answers. Public as well as private spaces of contestation and contradiction opened up as prescriptive discourses failed to reflect the messiness of everyday practice. Romantic love facilitated claims to autonomy on the basis of feeling. Expertise was embodied: it rested within the lover because the veracity of emotion was difficult to dispute. Claims to authentic love could pitch children against their parents and spouses against each other. The destabilizing power of love rested, at least in part, in its resistance to expert intervention even as it became an ever more ubiquitous aspect of popular culture and commerce.

* * *

The English in Love falls into three parts: Love, Courtship, and Commitment. Part One explores the nature of love. It describes what love meant to twentieth-century people and explains how everyday understandings changed across the period. Issues of authenticity are of particular interest as I weigh the relationship between love, pragmatism, and passion. The extent to which love was embedded in social relations is another major theme. Part Two shifts attention to patterns of behaviour, by examining the mechanisms through which people found love. Like historian Beth L. Bailey, I use a broad definition of courtship to include 'a wide variety of conditions, intentions, and actions, for men and women woo each other in many ways not all of which lead to marriage'.[75] Particular attention is paid to flirtations and introductions; tensions between public display and private intimacy and financial and sexual exchange in courtship. Part Three focuses upon emotional investment and commitment. It describes how attachments were formalized and explains how this altered everyday lives. Contemporaneous concerns about hasty, youthful and bigamous marriages are addressed as I survey state-sponsored strategies for bolstering marital commitment in the face of rising expectations. Along the way I also uncover the ingenious ways in which some people subverted societal and legal restrictions on their behavior, creating their own forms of commitment and building emotional intimacies on their own terms. Ultimately it is the exercise of emotional agency by ordinary people that drives the narrative of this book. Underpinning the whole story, however, is attention to the material worlds that people inhabited. Material circumstance both shaped and constrained, but always framed, the ways in which people crafted their emotional worlds. In this respect *The English in Love* suggests—to borrow from Marx—that whilst lovers made their own romantic histories, they did not make them entirely as they pleased, 'but under circumstances directly encountered, given and transmitted from the past'.[76]

Part I: Love

I-love-you has no usages. Like a child's word, it enters into no social constraint; it can be a sublime, trivial word, it can be an erotic, pornographic word. It is a socially irresponsible word.

Roland Barthes, *A Lover's Discourse. Fragments* ([1979] London: Vintage, 2002), 147.

The word *love* has by no means the same sense for both sexes.

Simone de Beauvoir, *The Second Sex* ([1953] Harmondsworth: Penguin, 1972), 652.

I

An Emotional Revolution

Early in 1930, a 27-year-old spinster placed a short advertisement in the pages of a popular contact magazine with the hope of attracting a suitor. *The Matrimonial Post and Fashionable Marriage Advertiser* had been established in 1860 and claimed to cater for all classes. It assured readers of its serious purpose by emphasizing that 'this paper is not published for a joke'.[1] Each eight-page monthly edition carried advertisements from bachelors, spinsters, widowers, and widows to which readers could respond via the Editor. Divorcees also featured on its pages, but only after the Second World War. Readers unable to see a suitable match were encouraged to send their requirements to the Editor who would endeavour to arrange an introduction with one of his many other clients, all in the strictest confidence.[2]

The personal attributes specified by our 27-year-old woman suggest precise and self-consciously realistic expectations: 'Spinster, age 27, height 5 ft, RC, fair complexion, dark brown hair, in business, fond of music, quiet, daughter of a farmer, desires to meet clean, and if not good looking, at least pleasant man, earning about £5 per week.'[3] What the modern reader might see as endearingly modest romantic aspirations were not unusual amongst *Post* clients in the 1920s and 1930s. The successful execution of gendered roles was of apparently more importance than looks and the capacity for passion. A 5 foot 6 inch tall widower felt it important to include his skills as a motor car driver, pony and pig breeder, and experimental fruit grower before self-describing as 'kind and cheery...and not too ugly'.[4] A commitment to domesticity was paramount: both spinster and bachelor clients requested 'homely' individuals. Steadiness was a much sought-after attribute.

After the Second World War personality traits became more important within the pages of the *Post.* Women clients now looked for a sense of humour, loyalty and kindness whilst men requested affectionate and loving women. 'Normality' and 'ordinariness' was also much in demand. By 1955, the language of emotional intimacy had shifted. It was not unheard of for those who advertised to suggest that they were looking for a soulmate.[5] We can begin to discern a more introspective model of romantic taste which placed emotional connection at its heart. Changed understandings of love—of its everyday status, meaning, and power—underpinned this model. Within this context, love had the capacity to transform the self. Indeed, a capacity for transcendence came to be a marker of emotional authenticity. Private life provided a testing ground for new models of selfhood which prioritized self-fulfilment over self-control.[6] The meanings and uses of love had changed.

* * *

An image of mid-century England as morally conformist and socially well-ordered has long provided a counterpoint to the apparently more unstable decades that were to follow. Emotional restraint plays an essential part in this portrait, and superficially at least, underpins the great romantic films of the period. David Lean's *Brief Encounter* is a classic example. And yet attention to everyday emotional worlds suggests a different picture.

In the central years of the twentieth century a very precise and historically distinctive form of love was established as the pre-eminent reason for courting and marrying across social classes. As living standards improved, more practical matrimonial considerations were increasingly sidelined. 'What teenagers are really looking for is love,' suggested Charles Davey at the beginning of the 1960s.[7] According to marital experts, love was an increasingly dominant requirement within spousal selection; the factor to which all others considerations should give way. Chair of the Marriage Guidance Council, Reverend Herbert Gray, expressed this position with absolute clarity in 1949:

> The only sufficient reason for marrying is that you have come to love somebody of the other sex. Life must always have troubles in it. Married life has its own peculiar trials, for men are queer creatures, and so are women. It needs love, needs strong and loyal love, to carry a couple through. Love can solve a hundred petty problems, and make light of larger ones. It can make marriage a joy in spite of narrow means, in spite of carking cares and poignant anxieties. But nothing else can.[8]

Some went further, suggesting that love was an essential component of everyday life. According to the advice author R. Edynbry, 'Every feeling of life's happiness rests in love. This is sensed intuitively by nearly all men and women who realise that existence, without someone upon whom their affections can be centred, would hardly be endurable.'[9]

Modern mass culture offered a continually expanding resource out of which individuals could fashion a sense of themselves in love.[10] Films, novels, and magazines of the period offered fictional scripts which could be applied to the making of actual emotional lives. Sometimes these offerings were straightforwardly advisory. *Modern Marriage*—'the magazine for the engaged girl and the young wife'—was launched in 1931 with a free string of 'Parisian pearls' for readers.[11] The magazine was packed full of emotional, sexual, and practical advice for the bride to be. Honeymoon suggestions (Cornwall was highly recommended), astrological guidance, and wedding day beauty tips (spray perfume in your hair), sat alongside more general household advice. Romance fiction was perhaps

FIGURE 3 *Modern Marriage*—'the magazine for the engaged girl and the young wife'—was launched in 1931.

more baffling. A piece in *Woman* magazine called 'Wide-eyed and Innocent', for example, centred on Jill who was loved by one man, but was in love with her boss, who was in turn in love with an actress. Conveniently, they had all ended up on the same romantic cruise.[12] Advertising fed the emotional fire. Wincarnis tonic wine promised to rejuvenate the 4 out of 5 women aged over thirty that it claimed were 'starved of romance'.[13]

Not everyone approved of the new romantic scripts, however. Sociologist Pearl Jephcott recommended expert training in love for the working-class girls she surveyed. 'They have to be made aware of the magnitude and of the scale on which "love" may operate. For that, they must begin to make contact with the real as opposed to the Hollywood exponents, which means that they must become acquainted with what "great" people, the poets, the scientists, the painters and the saints have to teach.'[14] According to Jephcott, commercial leisure offered nothing but bad advice and fakery. The Mothers' Union shared Jephcott's concerns: 'the devil, who was

FIGURE 4 Love, romance and matrimony were increasingly harnessed to sell a wide range of commercial products.

once credited with all the best tunes, has now appropriated the glossiest, best-produced weeklies, the liveliest and smartest radio and television programmes, and the most popular newspapers. And the one subject they all blare, croon, shriek, purr and smirk about is what they call "love".'[15]

Romance was an important element in the reframing of everyday love but the transformation did not stop there. Love was increasingly credited with the power to change people and society. The revolutionary potential of love was well-understood by interwar radicals such as Dora Russell and Naomi Mitchison.[16] For writers like these, as historian Stephen Brooke explains: 'Love—whether physical or emotional—was...perceived as the catalyst of a new society.'[17] In the years after 1945, a more widely spread belief that love could lay the foundations for a better social order was indicative of a social optimism which went hand in hand with the fear and anxiety of the atomic age. If properly embedded within the broader project of family reconstruction and material improvement, love was held to offer an antidote to the brutality of war, acting as social cement. Love also suggested a solution to the new and disconcerting ideas about sexuality raised by Freud and other psychoanalysts. Happy nuclear families bound together through conjugal—and indeed maternal—love seemed to provide a bulwark against all kinds of unsettling social change. The emotional intimacies of private life were explicitly drawn into public policy discussion. A growing body of state-sponsored, as well as commercially located, experts worked to provide guidance on how to get the most out of love. This distinctive development contributed to a blurring of the boundaries between public and private life.

Autobiographical accounts also point to significant shifts in understandings of heterosexual love across the twentieth century. Here the Second World War again acts as a boundary marker. Mass-Observers who reached maturity before this watershed were quick to offer definitions of love which accentuated respect and affection and downgraded attraction and passion. 'I think love is a lot of things and a lot of it is nothing to do with sex,' one such woman explained.[18] In contrast, those who reached maturity after the war had a greater tendency to emphasize the physicality of love, its instinctual character and the existence of 'chemistry'.[19] Crucially they seem to have expected significantly more from emotional intimacy than had the older correspondents. A woman born in 1936 recalled:

> The edgy excitement of meeting someone new, not being able to eat in front of them for the first time, wondering what sort of person they really were, talking about them too much to family and friends, or indeed anyone who'd listen. Long phone calls, blushing etc. etc. What is love? What a question! Love is overpowering sexual excitement in the beginning and eventually respect, warmth, companionship, loyalty and the all-embracing word of love covers all those aspects. To put it briefly love is long term or in romantic terms, forever and ever.[20]

For this individual love had profound, and overwhelming, physiological, emotional, and cultural meanings. It was both incredibly simple—'forever and ever'—and wildly ambitious—'the all-embracing word of love covers all those aspects'. 'As a younger person I had to "fancy" someone—they had to be able to "turn me on",' another writer recalled. 'I didn't then give much thought to the money situation, or whether or not we had much in common.'[21] A woman born in 1949 explained that, '[i]n possibly typical twentieth century style I have fallen in love romantically, gone with it and followed my instincts, and I wouldn't change any of it!'[22] Looking back on her life from the vantage point of 2001, this woman had a clear sense of the historical distinctiveness of her own approach to love. She also laid claim to its typicality.

The loading of love with new expectations—be they of a political or personal nature—was not a guarantor of stability. Love, particularly when tied to 'chemistry' and romance, proved to be a capricious basis upon which to build actual marriages. It had a tendency to seep beyond the confines of matrimony. The nature of heterosexual love was therefore much discussed, argued and agonized over during the golden age of marriage. Was falling in love easy? Was it a unique or a repeatable experience? Was it possible to love two people at the same time? Could a love affair alone lead to self-fulfilment? Was love more compelling than sex? These questions emerged because there was—according to historian Jane Lewis—'a logical inconsistency at the heart of arguments about love, sex and marriage'.[23] They suggest a context of emotional instability—perhaps even emotional revolution—rather than unquestioning conformity and affective calm.

* * *

Within mid-century stories of everyday love, two elements were particularly striking: the principle of 'true love' and the phenomenon of 'love at first sight'. Both were evident across cultural and autobiographical texts; neither went uncontested as ways of understanding emotional life. Writing on the cusp of war, relationship expert Rennie Macandrew believed that it was 'almost invariably the case' that men fell in love at first sight. He cited the Polish proverb, 'Love enters a man through his eyes, a woman through her ears' as his evidential base.[24] Psychiatrists Slater and Woodside also suggested that men were more likely to fall in love at first sight than were women, although their evidence indicated that the phenomenon was in fact a 'comparative rarity'.[25] Love at first sight stories were a recurrent feature of the post-war tabloid press. For example the *Daily Mirror* reported that blue-rinsed pop star, Larry Page, had met his first wife on the set of the BBCs first Rock and Roll television programme, *The Six-Five Special.* They were engaged within eight hours. 'What's the point in waiting around when we love each other,' his enthusiastic typist fiancée proclaimed.[26]

Love at first sight is a much repeated device within the stories people tell about love in the mid-century—women as well as men. Within autobiographical accounts it is favoured by those who found

FALLING IN LOVE 135
"Love at first sight" is by no means only the ideal of the novelist. If it is experienced by sane and balanced young people it is the happiest and truest kind of love, and may endure for a lifetime; on the other hand, with unstable people it often proves an illusion.

FIGURE 5 Love at first sight was a particularly striking element within mid-century love stories.

love in the 1950s and 1960s. 'I think my wife had hooked me from the moment we first met,' one man's account began:

> I remember seeing her home from the dance and then making my own way home knowing that I had met someone special. In no time at all I was her slave. My mother was not all that impressed, a grown man so moonstruck! About three weeks after we had met we went out in the car one night and she was so edgy. For a brief despairing moment I thought she wanted to call things off, but she hastened to re-assure that was not so. Then the truth fell upon me like a ton of bricks. She felt the same way as I did.[27]

A woman born in 1930 met her husband on a blind date, 'as soon as I saw him I knew he was the one for me'. They married when she was 22.[28]

Those who reached adulthood a decade later were even more likely to frame their emotional life stories around love at first sight. This provides an instructive counterpoint to interpretations of the 1960s which foreground sexual libertarianism. It suggests that the decade witnessed the deepening of existing constructions of everyday love rather than the acceptance of new models. 'We expected to meet someone who we would love and be loved in return, get engaged eventually and be several years in this state of limbo until we had saved enough for a house or found one to rent, and then we got married,' recalled one woman.[29] In fact she met her husband at Christmas 1965 and married in September 1966, recalling: 'I waited a long time before I found the right partner (I was twenty six when I got married) but I knew I had found the one person for me because we have now been happily married for thirty four years.' Emotional authenticity at the time is here retrospectively proven by the length of the marriage. Another writer married her husband exactly a year after meeting him at a wedding in the late 1960s: 'we knew this was "it." Looking back I'm amazed at my certainty. The following weekend he came down to see me...and asked me to marry him.'[30]

Within romantic fiction and non-fiction, the love at first sight trope was used to deny the influence of social identities and individual pragmatism on love. It denotes the triumph of feeling over rational assessment and suggests the intervention of fate—in the shape of a serendipitous meeting—in assuring long-term happiness. Love at first sight was, in fact, at odds with the more careful calculations about character which women had long been encouraged to make when selecting a spouse. Because of this, acting on love at first sight was more likely to be retrospectively construed as a catastrophic failure of judgement if things did indeed go wrong. 'I fell in love at first sight but from the beginning life was difficult,' admitted a woman who met her future husband in 1947. 'With hindsight I should never have gone ahead with this marriage. His treatment of me gradually wore away any love I had for him.'[31] Slater and Woodside found that 'dislike at first sight' characterized the experiences of a proportion of the working-class women they surveyed in the 1940s. Mrs N., for example, 'didn't like the look of him at first—he was big and ugly. And to "tell you the truth, he thought I was a prostitute, or one of those good-time girls". She supposes she agreed to go about with him because "I was lonely" and she got fond of him.'[32] Very few of the men they talked to felt this way. Robert N. was an exception, although his views changed with surprising speed:

> 'I hated the sight of her when I first met her.' However, at the next meeting he took her to the pictures and on the third meeting when he took her to Cardiff for the day he asked her to marry him. 'I had a big physical desire for her. I asked myself would I like to sleep with her often; would I like to see her opposite me at table in the mornings; would I like to support another man's daughter; and I thought it was a good idea.' He knew her for only four weeks before marriage, and had to ask her parents' consent as she was under twenty-one. Pre-marital relations occurred, though 'I had to promise I'd marry her before she'd give way.'[33]

In both of these cases rational calculation, rather than instantaneous emotional response, played a determining role in the decision to marry.

Love at first sight stories often constructed love as a once in a lifetime phenomenon—whether or not the relationship actually developed into a marriage. The notion that one 'perfect partner' existed is certainly evident in autobiographical writings. 'I think I was about 18 when I had sex for the first time with my one and only love,' wrote one, 'I'm now married to someone else (see previous directive full of pain and anguish!) and if I had my time again . . .'[34] Everyday love expert R. Edynbry explained with brutal simplicity that if a woman mistook mere affection for love, 'she might suffer greatly should her "real partner" ever come upon the scene'.[35] In fact the very idea of 'true' love encouraged careful consideration of the possible repeatability or conversely uniqueness of this emotional state.

There was not universal acceptance of the true love ideal, of course. 'Is there really some boy waiting just for you? Or do you believe that love is something that just happens?' teen magazine *Boyfriend* asked its readers in 1963.[36] According to true love enthusiast 'Pauline', 'There's only one man for you and me and someday we'll meet him.' In contrast 'Janice', whilst no less enthusiastic about the general love project, advanced what she held to be a more 'scientific' approach: 'Frankly if there is only one, I think we've got fat little chance of finding him. But don't get all steamed up girls, because I've got news for you. There isn't only one! There are millions and millions of the lovely beasts. And there are any number who will suit you.' A decade earlier anthropologist Geoffrey Gorer had identified 'two groups in the population, one of which believes that falling in love is a unique experience in life, normally culminating in marriage, and the other that falling in love is a repeatable experience'.[37] By the time of his 1971 publication, *Sex and Marriage in England Today*, a sizeable minority of his respondents—23 per cent of men and 25 per cent of women—said that they had fallen in love more than once, and 39 per cent of men and 44 per cent of the women felt that it was possible to 'really fall in love' more than once.[38]

Most interesting amongst Gorer's findings is the high percentage of both men and women who felt that it was possible to love two people simultaneously. Writing in 1974, feminist Lee Comer argued that 'monogamy has come to be the definition of love, the yard-stick by which we measure the rest of our emotions. "Real" love is only that which is exclusively focused on one person of the opposite sex—all else is labelled "liking". Like so much butter, romantic love must be spread thickly on one slice of bread; to spread it over several is to spread it "thinly".'[39] 'But experience is always at odds with the principle', she added, tellingly. 'I am in love with two boys and I can't decide which of them I want to marry...Do help me choose between them', begged a reader of Leonora Eyles's 'Life—and You' column in 1934.[40] 'Which one would get on your nerves least?' Eyles replied. By the late 1960s 40 per cent of Gorer's respondents believed that a man could love two women at the same time and 40 per cent of men and 34 per cent of women believed that a woman could 'be in love with two men simultaneously'.[41] Such views were most strongly held amongst the middle classes suggesting that economic security was a factor. These findings in particular suggest a disjuncture between the models of emotional exclusivity and relational 'honesty' promoted within prescriptive literature and evident in some autobiographical accounts, and the everyday experience and attitudes recorded contemporaneously. In short, as love became more central to the way men and women constructed their lives, it also became rather messy. Gorer's findings suggest that the British were more libertarian in their views on emotional intimacy than in their approach to erotic practices. An emotional revolution not only predated any sexual revolution; it provided the necessary conditions for such change.

Within this context gender continued to play a role in framing understandings of love. According to medieval historian Catherine

Cubitt, 'the emotions and their expression have always served to delineate gender difference.'[42] Popular magazines portrayed male and female love as essentially different: 'The love of a girl or woman was described as deep and permanent. Male love, in contrast, was often shallow, more easily controlled and redirected.'[43] The authors of advice literature of the period were convinced that men and women experienced love differently. Their analyses sometimes challenged the long-established assumption that women were innately more 'emotional' than men. In part this was because they often disentangled love from sex when addressing women and conflated the two when appealing to men. Rennie Macandrew, for example, advised that 'the sight of a man's body, however perfect, creates practically no sexual excitement in a young woman'.[44] Instead, he suggested, she 'is usually more attracted by the psychological aspect of a man'. According to Macandrew this had the advantage of making her 'less susceptible, for she considers the dependability of the protector and bread-winner before the physical attractions of the love mate'. However although a woman was prone to fall in love less immediately than a man, she was ultimately 'more deeply engulfed'. Her love was more robust because it was 'built on a more lasting basis. She did not love him primarily for his figure; her attraction was more an affection of mind.'[45] In contrast 'the man's "love" is at first possibly no more than a body urge which he can switch over to another girl if the first doesn't come up to expectations'.[46]

The complex relationship between physical attraction and affection could be a source of real anxiety for men as well as women. 'Can a mere man come to you for advice?' Helen Worth of the *Modern Marriage* 'Heart-to-Heart Bureau' was asked in 1931:[47]

> Can a man love a girl for some things and hate her for others, and is it right to marry a girl who rouses such feelings? I am engaged to a distractingly pretty girl but I can't help seeing her imperfections. She is not at all nice to her mother and sisters and she is lazy and not at

> all fond of home life. I feel so angry sometimes that I could shake her and at other times she is so attractive and sweet that I am fascinated by her. Is this mere physical attraction?

Mrs Worth was uncompromising in her response: 'If you marry her you risk terrible unhappiness. She will enslave you with her prettiness and torture you by her selfishness and emptiness.' More generally the suspicion that men loved lightly because they were driven by a physical response posed questions about whether their love was 'real'—something we will explore further in Chapter Two.

If men were accused of loving lightly, or mistaking physical desire for emotional connection, women were more likely to be charged with bestowing their affections indiscriminately. In her post-war study of personality development in England, *The Deprived and the Privileged*, the female psychologist B. M. Spinley suggested that the engaged underprivileged girls she surveyed were 'not in love with *the* man but with *a* man'.[48] 'It is as if a girl is determined to attract a partner, and when one is attracted she is prepared to fall in love with him; there is little evidence of deep, permanent, and tender emotional involvement.' She added that 'This falling in love with the available man is not uncommon of course in other sections of the broad culture.' Set alongside Slater and Woodside's findings this evidence implies that love itself was more malleable for women than for men, reflecting the continued, but gendered, importance of pragmatism in partner selection. It also, however, points up middle-class views of the affective capacities of working-class women. In fact the distinction between the love match and the practical choice was not always so clear cut. The way in which love was subjectively 'felt' was rooted in material and cultural, as well as emotional, considerations. As we will see in Chapter Three, pragmatism could itself inform narratives of 'falling in love'. Nonetheless a major post-war development was the gradual disentangling of love from practicality as the necessity of making the sensible choice and tailoring one's affections accordingly declined in the face of welfare state security and a 'very brief' golden age of affluence.[49]

* * *

Expectations, as well as understandings, of love shifted in this period. Whereas in the first half of the century 'to love' might mean to 'take care' of a partner, in the second half of the century it increasingly meant understanding them and cultivating their self-development. Crucially it also meant expecting them to do the same for you. Psychic transformation as well as personal satisfaction lay at the heart of the new-style emotional intimacy. For one woman born in 1936 love was 'the embodiment of understanding, desire, need, humour and soul mate'.[50] Another described it as 'a very strong attraction, mentally and physically. A sense of belonging—of being "at home" with. A strong desire to be always with the loved one. An overwhelming warmth. A longing to be at one with. A feeling that you have found perfection.'[51]

As emotional intimacy became increasingly valorized as the key to happiness, romantic love was endowed with extraordinary powers beyond material advancement and mutual care. 'In its highest form "love" transforms the individual...' claimed one Mass-Observer.[52] 'True love should be the fulfilment of a person through association with another,' asserted another.[53] Elsewhere an almost religious imagery of ecstatic lifting up and transformation was apparent with love represented as a 'transcendental experience'.[54] Mid-century love promised self-fulfilment and well-being. Matrimony appeared to be the context within which this promise could be best realized. In fact the institution of marriage proved ill equipped to withstand the challenges these expectations posed.

For some the promise of self-development through love was indeed an empty one. A woman who married aged 19 in 1960 and divorced 24 years later encapsulated the disappointments that post-war relationships could engender for women:

> In 1960 you knew you would marry, sooner rather than later, in church, have a baby after 2 years and live happily ever after. The script had already been written, down to the last stitch in the curtains, in the women's weekly magazines. It had become possible for a woman to continue her full-time job after the wedding, and this created a false sense of equity. We would be different from our mothers—equal partners, with economic and social independence. Marriage was a disappointment; an unimaginable curtailment of freedom—not only freedom to do, but freedom to be. Obligations to in-laws, social functions, entertaining people you didn't like. Accountability for everything. The impossibility of spontaneous action. And above all, the differences between men and women: husbands had rights and privileges; wives had obligations and duties.[55]

Men too could feel let down by love. Writing in 2001, one man reflected on a marital relationship that spanned the second half of the twentieth century:

> We get along but there is nothing deep for either of us, we love our children, I'm sure life could be much worse for us both and we look after each other. How many married couples are really happy being with each other, in my experience and observation very few, and second marriages it appears are very successful, or, even more of a let-down than the first...I am very much against divorce where there are children and I think men who walk out on the Mother of their children, often after years of marriage, for a younger slimmer model, like buying a new car, are total shits. But it is a lot to expect to get along happily with someone after ten years, let alone fifty.[56]

For many people the longevity of a marriage acted as the ultimate proof of love allowing them to identify emotional continuity over a period of many years. This example suggests that longevity did not always denote depth of feeling.

For others love really did deliver, offering a transformation that mirrored that of a religious conversion, or at the very least the opportunity to attain what was frequently articulated as the 'real' self. One such example is a man who married in 1950 and described meeting his future wife as 'The day my life became worth living'.[57] 'To me, being married to my darling wife has given my life meaning. Previously it wouldn't have mattered to anyone if I was dead.'[58] Another is a woman who struggled to convince her family of the authenticity of her youthful love affair. When she married in 1950 she was 20 years old. Writing for Mass-Observation in 1990 she reported that

> This September my Hubby and I celebrate forty years of married bliss. We both 'fell in love' at the age of sixteen when we met at our church fete. From then on, we hated to be apart and were determined to marry each other as soon as we were allowed to. When we were both eighteen, we asked my parents' permission to marry, but were told that we were 'too young'. However, we became engaged and finally convinced my parents that we were 'in love' and married with their consent when we were twenty years old. How did we know that we were in love? We only knew the longing (when we were apart) to be together was all consuming. Nothing could console our despair when the Army conscription caused us to part for two years...But we overcame all obstacles and here we are, forty four years on, and still very happy together, it must be 'LOVE'.[59]

2

Love, Passion, and Pragmatism

In 1937 the *Every Woman's Book of Love and Marriage and Family Life* attempted to prepare its readers for what it described as 'the very crown of love'—marriage. In so doing it undertook a somewhat ambitious definitional task. 'What is this deep and powerful emotion which is urging you on?' it asked. 'What is this love which demands the surrender of your whole self to the tender keeping of another?'[1] The answer, apparently, lay in an embodied fusion of passion, mutuality, and good citizenship. 'It is a bliss and ecstasy that cannot be described but only felt in every fibre of body and soul; it is sex attraction, friendship and companionship, and it is also Nature's method of ensuring that the race shall carry on.'[2] Notwithstanding the enthusiasm with which it promoted such high expectations of love, the *Every Woman's Book* frankly acknowledged the difficulties some might face in judging the authenticity of their emotional state. Whilst 'the happiest lovers feel sure that it was "fate" that brought them together—and they are saved much heart-searching and worry', others, it was suggested, were less secure in their feelings of love. In these circumstances a 'simple test' was prescribed.

> Arrange not to see each other for a stated period, and see how you get along. If your feelings are deeply genuine, they will survive the separation and be stronger than ever at the end of it. If there is a mutual attraction only depending upon kisses and caresses—which can be so deceptive, and can so easily impersonate Love because

> they are so wrapped up with the real thing—separation, if long enough, will break the spell and destroy the glamour, restoring your clear-sightedness. But even those of you who are sure would do wisely to ask yourselves very honestly the following 'test' questions. Is your feeling deeper than the mere passion which is a part of sex attraction?...Is he—or she—the sort of person you can value as a *friend*? That is to say, have you anything in common? Do you appreciate the same sort of things, laugh at the same jokes, share the same sort of ideals, and like the same set of friends? Do you think the same on the biggest topics of life and love and religion?...Another point of immense importance is the attitude of both regarding children...Do you love each other enough to make ANY sacrifice—to share poverty, ill health, and misfortune gladly together? Would you rather have each other with any misfortune than live carefree apart?[3]

If the answer to this rather taxing list of questions was yes, the reader could, without further concern, be sure of love.

The growing stature of love within models of intimacy brought problems. These stemmed from the difficulty of judging the veracity of any particular romance. To what extent was it possible to know whether you were really in love? Emotional authenticity mattered because love and marriage were entangled as never before. If real love should lead to marriage, then a real marriage was founded upon love. In this context it was increasingly important to ensure that love was genuine. The difficulties of getting a divorce until the Reform Act of 1969 meant that marriages could last a very long time. 'I grew up in an age and in an extended family where a marriage really was for life,' confided a Mass-Observer born in 1930. 'To me that meant being very careful not to have to end up having to marry the wrong girl. When it did begin to look as if a "courtship" might lead to something I would ask myself do I want to spend the rest of my life with this girl?'[4]

The authentication of love demanded consideration of its relationship to both passion and pragmatism. 'Is love real?' one young

FIGURE 6 'What is this love which demands the surrender of your whole self to the tender keeping of another?'

woman asked the *Woman's Own* agony aunt, Leonora Eyles. 'I am engaged to a boy who is very passionate and, though he has never tried to do anything wrong, his life seems to be one long fight against temptation. Are all men like this? It makes me feel that love is nothing but desire.'[5] Eyles offered to write privately to the girl to provide the advice which presumably she—or the magazine editor—deemed inappropriate for public consumption. Another reader, enquiring as to the difference between 'real love' and 'infatuation', received a somewhat less helpful reply. 'The symptoms are almost identical—the difference is that infatuation doesn't last and love does', suggested Eyles's post-war successor, Mary Grant.[6] Adjudicating between love and pragmatism was no less problematic, as role-based and emotion-based models of matrimony overlapped. 'For some time I've wanted to settle down,' confessed a young man from Lincoln. 'Should I pick a girl who can cook, sew and be a good housewife, or must I wait until I meet the girl who will make my heart thump?'[7] The *Daily Mirror*'s Mary Brown optimistically suggested that he might meet someone who could do both. Amongst women too, pragmatism vied with emotion in the negotiation of future lives. The turn to emotional intimacy did not bring the wholesale rejection of practical considerations such as economic security, but the balance between these factors was decisively re-drawn. Along the way the tensions between love, passion, and the sensible choice became more sharply accentuated and publicly discussed.

* * *

As we have seen in the pages of the *Every Woman's Book of Love and Marriage*, mere mutual attraction could 'impersonate' love. The dangers of confusing the two were believed to be considerable but the distinction between them was actually quite difficult to draw. Writing in 1949, Marriage Guidance Council chair Herbert Gray advised that:

> It must be remembered that 'falling in love' may be the joyous beginning of life-long love and successful marriage, but equally it may not. It may be almost entirely a physical attraction, the result of some physiological or even 'electric' affinity. There may be behind it no real appreciation of each other's natures and temperaments. Such an attraction will indeed at times spring up between two people who are really profoundly unsuited. It should be remembered, therefore, that while physical attraction is necessary, it is not in itself an adequate basis for marriage. Marriage involves so much more than the interchange of caresses. It cannot be built merely on a succession of passionate interludes; a married couple are not always making love; there must be also solid friendship.[8]

For Gray, the relationship between desire and love was a potential minefield: physical attraction could be an expression of love between the profoundly unsuited. His marriage guidance colleague, David Mace, went further. '[T]he sex-stained tinsel which people are calling "love" today is by comparison so mean and tawdry that it's just about time we found a more appropriate name for it.'[9] Such commentators tried to draw a distinction between necessary physical attraction rooted in love and dangerous unbridled passion rooted in desire. As love and desire became increasingly entwined within everyday lives, this was a distinction that ceased to make sense.

The relationship between passion and love troubled other people too. A concerned young woman wrote to *Woman's Own* in 1945 that 'I heard a talk on the wireless lately saying that if you marry simply because you are violently in love, your marriage may fail. My boyfriend and I are passionately in love, and now I feel worried in case we are making a mistake.'[10] Another wrote of a boyfriend who felt they should part despite loving her 'intensely' because 'he always feels he must do wrong when he is with me'.[11] One reader even wondered whether it would be best to give up her boyfriend completely, because 'I find it hard to control my emotions when I am with him'.[12] Here we see people driven by emotions; desperately trying to keep their feelings under control—but failing. The intensity of the experience posed a profound challenge to models of emotional control. Former headmaster of Rugby School, Hugh Lyon, suggested that the strength of such emotion 'degraded the very name of love and [has] driven many in despair to approve the arranged marriage where violent emotion is out of account'.[13]

Within women's magazines the *control* of passion rather than its expression was held to authenticate love before marriage. Unbridled passion was a threat on a number of fronts: emotionally, socially, and sexually. 'My fiancé and I have been engaged for a year and cannot marry for two more years because of financial difficulties. The problem is that we are very passionate and my health is suffering—nerves, loss of appetite. Would lovemaking help or complicate things?' one reader asked agony aunt Mary Grant. Her reply was predictable: lovemaking would only make things worse.[14] The tensions between love and desire seemed particularly vexing during wartime. The popular problem pages were littered with fears concerning the consequences of 'losing one's head' and 'giving way' to a loved one. Intrepid travel writer and divorcee, Rosita

Forbes, advised *Woman's Own* readers on how to 'be a success!'—an important factor was the avoidance of pre-marital sex even in the face of overwhelming love:

> It's not romantic. It's not grand and unusual and altogether up to date. It's not even kind to the man. You can love him with all your heart and yet have sufficient courage to wait. Of course it's hard. You do agree, don't you, it's up to you to give him the best. So give him faith and honesty and courage. Give him love that is going to last, that he can look forward to, and that he can trust for the rest of his life.[15]

Nonetheless no wartime problem page seemed complete without a story of a woman who had apparently mistaken attraction for love. Often the objects of desire were foreign nationals who, according to Leonora Eyles, posed a particular threat. 'My dear, please try to realize that this was not love; it was sex attraction, novelty, and the man's foreign charm,' she impatiently advised one young woman.[16] In fact men also needed guidance in sifting true love from mere attraction. 'Marriage is one of the few things the war has not knocked sideways,' wrote *Woman's Own* in 1940. 'It flourishes in wartime, and men find it as difficult as women do—in these days of nightmare fact and dreamlike happiness—to be sure of themselves. "Am I really in love with her?" "Is it just infatuation?" "Is it because life's so damned uncertain?"'[17]

Of course the primary responsibility for controlling passion and thereby safeguarding love lay with the woman. 'I *like* Bill and he *is* a squadron leader and all that, but I simply can't face the coping I have to do every evening,' was how one member of the Women's Auxiliary Air Force put it.[18] When an 18-year-old, 'very much in love with a boy', asked Leonora Eyles how she should deal with his 'frightening' and 'disgusting' behaviour, she was firmly warned: 'If you do such things to keep another's love you will lose it and your self-respect with it.'[19] Another who asked whether it was possible to 'want to make love when you don't wish to marry' was urged to 'find someone with whom you are friendly first and passionate second'.[20] And yet the language of love was not a little confusing. In response to a girl who had suffered unwanted sexual advances Leonora Eyles explained that:

> I am afraid there are some boys like this. This love-making was to please himself; he couldn't be in love with you or you with him until you know one another. There isn't any harm in going out with boys like this as long as you can keep your head, but do remember that there are other men, quieter, not so obviously amusing, who respect a girl and wait until they know her and love her before they make love.[21]

As Peter Bailey recalls in his account of coming of age in 1950s Coventry, '"Make love" was [an] omnibus signifier, an elastic term implying everything from larking to fucking.'[22]

The tensions between love and sex were perceived to be more dangerous to women than to men in part because the sexual double standard attached gendered meanings to sexual experience. Without access to reliable contraception or legal abortion, the possibility of pregnancy was an even more pressing factor. The opprobrium heaped upon the unmarried mother throughout the period ensured that a fear of 'getting into trouble' or 'losing one's head' underlined intimate relations for women. Conflating love and desire could have life-changing consequences. 'Talk about "Romantic love"—this was a prime example of it. Unfortunately it was more a matter of lust than love, and we were all the time looking for places where we could make love,' recalled one woman who met her husband at a dance during the war.[23] She was pregnant when she married him three years later at the age of twenty.

If the representation of unmarried passion as potentially injurious to love was a constant across the mid-century, sex *within* marriage was increasingly celebrated. The erotic dimensions of love, and the romantic aspects of marriage, were central to the model of intimacy promoted by Marie Stopes in her seminal 1918 text

Married Love. In the years that followed a whole series of marriage manuals emerged which drew upon and sought to popularize the ideas of sex theorists such as Havelock Ellis and Freud. Clergyman Herbert Gray, for example, emphasized the sexual dimension of married love as early as 1923.[24] These texts encouraged the sexualization of marriage, emphasizing in particular the female potential for sexual pleasure within matrimony.[25] While historical studies by Elizabeth Roberts and Natalie Higgins have demonstrated how inconsistently the 'modern marriage' chimed with the specific experiences of working-class couples in the years before the Second World War, the idea that marriage should include love *and* sex was widely propagated.[26] The 'companionate' marriage, founded upon emotional and sexual satisfaction, and located within an increasingly privatized home, thus emerged as an ideal model in the inter-war years.[27]

Both love and sex played a role in everyday marriages well before the Second World War of course, and have long constituted a corner-stone of personal happiness within and outside both matrimony and heterosexuality across social classes. Many of the letters Stopes received following the publication of *Married Love* modelled loving relationships, based on mutual care and spousal devotion.[28] 'I love her so', Mr W. B. declared in explanation of his request for advice on how to prevent his wife falling pregnant again.[29] Mr T. D. similarly wanted a 'safe, simple and cheap method of Birth Control', stating that:

> I *myself* am a Labourer, have had to work for my living since I was Twelve, and eventually Married my present Wife when I was 19, she being a few months younger than me, we have been really happy together all this time, though being in very poor circumstances, financially. We have Eleven Children living (and 7 Children Dead) the youngest living now is 3 months old, I will be 43 next August, and my wife is 43⅔, we deeply Love each other, equally as much as when we were first married, but we have an extremely hard time with such a large Family, and insufficient means to maintain, but are

> quite satisfied to do our duty for them as far as is humanely possible for us to do, but we do not know how to avoid bringing any more Children into the world (that is of course, and live our Married Life as usual).[30]

Sex wasn't absent from this marriage but neither was it a source of unmitigated joy. Rather, in the absence of reliable contraception and where material resources were limited, sex was a strain on love. Unplanned children brought physical and financial costs that might destabilize a happy marriage. In this context—as historians Szreter and Fisher have demonstrated—the 'caring' aspects of marital love could be powerfully expressed through sexual abstinence and moderation.[31]

In the early years of the twentieth century sex could pose a threat to love during, as well as before, a marriage. By the middle of the century, married love and sexual pleasure were profoundly linked. Female sexual pleasure was placed centre stage and passion was transformed from potential danger to indicator of emotional authenticity. The absence of physical attraction increasingly seemed to suggest the absence of real love, even before marriage. At the beginning and at the end of the twentieth century sex and love constituted separate, though often interlocking, spheres. The mid-century achievement was to entwine them.

If love and sex were increasingly interwoven within mid-century marriage, the link between sex and reproduction was unravelling rapidly. Although the Catholic Church remained hostile to artificial contraception, the Church of England accepted the principle of family limitation—according to 'Christian principles'—as early as 1930. Within this context it was love, rather than procreation, which legitimized sexual appetites. 'The sexual act is humiliating unless it is accompanied by love', a headmaster told Mass-Observation's 'Little Kinsey' investigators.[32] D. H. Lawrence's *Lady Chatterley's Lover* was, in part, defended against the charge of obscenity on the grounds of love. As a supporter of the novel's publisher, Penguin, informed *The Times* in 1960: 'Lawrence wrote supremely well about sexual intercourse as an act of love: it would be supremely irreverent to silence him.'[33] In contrast, sex without love was deemed dangerous and even potentially violent. In her 1955 trial for murder, Ruth Ellis was explicitly asked whether she was in love with the man she shot dead. Her reply of 'not really' damned her as a woman willing to enjoy sex without love.[34] Within marriage a mutually satisfying sexual relationship became *the* signifier of love. A National Marriage Guidance Council manual published in 1953 opened with the rather menacing statement that 'a normal woman should enjoy sexual intercourse with her husband'.[35] And yet once sex and love were so firmly tied together *within* mid-century marriage they proved difficult to contain there. A degree of non-penetrative sexual activity was increasingly accepted as part of everyday courtship. Reverend Gray of the National Marriage Guidance Council was forced to admit that some unmarried couples might ask, 'why all this talk of going so far and no further? Why should we not have complete sex intercourse, if we know that we love each other, and are going to get married as soon as we can? We hate the idea of sexual relations without love, but we have all the love that is needed to make them beautiful and happy.'[36] For Gray this question could only be answered with reference to the exchange value of virginity and the unpredictability of men who 'change their minds—even men who have seemed to be very much in love. Then the woman finds that she has given away something that she really wants to keep for her future husband.'[37]

The difficulties of negotiating the physical dimensions of love were pronounced. And yet love also had the capacity to drive sexual change. It was a powerful lever in the negotiation of degrees of intimacy between individuals and was increasingly used to legitimate pre- and extra-marital sex. Although feminist thinkers such as Simone De Beauvoir and Shulamith Firestone have rightly emphasized romantic love's capacity to enslave women, it was also a sphere in which women could exercise agency.[38] While popular culture provided a plethora of usable romantic scripts—'film crooners, advertisements and "romantic novels" keep on telling girls that passion and rapture lie around the corner'—and while parents and experts offered their own advice, ultimately the state of being in love was one which only the individual him- or herself could properly authenticate.[39] As the National Marriage Guidance Council acknowledged in a 1964 booklet: 'If a boy and girl know each other well and feel they really are in love with each other, it is only natural that the day may come when they ask, how far should we go?'[40] In his survey of *The Sexual Behaviour of Young People* published a year later, Michael Schofield found a 'strong association between those who have been in love and the level of sexual activity'.[41] The teenage girls he interviewed were nearly twice as likely as the boys to say they were in love.

Pre-marital experimentation was discouraged by the everyday experts until at least the end of the 1960s. Within the pages of *Woman's Own* shared hobbies were suggested as a way of taking one's mind off lovemaking. But the letters published over time demonstrate a clear shift away from a sense of passion as dangerous to a suggestion that it could be an expression of love *before* marriage as well as within it. This is keenly evident in the shifting language of intimacy. 'My boyfriend and I have often made love and have no regrets' began one letter from a 17-year-old to Mary Grant in 1965, 'Why are we condemned for doing this when we are only expressing our love for each other?'[42] Here sexual intercourse is not an end in itself. Rather it actually expresses something else—as if it were words or a gift. It acts as the signifier of authentic love. Although Grant rallied her arguments in defence of sexual control, continuing to suggest that unmarried love could be authenticated only through the denial of sex, the tide was clearly turning. Whilst Grant continued to suggest that 'Almost every woman wants security and romance. The two rarely mix, for the glamorous lover cannot be the steady husband', by the late 1960s passion was neither a danger to love, nor an impostor. Rather it was constructed as an integral part of everyday intimacy as both love and sex escaped the bounds of matrimony.

* * *

The central character in Powell and Pressburger's 1945 film *'I Know Where I'm Going!'* is a young woman with expensive tastes and a determination to marry well. Beautifully played by the Oscar-winning actress Wendy Hiller, Joan Webster's passage towards marrying the wealthy Laird of a remote Scottish island is fatally compromised when she falls in love with naval officer Torquil MacNeil. In this way the film provides a classic representation of the battle between love and pragmatism: one in which love, unsurprisingly, triumphs. *'I Know Where I'm Going!'* is also a film about authenticity. 'Stop acting', Wendy's bank manager father demands of her early in the film. Ultimately it transpires that the incumbent Laird has merely leased the title from its rightful owner. That owner—the real Laird of Kiloran—conveniently turns out to be MacNeil.

Within mid-century film, pragmatic considerations rarely derailed love, although it helped if the apparently penniless suitor turned out to be rather rich. The 1953 Monroe, Grable, and Bacall vehicle *How to Marry a Millionaire* is the most celebrated example of this happy outcome: the three female characters literally fall off their seats when the truth about Tom Brookman is revealed. In contrast—as historian Christine Grandy has shown—women screen characters generally traded job, status, and wealth for love: only in so doing could they reveal their true self.[43] Personal success was, for a woman, an active impediment to love. While Greta Garbo's *Queen Christina* (1933) ultimately gives it all up for love (even when her lover is already dead), the princess played by Audrey Hepburn in the 1953 film *Roman Holiday* cannot do this and therefore sacrifices her love affair.[44]

Away from the silver screen the dilemmas of love were no less pressing. The relationship between love and pragmatism was just

FIGURE 7 The 1945 film, '*I Know Where I'm Going!*', placed the battle between love and pragmatism centre stage.

as complicated as that between love and passion. 'Gold-diggers' were castigated for the calculation they brought to affairs of the heart but good judgement and prudence had a role to play in everyday relationships too. As we have already seen, both men and women looked for spouses able to fulfil clearly gendered roles—notably so in the years before the Second World War. For men this entailed finding a good homemaker. For women this meant a husband capable of providing reliable financial support and a home within which to bring up a family.

With this in mind, it is clear that some women explicitly rejected romance in favour of domestic security. The limited earning capacity of married working-class women in particular, ensured that pragmatic considerations could not be ignored when making life choices. As historian Judy Giles explains: 'in the 1920s and 1930s the acceptable response to the longing expressed in romantic fiction was to read these as "silly", "perverted", and "immature", marginal and potentially threatening to the "real" experiences of a woman's life which consisted of prudential marriage and the provision of a comfortable, hygienic home in which to sustain a male breadwinner and rear healthy children.'[45] The *Woman's Own* problem page regularly received letters from readers wondering whether or not to marry men they did not actually love—they were never entirely discouraged. Some actively disliked men but nonetheless wished to marry one. 'I am very anxious to get married some day and have a husband and children, but I don't really like men at all', worried a magazine reader.[46] The desire for home could persist in the face of terrible romantic misfortune. A 34-year-old explained how she had twice been let down by love. 'The first one turned out to be married, and I only discovered it a month before our wedding. The next one took all my savings to put in the bank towards a home and then cleared out. Another man has now asked me to be engaged to him, but I feel frightened. I do so long to be married, as I hate not having a home of my own.'[47] At a time when married life remained their primary destination, young women endeavoured to make the best possible life choices within a limited range of options.[48] Romantic love was not always seen to be the most sensible basis upon which to build the future. Those who did not marry could find themselves in a precarious economic position.

In the mid-1930s at least one insurance company—Britannic Insurance—sold a policy which offered protection 'in case you don't marry'.[49]

Wartime conditions provided a distinctive context for the weighing up of pragmatism and emotion in the making of relationships. The everyday experts were keenly attuned to potential wartime pitfalls. Leonora Eyles urged her readers to resist the temptations of marrying without love:

> In war-time, even more than in peace-time, a man needs a wife who loves him and will sacrifice herself for him; whether he is in one of the forces or working hard at home. A girl who has married him so that she can be called Mrs. won't give him the happiness he needs and deserves, and won't be happy herself. May I beg of you to wait until you meet the man you really love, and even if you never do, being an old maid is not such a terrible thing.[50]

Identifying a good match was in any case problematic when future security was under daily assault. There were, however, short-term practicalities which might be considered ahead of romance. First, the existence of the serviceman's wife's allowance might be a pragmatic motivation to marry in wartime. Second, unmarried women—conceptualized as mobile labour—might marry in order to avoid being moved into war work. 'Marriage is treated as a loophole to conscription and girls are willing to risk the prospects of an unhappy marriage to a job in the services or munitions. On the whole it can be assumed that marriage is a means to an end in wartime but not the means originally intended for it,' suggested one cynic.[51] Another observed that, 'even in my small circle of friends and acquaintances, there have been quite a few war weddings. One of these at least has been to secure the married soldier's allowance with which to furnish a home, for the wife has continued working without an interval. In other cases I am told the marriage has taken place to immobilise the wife.'[52] In both views it is practical home front concerns which are perceived to be driving decisions about commitment. In wartime as in peacetime, then, pragmatism could triumph over love in the making of relationships. This did not always ensure future happiness, as Slater and Woodside discovered.

> Mrs G., twenty-six, looking back now, remembers that even after she was engaged she had her doubts. He was moody, sulked, was terribly jealous, never liked her to have friends. She thinks, 'I may never have loved him?' However, she hoped he would improve. To be frank, it was marriage instead of the services; she didn't want to be conscripted. Their marriage has been a disappointment.[53]

In the 1950s and 1960s—against a backdrop of affluence and welfare state security—the balance between love and pragmatism shifted. Love became the primary basis for lifelong partnership. 'Slightly more than three-quarters of the total English population and nearly 90 per cent of the married, consider they have been "really in love"', anthropologist Geoffrey Gorer recorded, continuing 'the meaning of this phrase is far from precise...but whatever the understanding the English give to it, it does represent an important emotional event in the lives of the greater part of the community.'[54] This is not to say that pragmatic considerations vanished completely. Affluence was a patchy experience and women's characterization as economic dependants continued into the welfare state era. According to Gorer, 'the hope for future falling in love increases steadily with income...the poorer one is, the less hope one has of a future "falling in love".'[55] Sociologist Ferdynand Zweig claimed that 'Young girls expect or hope that they will be able to cross the borderline of their class by marriage', and that 'Marriage, not work or study, is the main door of escape from class membership.'[56] Walt Disney's animated version of the Cinderella story appeared, in 1950, to breathe new life into the fantasy of marrying well, while the creative output of the Angry Young Men showcased male matrimonial pragmatism alongside their social mobility.

And yet the emphasis had shifted. While too little attention to practicalities might previously have explained relationship failure, too little attention to love was now more likely to be the causal factor. Cinderella's marriage to a prince was as much aided by her aristocratic birth as it was by a fairy godmother in league with a number of unusually helpful animals, but she was also very much in love. In John Braine's *Room at the Top* Joe Lampton's determination to marry his way out of the working-class, spurning the woman he really loves along the way, ends in tragedy.[57] Privileging pragmatism over love was increasingly represented as a recipe for unhappiness and where stories of 'marrying up' were showcased, their romantic underpinnings were emphasized. In 1967, for example, 19-year-old Shirley Williams married 25 year-old Malcolm McDonald. According to the *Daily Mail*, 'HE was a director in his father's electronics firm at Old Hill Staffordshire. SHE was in the typing pool.'[58] Her father drove a lorry for the firm and explained how the romance had flourished. 'Malcolm just became one of our family. He turned up for tea every Sunday—his car caused a bit of a stir in our street. I was not surprised when he asked me if he could marry Shirley. They were in love and that was that.'

Shirley and Malcolm were the exception, rather than the rule. Whether through love or design, the likelihood of achieving actual social mobility through marriage was limited. Both pragmatism and feeling operated within boundaries. Most people continued to marry partners from a broadly similar social background to themselves. An analysis of the Population Investigation Committee Marriage Survey of 1959–60 suggested that in 48 per cent of mid-century marriages both partners were from manual occupational family backgrounds.[59] In 21 per cent both were from non-manual backgrounds. Within 17 per cent of marriages the sons of non-manual workers had married the daughters of manual workers, whilst in 14 per cent the daughters of non-manual workers had married the sons of manual workers. In her research on courtship in Swansea conducted during 1968–9, Diana Leonard found that most of her interviewees married someone of similar socio-economic status to themselves.[60] Moya Woodside concluded that

'Chances of unselective mating, as depicted in the "shop girl-married-boss" wish dreams of the cinema are negligible.'[61]

The relationship between love and pragmatism was not, of course, something of concern to individual men and women alone. Across the mid-century families also played a role in the material and emotional aspirations they had for their younger members—and might attempt to stymie a love match in favour of one 'with prospects'. In this way the independence of youth could come into conflict with various forms of family authority when it came to romantic choice. Parents shaped the romantic opportunities available to their children through the educational and social choices they made on their behalf. Some went further. 'My mother, being a devout Christian and churchgoer, fearing that I might get into the wrong company watched like a hawk, from a distance and hoped that I would restrict my choice to those "nice" girls who she knew from the church,' recalled one young man.[62] A *Woman's Own* reader explained how a love match was imperilled by her father's business concerns. 'I am a farmer's daughter and four neighbouring farmers have asked me to marry them. I like them all, but love one. Father is afraid it will go against him in business if I marry any of them, because, being so far away from towns, we depend on neighbours for almost everything.'[63]

Whilst this father's motivation was apparently rooted in self-preservation rather than a desire for enrichment, more aggressively self-interested meddling in the romantic affairs of children was not unheard of. Stanley Houghton's play *Hindle Wakes*, first performed in 1912, but filmed in 1927, 1931, and 1952, provides a compelling representation of the gold-digging mother keen for her daughter to marry into money. Lancashire mill-girl Fanny Hawthorne spends an illicit weekend with factory owner's son Alan Jeffcoate. He is already engaged; she works at his father's factory. When their behaviour is discovered both sets of parents insist that they marry. Her mother, in particular, sees an opportunity for financial gain. In a powerful scene Jenny refuses Alan's offer of marriage saying,

'Love you? Good heavens of course not. Why on earth should I love you. You were just an amusement, a lark!' Her mother is, unsurprisingly, furious.

* * *

Love and pragmatism were not always opposing forces within intimate lives, just as love and passion were not always at war. 'I am in love with two boys and I can't decide which of them I want to marry,' wrote a young woman to *Woman's Own* in 1934. 'My parents have just died and I need a home badly, as I am unhappy alone. One of the boys is very well off and can give me everything I want. The other is quite poor and has no prospects. Do help me to choose between them!'[64] In the absence of a definite emotional preference the choice was probably not that difficult. Anyway, it was not always easy to disengage love from pragmatism: the latter could actively inform the former. Writing on the eve of war, one woman offered a clear indication of the malleability of 'love' in relation to future prospects:

> I went to a party and was introduced to two men. Both seemed equally presentable to me at first until I heard that one was a printer and the other a medical student in his last year. I liked them both to begin with but am now in love with the student. At first it was because I liked the idea of being a doctor's wife better than a printer's—though the latter will probably have a better income. The doctor seemed to belong to a higher 'class' than the printer, though socially they move in the same circle. This I think was the fact that made me think more about the student, though now of course he genuinely means a great deal more to me than the printer.[65]

Within this story, status triumphs over income. An emotional investment was made only after a pragmatic decision had been arrived at. In this respect the head may have ruled the heart, but the heart was not entirely absent. Cases such as these suggest that the way in which love was subjectively 'felt' was rooted in material and cultural, as well as emotional, considerations, a point that I will develop in Chapter Three. Whilst pragmatism did indeed loom large in spousal selection this was not necessarily a counterpoint to romantic love. Pragmatism could itself inform narratives of 'falling in love', just as sexual desire could be a mark of emotional authenticity.

Mid-century love was rich and multifaceted, infused with complex hopes and troublesome desires. Physical, material, and emotional needs often collided, and sometimes coexisted, as the status of love in everyday lives grew. A pattern of historical change is nonetheless clear. As love and passion became increasingly more entwined, love and pragmatism were pulled apart. By the end of our period love alone was widely expected to determine the decision to commit for life. Thus love acquired significant power over how ordinary people ordered their lives: the problem was that the veracity of love remained so difficult to test.

3
Suitability

In September 1943 Mass-Observation's volunteer panellists received their usual monthly directive. The questions posed this time round, penned at the height of wartime mobilization, ranged across politics, inter-allied cooperation, general war strategy, and the BBC. There were also questions about marriage. 'What do you consider the foundations of a successful marriage? Discuss in detail factors that appear essential to you.'[1] A 36-year-old married Royal Air Force clerk addressed the topic with enthusiasm:

> I should say that the first essential is similarity of outlook. I think that husband and wife must hold the same fundamental views—their ideas must agree on the having and upbringing of children, on health and social matters, and on the way the world is governed. I think that this must be realised before marriage, otherwise, when the presumed novelty of sexual intercourse has worn off, it will only be the fact that the man has an unpaid housekeeper and that the woman is usually provided with a home, that will keep them together.[2]

Similarity of outlook was not the only factor that this man considered essential to marital success. Age was also important with less than five years' difference between husband and wife apparently ideal. If the age difference had to be wider it was best that the older spouse be the man, 'since I think that both physically and mentally, men age less rapidly than women'. Education and, by implication, social class were also key considerations:

> Husband and wife should come roughly from the same level. I don't mean that a Council schoolboy shouldn't marry a girl with a High School education, but a boy with a Public School education would probably not make a 'do' of it with a wife brought up in working class conditions. They would never understand each other's point of view, and one would always be the senior partner. I think that in a successful marriage the personalities should be equal.

It is impossible to approach mid-century emotional worlds as if they were divorced from social context and social distinction. Matrimonial success—according to our RAF clerk—was rooted in similarity of background and shared cultural capital. We have already seen that pragmatic, materialist concerns could vie with love in the making of relationships. In this chapter I map the parameters within which romantic taste and spousal suitability operated. These parameters were emotional as well as spatial, personal as well as societal. While models of 'true love' infer that an emotional attachment can transcend all forms of difference, we will see that in mid-century England a range of factors influenced the opportunity, and inclination, to fall in love. Age, religious affiliation, nationality and ethnicity all had a part to play. Above all social class operated as a mediator of partner selection, influencing notions of attractiveness and suitability. These elements point to the limits of individual agency and suggest that personal preference was socially located. Mid-century love was not blind. It was not even deaf. Instead it was carefully attuned to social differences—at times simply reflecting them and at others actively rejecting them but rarely ignoring them.

* * *

Originally published in 1935, *Every Woman's Luck Book* offered numerous strategies for securing good luck and good fortune. Training in the art of tea, card and palm reading was offered, the mysteries of lucky stones were explained, and basic dream analysis was performed. Mechanisms for delivering romantic good fortune—and reading authenticity—were emphasized. 'It is unlucky to kiss on a staircase, or to look into a mirror together,' readers were told. 'A love-letter should never be written in red ink, or there will be a quarrel. An engagement is luckiest if announced on a Saturday.'[3] The book provided a range of tips on how to choose a good husband including the analysis of features and deportment. Women were instructed in the art of head, hair, eyebrow, eye, nose, mouth, chin, ear, neck, and hand analysis. They were also taught how a man's walk and style of sitting could betray his character. 'Best of all is the man who can sit quietly, easily and comfortably,' the manual advised. 'There is nothing extreme about him; he is the all-round good sort who will make a splendid life partner.'[4]

For those who saw limitations in the *Woman's Luck Book* approach, there was no shortage of alternative advice. From Valentino to Elvis, popular culture offered ever-changing models of desirable masculinity. Gary Cooper was the nation's most popular male film star in 1937; by 1946/7 it was James Mason.[5] Margaret Lockwood led the way amongst women that year. The emergence of the 'pin-up' image offered new models of femininity. Writing in 1957, Richard Hoggart believed such posters to be 'the most striking visual feature of mid-twentieth-century mass-art', adding rather darkly that 'we are a democracy whose working-people are exchanging their birthright for a mass of pin-ups'.[6] The rights and wrongs of romantic taste were dissected by everyday experts and ordinary people alike. Advice filled the pages of magazines and the shelves of local libraries, for example. Rennie Macandrew, writing before the war, urged couples to privilege affinity of character, to 'think twice' before getting involved with an only child, to avoid the 'emotional adolescent' and to 'view with suspicion the man who is a woman-hater and the woman who is a man-hater'.[7] A good husband would be 'a manly fellow', a good wife should not be 'over clever'. The context of war introduced different models of desirability.

In a report sent to Mass-Observation in 1942, a member of the Women's Auxiliary Air Force claimed that 'to get a man is not sufficient. It's easy to get a man: in fact it's difficult not to. Competitive factors in the Great Man-Chase are under the following headings: quality; quantity; intensity. The decisive qualities are rank/wings; looks; money; youth in that order.'[8] She continued, 'Rank is unbelievably important. There's a Wing Commander here whose only redeeming feature is that he's young. He isn't good looking, he's owned to be a great bore; and he's extremely "fast" (which is not a recommendation...). Yet he could go out with any woman on the station he cared to ask: no-one would refuse. And all this rests purely on his 3 rings and wings.'[9] After the war the state proffered advice about suitability: directly through committee reports and legislation and indirectly through its financial support for the National Marriage Guidance Council. Writing at the height of postwar anxiety about the viability of family life, the Council chair, Herbert Gray, advised that mutual good health was essential for marital success.[10] He also had views on age, race, and religion. In each case significant differences were seen as an impediment to successful partnership.

A slight disparity in age—with the husband a little older than the wife—was generally encouraged. Even a significantly older husband was not too problematic. Leonora Eyles advised a 17 year-old woman that a 9-year age gap was fine, 'if you are really friendly and happy together. I should marry him, if you care for him enough and like the company of people older than yourself.'[11] This gendered take on matrimonial age difference reflected a long-established notion of the husband as sexual educator and more experienced guardian, and is evident in the requirements of both spinsters and bachelors advertising in the matrimonial press. After the war this age disparity also accommodated the disruption which national service caused to the male life cycle. Once the last national servicemen were discharged in 1963, the age difference between husbands and wives narrowed.[12]

The older wife, however, was more of a problem. Leonora Eyles bluntly informed a twice married 46-year-old that the 22-year-old man she was courting was simply infatuated: 'when he grows out of it you will both be miserable.'[13] According to Gray:

FIGURE 8 Age differences—actual or imagined—were not always so easily resolved. Nonetheless an older husband was generally believed to be preferable to an older wife.

> For a woman to be a year or two older than the man may not matter at all, but if she is a good deal older it matters considerably. When the difference amounts to seven, eight or ten years serious difficulties are likely to arise. The trouble will not develop at first; when the man is in the twenties and the girl still in the early thirties, both feel that they are still in the same stage of life. They are both full of vigour and can keep step with each other. But fifteen or twenty years later this is no longer the case. The man is still young and vigorous, but the woman is becoming elderly, her pace is slowing down, and she is experiencing those changes that mark the end of the reproductive period.[14]

Gray's grim prognosis was that the older wife risked losing her husband to a younger women whose 'gaiety and quickness' he would find difficult to resist. While happiness for such couples was not definitively ruled out—after all 'a man need not be the victim of his passions'—age complications such as these were, apparently, much better simply avoided. In fact they increasingly were. As historian Michael Anderson has shown, a modern life cycle emerged after 1939 'which had a number of clearly demarcated stages through which most of the population passed within a relatively narrow band of ages'.[15] The apparent homogeneity of this pattern of living left those who did not conform increasingly exposed.[16]

If age difference was potentially problematic then so too was religious and ethnic difference. Advertisers in the matrimonial press occasionally ruled out whole groups of potential suitors on principle: Catholicism and Judaism were the most often cited grounds for exclusion. A 34-year-old nurse wished to marry a 'bachelor, tall and clean shaven (not a Jew) aged 34–50' in 1922.[17] In 1943 a 38-year-old bachelor clerk apparently interested in general affairs wished to meet a reasonably intelligent, broadminded, affectionate home-lover. He did not object to a childless widow but specified 'not R. C. or Jewess'.[18] It was more common for advertisers in such publications to specify a definite requirement however. For example, a 'spinster, aged 38, good-looking and good figure', desired an introduction to a 'homely man, not too stout, well educated, and of sober habits. Must be Church of England and possess about £350 per annum'.[19] After the war, explicit references to religion were rare. Where they did exist, 'not R. C.' predominated. In 1955, for example, a Kent-based teacher who had 'no objection to Continental lady if language not a problem', added, 'Not divorcee or R. C'.[20]

For the Reverend Herbert Gray the most problematic of religiously mixed marriages were indeed those that involved the established church and Roman Catholicism. The difficulties were apparently 'almost insuperable'.[21] Roman Catholic rules on interfaith marriage were strict. Such marriages had to be celebrated in a Catholic Church by a Catholic priest; both parties had to promise to raise their children as Catholics and conversion of the non-Catholic partner was recommended. Moreover, church teaching on artificial contraception, reaffirmed in Paul VI's 1968 encyclical *Humanae Vitae*, posed an additional difficulty in an age when family limitation was widely supported in Britain. In their 1951 study, *English Life and Leisure*, Rowntree and Lavers outlined the case story of Miss M., 'an attractive Irish girl of strikingly good looks' who was 'far from happy because of a love affair'.[22] Having decided to marry her Methodist sailor boyfriend, the mother of this practising Catholic enlisted the help of a priest to prevent the union:

> The priest stopped her in the street one day when she was walking with some friends and caused her great embarrassment by calling her over and walking home with her. He cross-examined her about her life in London and her observance of the Catholic faith, and warned her that she would burn in Everlasting Hell if she gave up the Roman faith to marry a Methodist.
>
> As she refused to promise to give up the idea of marriage, the Priest told her various sad stories of the disastrous ending of mixed marriages.
>
> By this time the sailor had gone back to his ship but he and Miss M. exchanged daily letters. Some ten months later the sailor stopped writing and, in reply to an enquiry from Miss M., revealed that her

> mother had written to him asking him to give her up as if he did not do so it would estrange her from her family and make a great many people unhappy.

According to Rowntree and Lavers' account, the result was that she took to drink, tried to commit suicide and ultimately gave up both church and her family.

The prejudice against inter-faith relationships worked both ways. A Mass-Observer born in 1941 admitted that she felt pressured to end a relationship with a Catholic because of parental disapproval.[23] Even if outside pressure was not forthcoming individual reservations could be powerful. 'She was a Roman Catholic which disturbed me though I agreed if we had children they would be brought up as RC', wrote another man of the woman he was engaged to in the 1950s:

> In the end my worries got the better of me and I sent her a letter laying out my concerns, in reply and to my surprise she returned her engagement ring and the letter which had, obviously, from her reply, deeply offended her. It was a blow, I wanted to marry her and expected to but religion as it so often can messed that life up and it was not to be. I still regret sending that letter, it was stupid of me...On the rebound I met my wife, and for her it was the same, you had wanted to marry, you meet someone and in haste you do so. We'd known each other for several years to say hello to and pass the time of day and once I'd asked her out but she'd declined...We walked out with each other in September and married the following January.[24]

For this man the complexities of religious difference inverted the post-war narrative that emotional authenticity could be evidenced through the speed of a courtship. Having unwittingly sabotaged a relationship based upon long standing knowledge and understanding, marriage on the rebound necessitated lifelong pragmatism rather than romance. It also brought a lifetime of regret.

In fact, as historian of religion Callum Brown has shown, the number of mixed faith marriages grew throughout the 1950s and

1960s, 'perhaps a quarter of all Catholic weddings in 1955 and a third by 1960'.[25] When pollsters inquired about attitudes towards marriages between Catholics and Protestants in 1968, 61 per cent approved and 24 per cent disapproved.[26] By 1973 the figures were 71 per cent and 15 per cent.[27] Comparable figures for marriages between Jews and non-Jews were 50 per cent approval and 23 per cent disapproval in 1968 and 61 per cent approval and 16 per cent disapproval in 1973. Attitudes were moderated by class and age. In her study of girls *Rising Twenty* Pearl Jephcott found that amongst the working-class girls she surveyed differences of religious background were of little consequence, 'almost on a par with such another handicap as that the boy cannot dance'.[28]

Social attitudes towards nationality and intimacy were rather more deeply entrenched. Recalling her two years at Clarks commercial college in the early 1930s one Mass-Observer wrote that there were 'lots of foreigners there and about the only objection my parents had to my going out with boys was *no foreigners*, a shame because they were so charming'.[29] Foreigners of all stripes were treated with suspicion within the pages of women's magazines even as cross-cultural relationships became a popular trope within middle-brow fiction and film.[30] A young school teacher 'wildly in love' with a Sicilian she had met on holiday was firmly advised to drop the relationship.[31] 'This is a dream of romance from which I urge you to wake up,' Helen Worth of the *Modern Marriage* Heart-to-Heart Bureau intoned. Perhaps surprisingly Worth did not object because it was a transient holiday romance. Instead she drew attention to national difference. 'Sicilians have very old-fashioned ideas and ways of living; you would be under the thumb of your mother-in-law, never allowed out without escort by some older woman, have to cope with different ideas and modes of living, and be bored to death doing nothing all day.' Just in case her correspondent failed to get the message she hammered it home. 'You cannot imagine what your loneliness would be, nor can you imagine how differently foreigners regard their marriage bonds.'

During wartime it was the unfamiliarity, as much as the glamour, of foreign soldiers that was believed to account for their attractiveness to British women. Agony aunts consistently warned their readers of the threat posed by charming foreigners. On requesting advice about how to choose between a Pole and a Frenchman both of whom could be the father of her child, one young woman was told: 'your feeling for neither of them is love, but something much less sure and valuable. Your head was turned by their unfamiliar accent and charm, that's all.'[32] Another woman was assured that she was merely fascinated by an allied soldier's 'difference'.[33] Historian Marilyn Lake points to the particular appeal posed by uniformed Americans, already coded 'as lovers, as sexual and as objects to be looked at' by Hollywood film.[34] To add to the confusion, actual American film stars such as James Stewart spent time stationed in Britain during the war.[35] The fact that the Americans were better paid than other allied troops may have further contributed to their desirability.[36] Nonetheless, British women were warned off: they were repeatedly reminded that they would lose their nationality if they married a foreigner. Until 1948 this was in fact the case although it failed to put a brake on such unions.[37] By the end of the war there had been four thousand Polish–British marriages, for example.[38] Polish pilot Zdzislaw Langhamer married Marie Black in 1941 after they had spent just four leaves together. An estimated forty thousand British women became GI brides by the war's end, benefiting from the comparatively generous marriage allowance that US troops received.[39] Most moved to the United States, transported in special war bride shipments.[40] Canadians proved particularly matrimonially attractive to British women. Although there were significantly fewer of them stationed in wartime Britain, they contracted even more marriages than the Americans. Around forty-five thousand Canadian servicemen married whilst serving in Britain.[41]

* * *

Pearl Harry met her future husband Jeff McKay in 1941 whilst living in Jamaica. Nine months later he departed for England as one of many volunteer servicemen from the Caribbean. Within two years she too had made the move and joined the Women's Auxiliary Air Force. Like many wartime couples they corresponded daily but did not meet again until the week of their wedding in 1945. Writing from the vantage point of 1970—twenty-five years after the war had ended—she recalled that the army was initially reluctant to accommodate their marriage plans. 'In 1945 many troops were coming back to England on all sorts of grounds. The army may have thought he was going to marry a white girl. Anyway, his posting was refused. When it was realised I was coloured, my boyfriend was posted to England, arriving on VE Day.'[42] The couple stayed in Britain for the rest of their married life.

As the initial army response to Jeff McKay's posting request suggests, 'interracial' intimacy was strongly discouraged during the Second World War. But hostility to what has historically been termed 'miscegenation' spanned the years 1920 to 1970. Cultural theorist Stuart Hall puts it particularly well in his assessment of post-war imagery:

> It is as if in the middle of the vast number of ways of representing the Black presence, in words and images, one topic, virtually unspoken, lay at the centre of the discourse, driving those who contemplated it crazy, like a shadow across the collective unconscious. In the mirror of the imagery—screaming to be spoken: the trauma of black and white people, together, making love, finding their sexuality with each other and having children as the living proof that, against God and Nature, *It Worked.*[43]

In the aftermath of the First World War, interracial relationships had, according to cultural historian Lucy Bland, been conceptualized as problematic in three key ways. They were held to be a cause of racial violence; they were assumed to be grounded in sexual immorality of some sort; they produced offspring which were believed to be genetically inferior.[44] Social historian Tony Kushner's study of the racial attitudes of wartime Mass-Observers shows that interracial mixing was opposed, particularly on the grounds of possible offspring, even by those with otherwise egalitarian views on race.[45] 'However strong and sincere our aspirations after international fellowship may be, and however much we may feel that Christians ought to surmount race prejudice, there are certain facts which ought to be weighed carefully before the decision is taken to marry a member of another race,' wrote Herbert Gray in 1949.[46] These 'facts' included his belief that the children of such unions 'occupy a precarious and difficult position in any society, and many of them in their hearts must reproach their parents for having brought them into the world to face life on such difficult terms'. Apparently without irony he added that 'It is always the interests of the children that are the supreme consideration.'[47] Not surprisingly beliefs such as these framed everyday experience of actual intimacy.

During wartime, the presence of military personnel and volunteer workers from the Caribbean Crown Colonies, Dominions, and Allied powers extended the field of potential romantic encounters for British women. But where those personnel were black, parental and societal disapproval could be vocal. Those who developed relationships with black American GIs, were put under particular pressure to give them up.[48] Such women were likely to be 'branded as gender outlaws and disparaged as sociopaths'.[49] In the south-western parish of Worle, the vicar's wife presented parishioners with a six-point code for dealing with black soldiers. Advice included moving away from them in the cinema, crossing the street to avoid them, leaving a shop if they entered, and certainly never entertaining a romantic liaison.[50] Her sense of shared standards was presumably punctured by the reported fury of her audience. 'I was disgusted, and so were most of the women there', one woman told the *Sunday Pictorial*. 'We have no intention of agreeing to her decree.' Responding to a wartime letter regarding friendship with a black soldier Leonora Eyles was clear that such liaisons should not be encouraged. 'Although coloured people are just as good as white ones', she advised, 'you must see that marriage between you would stand little chance of happiness for either of you. The truth is that a white woman who marries a coloured man is more or less an outcast; his race does not like her, and her own people don't like him; friends are difficult to find, and if they have children they are often unhappy. I think you would be very wise to end the friendship.'[51] In answer to another letter asking whether it was permissible to be friends with black US soldiers she replied that 'it would be not be fair either to them or to you to form such a close friendship as might lead to romance. It is by no means a question of their being "inferior" but *different*, and, certainly to-day, only in the very rarest cases do such marriages succeed.'[52] It is important to note that Eyles's advice did not go uncontested: 'Why aren't they as good as anyone else? And why say that they ought not to marry white girls?' one critic demanded.[53]

Patterns of post-war immigration provided another testing ground for the much vaunted blindness of love. In 1949 *The Report of the Royal Commission on Population* was published. Compiled at a time when the main source of immigration was the European Volunteer Worker scheme, it was published after the 1948 British Nationality Act which recognized the right of all Commonwealth citizens to settle in Britain. The Report mused on the problems that such immigration might bring. Its eugenicist underpinning was striking. 'Immigration on a large scale into a fully established society like ours could only be welcomed without reserve if the immigrants were of good human stock and were not prevented by their religion or race from intermarrying with the host population and becoming merged in it.'[54] Five years later when Trevor Philpott posed the question 'Would you let your daughter marry a Negro?' in *Picture Post*, he demonstrated that romantic encounters carried a symbolic, and very public, significance beyond the actual individuals involved.[55] Post-war films such as *Sapphire* (1959) and *Flame in the Street* (1961) portrayed the hostility such relationships could encounter whilst simultaneously reinforcing racial stereotypes. *Flame* explored reactions to the relationship between a white woman, played by Sylvia Syms, and a black man, played by Johnny Sekka. The relationship was played out against a backdrop of Notting Hill-style violence and a clear sense that immigration brought trouble.[56] *Sapphire*, directed by Basil Dearden, centred upon the death of a young pregnant woman initially thought to be white but subsequently found to be of mixed parentage. *Sapphire* is an odd film that marries the genres of melodrama, realism, and detective fiction. The police—themselves not immune to racist assumptions in the film—eventually identify the murderer as the boyfriend's racist and—it is strongly implied—sexually frustrated sister. Her declared motive is to save the family from the disgrace a 'mixed race' child would apparently bring.

Eugenicist ideas had currency well into the post-war period. Dr Bertram of St John's College, Cambridge and the Eugenics Society pressed the case for immigration limitation on the basis that 'breeding with that which is different is more likely to lead to trouble than to happiness'.[57] Gallup polls of the period present a depressing picture. In 1958 only 13 per cent of people approved of marriages between white and 'coloured' people.[58] By 1968 approval had risen to 29 per cent but 57 per cent still disagreed with such marriages.[59] When faced with sociologist Clifford Hill's version of Philpott's question 'Would you approve of your sister, or your daughter, marrying a coloured person?' in 1964, 91 per cent said they would not.[60] 'The subject of mixed marriages generates more heat and rouses deeper and fiercer passions than any other aspect of the race/colour situation in Britain,' he concluded.[61] The migrant women Amrit Wilson interviewed in the 1970s were familiar with the disapproval meted out to mixed marriages. One of her older Indian interviewees described the difficulties she had experienced with her husband's family:

> To start with at the beginning, when my husband told his parents of my existence, my mother-in-law, he told me later, began to weep hysterically saying 'we had such hopes for you, now everything is

> spoilt!' My father-in-law's reaction was merely 'I don't really mind as long as she is not an African.' I did eventually get asked to the family home for Sunday lunch, where for the first time I experienced the ways of silent communication—of disapproval and guilt—which I know are typical of English families.[62]

After many years of such treatment she withdrew. 'The decision that I should stop seeing his family was one my husband and I took together because we both felt that our marriage would be safer outside the guilt-ridden arena of his family.'[63] Sydney Collins's post-war research into migrants from Yemen, Somalia, Egypt, Pakistan, and Malaya suggested that the majority married local white women. 'Most white women who marry these coloured men are from the lower class of English society, with a small proportion from the middle and estrangement from their parents frequently results, the degree of social repercussions varying with the woman's social status. Reconciliation is partial in some cases, complete in others, but unattained in the rest.'[64] More than a decade later *The Guardian* published Canadian Nadine Asante's moving account of living with her black African husband in Britain. 'I am resigned to having people label me "cheap" when I walk down the street with the man I love. He is resigned to having people believe he married me to "better" himself. One becomes resigned to these erroneous ideas but one never gets to like them.'[65]

* * *

> 'The world's roughly made up of two kinds of people—you're one sort and I'm the other. Oh we're together now there's a war on—we need to be. But what's going to happen when it's over? Shall we go on like this or are we going to slide back that's what I want to know. I'm not marrying you Jenny till I'm sure.'[66]

The 1943 British film *Millions Like Us* introduces another lens through which mid-century feelings were mediated: social class. When down-to-earth factory supervisor Charlie discusses marriage with upper-middle-class conscript Jennifer he is acutely aware that class provides a framework for romantic choice. While *Millions Like Us* has at its heart an optimistic People's War message of cross-class unity in the face of national crisis, Charlie and Jennifer do not marry, although other characters do. There is, nonetheless, a hope that in the post-war world such a marriage might just be acceptable.

Everyday experts before, during, and after the war paid keen attention to the awkwardness of love across social boundaries. 'Although you may be the least snobbish person in the world, it would grate upon your ears, as an educated man, to listen to badly phrased and ungrammatical speech all the time, and even more so in the presence of cultured acquaintances,' advice author Edynbry suggested.[67] Constructing social difference in both cultural and genetic terms, he explained that:

> Your pride would be put to some very severe tests and might not always stand the strain. You would also find it difficult to get a servant to show the proper respect for a mistress who had evidently little good breeding. Another snag would be the relatives, who, as deficient as your wife, might not always possess her good qualities. The situation would be further complicated if you had children.

Co-founder of the National Marriage Guidance Council Edward F. Griffith put it more succinctly. 'On the whole we may say that each class has its own temperament, ideas, thoughts, and even speech, and it is very difficult for all these habits to be changed and modified in such a way as to fit in with a happy matrimonial existence.'[68]

In recent times academics have also pointed to the cultural and emotional dimensions of social class. 'Class is not just about the way you talk, or dress, or furnish your home; it is not just about the job you do or how much money you make doing it; nor is it merely about whether or not you went to university, nor which university you went to,' writes the academic, Annette Kuhn. 'Class is something beneath your clothes, under your skin, in your psyche, at the very core of your being.'[69] It is, in this reading, an aspect of selfhood. Historian Andy Wood suggests that class 'bleeds into all forms of human identities and relationships'.[70] The French sociologist Pierre Bourdieu has drawn attention to the ways in which judgements of taste and preference—romantic or otherwise—are actively rooted in social identities and reflect social judgements.[71] As we will see, this was undeniably the case within mid-century England. A recent study by Paul Johnson and Steph Lawler suggests this continues to be the case today: 'romantic love, desire and social class are mutually influencing factors in the formation and enactment of heterosexual romantic relationships.'[72] This is not to say that mixed-class couples did not exist: we have already seen that they did. 'I was an upper middle-class blue stocking. He was working class, from the worst slums of East Ham,' wrote a woman born in 1925, 'We have just had our Golden Wedding.'[73] But class as well as religion, age, and ethnicity informed the development of intimate relations. Unsurprisingly given the dynamism of class identity across the mid-century period and the shifting nature of emotional intimacies, the relationship between class and love was extremely complex.

On the eve of the Second World War, Mass-Observation asked its panel of volunteer writers to consider the relationship between social class and 'love', posing the question 'if you are married, engaged or in love, state the part played in this situation by considerations of "class".'[74] The majority of the correspondents initially denied the impact of class upon their love lives; some citing particular relationships as empirical evidence. 'I am married and married a working class girl. I considered myself good enough for her and she thought the same about me,' declared a train inspector living in South Africa at the time.[75] 'My boy's parents are wealthier and move in a higher social circle than my own, but it doesn't worry me in the least,' wrote a 20-year-old student from Newport.[76] Others wrote from a more theoretical perspective, advancing the notion that love should sit outside existing social structures. 'Love rises above class', and 'in love there should be only one consideration, that is, understanding' were not untypical responses.[77] A married woman from Liverpool suggested that authenticity was a factor: 'Being in love, one tends to forget any distinctions of "class"—that is, if one is really in love!'[78] She did, nonetheless, observe that 'when it comes to anything serious—money again is a premier consideration—one always wants to climb higher—and never go back a little even for a short time.' Indeed, taken as a whole, the directive is remarkable for the extent to which class considerations bled into mid-century intimacy right across the social spectrum. A 21-year-old wallpaper-manufacture apprentice was clear. 'I believe that "class" plays a very big part in practically all love affairs.'[79]

Some made direct reference to class as a marker of suitability. 'I married a girl of my own class,' admitted a 28-year-old, 'and I think it would have needed a considerable passion to have led me to marry anyone from a different class.'[80] A working-class clerk from Hull was particularly—and heartbreakingly—clear:

> I am married to a girl of my own class. She was not the only girl with whom I was acquainted, naturally, and one girlfriend in particular was of the lower middle-class. My friendship with this girl looked as though it might develop into something more, especially on her part. I realised that if we became more than friends and were married, that after the first infatuation had worn off and we came down to realities, she would be unable to adapt herself to restricted circumstances without friction and unhappiness. Rather than take this risk I cut off our friendship for the sake of both our happiness. Other experience and observation leads me to believe that as a general rule married happiness can only be found by marrying in one's social class.[81]

Another man of similar age mused that 'I shouldn't let a matter of "class" enter into consideration, though I suppose the other parties involved (parents, friends, and so on) certainly would. So actually, unless your beloved is, as free, legally and personally, as the wind, your choice is still nailed down to your own immediate circle.'[82] The use of the 'nailed down' image is both surprising and revealing, suggesting a lack of agency in the face of external obstacles.

Beyond these explicit references to class identity, however, there is a clear sense that class influenced feeling. 'Class has never had anything to do with my emotional affairs, largely because only women of my own class or outlook attract me', was a commonly made claim.[83] Social class—by which is meant status as well as wealth—is in clear dialogue with feeling in this statement. Educational level and, critically, cultural taste were an integral part of attraction and were presumed to be inherently classed. Here we see that the apparently neutral references to shared interests and outlook with which this chapter began were often simply coded ways of discussing social background. Some Mass-Observers were much more direct. 'One is most likely to find someone with similar tastes and amusements, one with a similar education and background, one with whom one thinks one could bear to live the rest of one's life with, among one's own class. An average factory girl would bore me stiff in five minutes.'[84] A female panellist explained that 'I should only consider accent, taste and education; I should not be attracted towards anyone who was deficient in any one of these.'[85] Another gave one of the more thoughtful replies characteristic of the Mass-Observation panel:

> This is an interesting point. I could fall in love with, say a plumber (and once did), but could never marry such a person because his ideas and outlook would be so completely different from my own, and I could never consider such a possibility. It is not easy for a person to remove themselves from the plane on which they have been living, and to try and accustom themselves to an entirely different one. I am not married or engaged and not really in love, but I am afraid that 'class' would have a definite influence on my choice—that is, if I was capable of looking at the matter dispassionately, which of course is not always the case. Love is a funny thing.[86]

This is a text full of contradictions as the author struggles to disentangle love from marriage. At first she succeeds—she could fall in love with a plumber but not marry one. The final sentence—'love is a funny thing'—also makes a claim for the autonomy of emotions.

And yet at the heart of her analysis is a sense that love, as well as marriage, is influenced by class.

Within the responses to this particular questionnaire, the challenges posed by actual cross-class relationships were more frequently articulated by women than by men. 'I would be more at home among wealthier surroundings,' claimed one unhappy woman. 'We are stuck through my husband while poorer brained women have forged ahead (through husbands) I want a fur-coat and a villa and a cat and a maid.'[87] It was not entirely about money. 'Marriage to my husband has been a continual drag-down,' wrote another. 'I have lived like a hermit to avoid letting people see him. Have not dared to make friends with interesting or cultured people because he will smoke cheap tobacco, murder the Kings English and behave like a fool.'[88] In both cases perceived social and cultural differences between spouses led to real marital disharmony.

Others were keen to avoid such disparities in their everyday relationships. 'Two years ago I was engaged to be married to a young man, very public school and solid middle-class,' a school teacher recalled.

> I had told him that my people were poor, but I don't think he took it in until he met them. 'Class' was not the only reason the engagement ended but the strongest one. Actually, I was not looking forward to marrying into his stuffy and rather unintelligent family, and would much rather have fallen in love with someone with the same history as myself. My brothers and sisters all thought him a snob, and stupid into the bargain, while he thought they were rather peculiar to be wanting to go to college instead of going out into the world and making money.[89]

The uneasiness of this relationship is not entirely explained by the response of the two families involved. The story is as much about feeling as it is about external factors. This educationally mobile young woman did not want to fall in love within her 'class' of birth. Rather she wanted someone 'with the same history'—the same mobility—someone with whom she could feel at ease. In similar vein another teacher wrote with absolute clarity about the benefits of being 'sprung from similar soil' but having a shared sense of social mobility:

> I am engaged to a teacher who has had the same sort of education as I have and is of the same origin. Her family is a very intelligent working-class family living in an industrial area. We fell in love before I knew anything of her family or she of mine; but I knew from her way of talking, her accent, her likes and dislikes and so on that she was of the same sort as I and sprung from similar soil. We did not of course think these things out, but they must have worked unconsciously for I would otherwise never have got to know her intimately. Incidentally she is of the same political opinions as I.[90]

For this man similarity of political viewpoint stemmed from similarity of background and was itself not inconsequential in framing romantic taste. Shared ideological perspective was valued by other Mass-Observers too. 'In choosing my wife I was influenced by her being a Unitarian (as I was then) and a Vegetarian and Socialist,' wrote an elderly man. 'It merely happened that she went to London daily to a sort of millinery factory. I should as willingly have chosen a University woman, a wealthy woman or even one of the nobility, but only if her ideas were simple and progressive. I really found I had a very limited choice.'[91]

Writing retrospectively in 2001 about her post-war courting experiences, one Mass-Observer described love as 'a sense of belonging, of being "at home"'.[92] Yet as sociologists Johnson and Lawler suggest in their study of contemporary love, feelings of being emotionally at ease and at home 'are themselves the products of social organization'.[93] The physical as well as the psychic importance of home was paramount within twentieth-century England. Indeed, 'for many families, their house was the crucial symbol of their social standing, often over generations'.[94] Housing type denoted cultural as well as economic capital. 'When I began to "court" my now husband, she [my mother] was really adamant that he was not "good enough" for me,' recalled one woman. 'True he came from a poorer home than mine, but his family of eight were very caring of each other. He lived in a rented house, whilst I lived in a newly built house with a bathroom. This was considered "posh" in those days. But true love won the day.'[95] In this account we see a powerful assertion of emotional autonomy. The claim to authentic love allowed her both to defy her mother and to assert a set of distinct social values. In contrast, another woman born in 1937 was less successful in mediating differences of status. Housing differences in this case symbolized her mother's view of appropriate and inappropriate marriage material.

> My first serious boyfriend was so gorgeous that I felt weak each time I saw him. We were very serious about each other and went to each other's houses for Sunday tea which I hated, due to being so nervous. We went out, on and off for about 1 year and did talk a lot about the future. My mother talked to me a lot, about how unsuitable he was because we lived in a modern semi-detached house, and he lived in a back-to-back terrace house, with no bathroom—also, his father worked for the council as a labourer. He thought that we were very posh people—I think my mother had a lot of influence over him thinking this. In the end we fell out anyway and I was heartbroken for a while, I still 'fancy' him even now, although I have not seen him since before I got married.[96]

Historian Selina Todd has argued that parents—particularly mothers—played a vital role in shaping young women's working lives in the first half of the twentieth century.[97] Carol Dyhouse suggests that mothers also played a decisive role in encouraging and supporting their children's university aspirations across the twentieth century.[98] Here it is clear that parents—especially mothers—also attempted to monitor, control, and regulate their children's emotional lives.

The relationship between taste, home and familiarity is apparent within the pages of the *Matrimonial Post and Fashionable Marriage Advertiser* too. A desire to meet someone from a particular social background was sometimes explicit—'professional man', 'working man'—and sometimes coded in class signifiers such as degree of education, ownership of capital, cultural interests, or characteristics such as 'steadiness'. In 1930, for example, a 26-year-old domestic servant wished to meet 'a good steady working man age up to 32', a 20-year-old secretary wished to meet 'a gentleman in every sense of the word' and a 33-year-old journalist requested 'a man with wide sympathies, thoughtful and intellectual, journalist or doctor preferred'.[99] During and immediately after the war, new codes emerged which emphasized ordinariness and familiarity as desirable attributes. These reflected the celebration of the ordinary which underpinned attempts to conduct a people's war. A 39-year-old bachelor wished to meet a 'homely working-class girl...fond of usual pleasures', another requested a 'working class girl fond of home life and usual working men's pleasures'.[100] Spinsters too made their social preferences clear. 'Well educated' men were much in demand as was professional status, breeding, nationality and military service. Working-class men were not ruled out:

> Spinster aged 32, height 5 ft, 5 in., Church of England, fair complexion, brown hair and good figure. Machinist, income, fond of all kinds of music, domesticated, fond of home life, children and the usual amusements, wishes to meet Working Class Man, aged 36 to 40, height 5 ft 9 in., fair complexion, dark hair, with similar interests, no objection to a widower. E309.[101]

and

> Spinster, age 30, height 5 ft 2 in., C.E. fair complexion, dark hair, ex WAAF, interested in music, cinema, theatre, dancing, fond of home life, children, domesticated, wishes to meet gentleman up to 40, average height, working class, loyal, honest, trustworthy, no objection to Widower without children. E285.

In both advertisements the quest for shared domestic and leisure interests apparently necessitated explicitly classed attributes. In these advertisements and those that follow a number of personality traits—honesty, loyalty, and trustworthiness—are implicitly ascribed to a social class identity. So, for example, a 41-year-old bachelor tailor wished to meet 'a lady, age 35 to 38, height 5 ft. 9 in., dark hair, medium figure, preferably working class, fond of usual entertainments, cinema, etc., able to cook'. A slightly older Foreman Engineer, 'fond of home life, and usual amusements', wished to meet a woman 'with normal working-class outlook, domesticated, affectionate, and particularly fond of home-life'. These descriptors, which place home centre stage, support sociologist Mike Savage's contention that a post-war working-class identity was positively framed around claims to an authentic 'ordinariness'.[102] Being ordinary denoted the absence of unfair advantage and wealth, and was a powerful marker of identity in a rapidly changing world.

As we have seen, cross-class relationships remained rather extraordinary within these years and were perceived to be uncomfortable—even after the people's war. Differences of taste and education continued to cause everyday awkwardness and occasionally visceral disgust. Women's bodies were often a focus. In 1950 the *Manchester Evening News* published a letter from a man who declared himself repulsed by the appearance of the typical Manchester woman—the 'superfluous hairs on her legs', 'the bizarre head scarf', 'the untidy way she had smeared her lipstick around the edges of her mouth', 'the lumpy effect of inexpertly applied make-up', 'the bright red varnish on her fingernails [which] turned a graceful hand into a thing of horror' and her 'shrill voice that could be heard across the street'.[103] Unsurprisingly the letter provoked a torrent of disapproval. 'He has (I suppose) had a better education than the ordinary working girl who so often offends his sensibilities,' one local woman suggested, 'but it has left him without her tolerance and lack of conceit.'[104] 'Maybe if he had finished his tour he would have found that this girl has brains,' asserted another.[105] Nonetheless as Zweig suggested in his 1952 study, *Women's Life and Labour*, 'the working-class girl suffers a great deal from snobbishness coming from other classes.'[106] The ways in which class influenced physique, style, and deportment—i.e. the way class was embodied—also provided a framework for the exercise of romantic taste.

Social differences were read in other ways too. Education was also a key marker: a powerful source of shame as well as motor for social mobility. 'Being a graduate,' admitted one Mass-Observer, 'I think that I couldn't have been happy with someone who had not had the benefit of this experience and it was, in the late 50s and 60s, a privilege granted to only a few.'[107] On the eve of the 1963 Robbins Report only 8.5 per cent of the relevant cohort was in higher education.[108] A man born in 1924 admitted that 'although I like to be thought of as "Liberal", I do think that if there is too much diversity of background a relationship is that much harder. For example to court someone who was illiterate would have been extremely difficult for me. The problem is that what one is used to is for you the NORM, a close relationship with someone who has a completely different NORM must be very difficult.'[109] Reader letters to *Woman's Own* show that perceptions of inequitable cultural capital fuelled tensions within relationships and could provoke embarrassment and shame. 'Although I am very much in love, there is one thing which worries me,' one woman confided. 'I can't help feeling a little ashamed of my fiancé. He has not been well educated and his speech leaves a lot to be desired. On social occasions he seems to have no idea how to act. He is doing well in his own business, but can we make a successful marriage?' Mary Grant's reply was characteristically direct: 'Feeling as you do I cannot think that your marriage could ever be a success. For the things that irritate you now will be a hundred times more noticeable when you are married. Unless you can overlook these things, you should break off your engagement now.'[110] Similar advice had been meted out eight years earlier when the following letter was published:

> I have been going out with a man for over three years and love him very much. The trouble arises over our education: he left school at fourteen and there is, frankly, a lot of difference between us intellectually. I am not superior to him in character but the difference in

> our interests and capabilities is very marked. When we are alone things are all right, but when I meet his friends I am bored stiff and when he is with my friends I do not feel comfortable, as we talk of things above him. I don't mean to be snobbish, but I can't see any solution except a parting, though it will hurt us both terribly, for we do love each other. You see, the awful truth is that when we are out together I am ashamed of him.[111]

Educational inequality had not stopped this woman from falling in love but the awkwardness that stemmed from difference cast a shadow over her feelings.

University students of the period also felt the pull of shared experience. Ferdynand Zweig's survey of Oxford and Manchester students—*The Student in the Age of Anxiety*—was published in 1963 and provides a window on student attitudes across a broad range of topics at the beginning of the 1960s.[112] He also asked about love and marriage: 'Would you marry beneath your class or level of education?'—a question which he believed would test the authenticity of their broader perspective on class differences.[113] Only a small minority felt they would marry beneath their educational level. The majority rejected the idea in no uncertain terms: 'I want my wife to be an intelligent and cultured person I can share everything with,' reported one; another observed that, 'It would show everywhere, the way you furnish your home, in tastes, in friends, interests and so on. I am sure it would not work.'[114] On the cusp of the 1960s expansion of higher education, many of these students viewed education, class, and intimacy as inherently linked: 'The ideal partner is the one with whom they can attain full understanding and have everything in common.'[115] Here we see the intense pressures and high expectations that accompanied the love-based model of matrimony. The ascendancy of love within erotic encounters did not, on this evidence, encourage its democratization.

In concluding his student study, Zweig suggested that: 'The conception of romantic love in marriage is widespread, but tempered by considerations of class, family background and level of education. A partner with a similar educational level and family upbringing is regarded as the right spouse.'[116] While romance and love might have been expected to widen the field of choice for marriage partners, high expectations went hand-in-hand with continued limits on who one might fall in love with. A wide range of factors—class as well as race, religion as well as age—persisted in framing ideas of suitability and hierarchies of socially acceptable matches across the mid-century. 'It wasn't an age difference that stopped me, but rather a class difference,' recalled one Mass Observer, 'Patricia was staff and middle class; I was a factory worker and working class. It was hopeless.'[117]

Part II: Courtship

During a 'courtship', both of you would treat each other with the utmost respect, you would never dream of letting him see you in your curlers or even putting on your makeup. This sense of mystique was a real and important part of the excitement. You almost lived in a sort of perfect paradise that had to be sustained until you were married and it gave you a lovely feeling of being cherished and envied. It also gave you a sense of independence from your parents, in particular your father who didn't dare criticize you once you were seriously courting because another, unknown force thought you were perfect and it wouldn't do to criticize you in any way. You became an important person in your own right.

(MOA, DR M1703, Summer 2001, woman born in 1947)

4
Meetings

When social psychologist Thelma Veness asked a group of 14-year-olds to write stories about their future in 1956, 69 per cent of boys and 94 per cent of girls anticipated marrying.[1] For the girls in particular, 'the husband must be found, and the finding is worthy of telling, if not the life spent with him'. The accounts are notably grounded in everyday detail, rather than grand romantic gesture. 'Going home one rainy day, I couldn't get my umbrella to open', one begins, 'and I didn't know what to do, as it was pouring so hard':

> Just then, a very good-looking young man came up to me, and asked if he could help me. I told him that I couldn't get my umbrella to open, and that I would get soaking wet. He tried to open my umbrella and he managed to. Then he asked me if I was going anywhere that night. I told him that I wasn't, except out to tea, when I got home. So he asked me if I cared to go to the Gaumont with him, and I said I would go. Well, after we came out I went to a fish and chip restaurant with him, and that led to other nights out with him. We got engaged about six months later.[2]

Once the actual wedding day had been described, the husband played no further part in the imagined future. In this respect the story was typical: in nearly a quarter of the girls' imagined futures the husband died in early life.[3] For these adolescent girls it was the initial meeting and subsequent courtship that really mattered.

Twentieth-century men and women, usually from age 14–16 upwards, met each other in a diverse range of haphazard and seemingly accidental ways. They might meet on the bus or train, in the street, sat in a café, watching a football match, enjoying a fun fair or whilst away on holiday. In Patrick Hamilton's fictional tale of swindling and seduction in inter-war Brighton—*The West Pier*—meetings take place on the sea front.

> The Pier was intimately and intricately connected with the entire ritual of 'getting off'. Indeed, without the Pier, 'getting off' would have been to some minds inconceivable, or at any rate a totally different thing. The Pier was at once the object and arena of 'getting off', and usually the first subtle excuse made by the male for having been so bold as to 'get off' was his saying that he thought it might be 'nice' to go on the Pier. An invitation to go on the Pier was like an invitation to dance; it almost conferred upon 'getting off' an air of respectability.[4]

Couples also met through social, religious, or political organizations and clubs, and through family, friends, school, university, and work.[5] Community and neighbourhood networks were particularly significant in the first part of the century. The autobiographer, Kathleen Dayus, first met her husband at a neighbour's party in 1919. Afterwards he walked her home.[6] Shifting educational and occupational patterns opened up new opportunities for contact: the move out of residential domestic service was particularly significant. 'I worked in service in a house in Lincoln and my day began at 5 a.m.' one of Maureen Sutton's interviewees told her, recalling the 1930s. 'We worked until 9 p.m. at night and the only time I got off was one Sunday afternoon in two weeks. I used to see young men with their parents and family at church on a Sunday evening but you couldn't get to speak to them.'[7] For some the war provided distinctive opportunities. 'I married in 1941', recalled one Mass-Observer. 'I was 23, my husband 34. I met him in an air-raid shelter five months earlier as I was doing my air raid warden duties. I don't know if we were "in love", I do know we both wanted to be married, at that moment, and saw the other as the most available and suitable.'[8] As might be presumed following the discussion in

Chapter Three, social class also exercised an underlying influence. 'With all the world from which to choose our mates,' noted Slater and Woodside, 'we take them from what is generally a narrowly limited class.'[9] Opportunities to meet were often implicitly, and sometimes explicitly, socially segregated.

Commercial leisure venues were particularly significant arenas for 'picking up'. The promise of romantic meetings was central to the attraction of particular leisure activities; the expansion of commercial, youth orientated, leisure provided more scope for romantic encounters. Eva Illouz has suggested that the new forms of leisure which emerged in the twentieth century were 'naturally' romantic.[10] As their earning capacity grew, young people were well placed to exploit the romance of leisure. This was not a one-way process: courtship was itself increasingly experienced as leisure, something to which 'all other activities must give way'.[11] Nor was this an exclusively British story. Writing in 1937, American sociologist Willard Waller observed that

> Whether we approve or not, courtship practices today allow for a great deal of pure thrill-seeking. Dancing, petting, necking, the automobile, the amusement park, and a whole range of institutions and practices permit or facilitate thrill-seeking behaviour. These practices, which are connected with a great range of the institutions of commercialised recreation, make of courtship an amusement and a release of organic tensions.[12]

Between the 1920s and the 1970s two commercial giants loomed large as arenas for 'picking up'. The dance hall and the cinema provided a location for youthful romance as well as cultural texts which placed love centre-stage. Dancehalls boomed in the years after the First World War. In his autobiographical account of working class Salford, *The Classic Slum*, Robert Roberts described how, 'At 6d per head (1s on Saturdays) youth at every level of the manual working class, from the bound apprentice to the "scum of the slum", fox-trotted through the new bliss in each other's arms.'[13] The Tower Ballroom in Blackpool was described by

Mass-Observation's investigators as a venue that 'sanctions the approach without introduction: "picking-up" and "getting-off" are accepted as normal behaviour'.[14] Florence Turner remembered travelling there from her home in Salford: 'Hair marcel-waved, clad in our long dresses and made up with "Betty Lou" face powder, and drenched in "Californian Poppy" perfume we would board the train with our "George Raft" look-alike escorts, all set to dance the night away in Blackpool Tower.'[15] A 1959 survey found that the dance hall was 'the most popular place for meeting one's life partner: over a quarter of couples had met in this way.'[16]

Of course not all young people went to dances, and not all dancers prioritized heterosexual romance. 'I seldom if ever go to dances now, since I have definitely adopted a masculine attitude to life, as I should not want to dance with men,' wrote one woman in 1939. 'If and when I do go it is either where I can wear slacks, and dance with my own women friends, or wear fancy dress and similarly avoid the necessity of dancing with men.'[17] Dance-hall culture between the wars could support homo-sociability, as well as hetero-sociability. The Royal Albion Hotel in Brighton hosted woman-only tea-dances; gay men rented working-class dancehalls in London for weekly events.[18] Whether gay or straight, dancers were not necessarily on the look-out for love. 'I like dancing for its own sake,' confided one young woman in 1939.[19] Dancing featured strongly in the pleasures sought by Blackpool holiday-makers just prior to the war but the motivation to dance was varied. The diary of one young woman demonstrated considerable stamina as well as a fairly relaxed attitude towards the week's dancing partners:

> Friday night. Visit the Tower, met two young men from Sheffield, went into the bar and had a few drinks, afterwards danced, then on the promenade, strolled on the sands, had supper at café (chips and coffee). Arrived back at digs at 12 o'clock... Saturday evening... went to the Tower dancing, from there to the Gardens and then back to the Tower, which we like best... Sunday... Monday, strolled along

> the prom with friends and met 4 Scotch boys, went dancing on the pier and drinks in the bar... Tuesday, went on the pier dancing, came off at 11.30, went up the prom... Afternoon, we went to the Tower dancing till 4.00, also had a walk in the aquarium and zoo... Night went to Palace dancing, then to Variety... Thursday... After tea went to Tower dancing with lady friend... Friday... Night went to Winter Gardens. Picked up sailor from New Zealand. Went and had a look round the amusements 1d. machines, he won me two bracelets and a powder box. We danced and then home.[20]

For this woman dancing was clearly a favoured activity and one which she was keen to pursue independent of any romantic inclinations. Young women were generally more enthusiastic dancers than men. Whilst the opportunity to meet women was the prime motivation for all but a minority of male dancers, the actual dancing was more often than not what drew women to the dance hall. 'The pleasure of movement which ones gets in dancing is definitely a sensual pleasure but not a sexual one,' recalled one woman of her experiences in the 1920s. 'When I danced often the partners I preferred were not those whom I found attractive in ordinary times and I would still prefer to dance with a woman professional than with a man who danced badly.'[21]

Even if the dancers themselves were not necessarily looking for love, however, romance was a dominant theme within dance hall music. The historian James J. Nott calculates that in 1935, 55 per cent of popular songs written for British audiences were love songs.[22] He detects a shift from more optimistic 1920s love songs such as *Sweet Georgia Brown* to darker, more sentimental 1930s torch songs and the intimate offerings of male crooners. During wartime love was a particularly important theme in a rapidly changing and uncertain world. The manager of the Aspin Hall dance hall in Bolton confessed in July 1940:

> The popular tunes are certainly NOT connected with the war. We had to scrap one or two—things like 'The Siegfried Line' and 'Somewhere in France with You'. It's not much good singing about

> somewhere in France now. There's not much point in playing that these days. We don't bother with tunes like 'There'll always be an England'. We feel it is better that they should be cheerful with tunes with romance and love, moon, June stuff you know. They were there before Hitler and they will be there after him.[23]

If love provided the soundtrack for the dance hall, soft lighting, sprung floors, and the fundamental physicality of dancing, contributed further to a mood of intimacy. Dance-hall rituals made introductions fairly effortless. 'Generally, men lined one side of the hall, women the other,' recalled Robert Roberts. 'A male made his choice, crossed over, took a girl with the minimum of ceremony from in among and slid into rhythm.'[24] Mixer dances enforced partner switching. 'I found it was a Paul Jones,' recalled one 25-year-old dancer in 1939, 'Ended up with a young man with spectacles who danced the next one with me—Lambeth Walk—and then stuck pretty close to me for the rest of the evening; never discovered what his name was.'[25] More rarely 'excuse me' or 'buzz off' dances allowed women to choose their own partners. The 'Blackout Stroll' introduced in late 1939 offered an enterprising solution to those in need of a dancing partner: 'You ladies called "wallflowers", fated to sit out all the dances, because, perhaps, your face isn't your fortune, or you aren't too good a dancer, or your figure isn't the cuddly kind... HERES YOUR CHANCE TO DANCE THE "BLACKOUT STROLL", LONDON'S LATEST STEP IS YOUR GODSEND.'[26] The novel aspect of the dance rested in the turning off of the dancehall lights mid-dance. Those at the sides were encouraged to use this opportunity to emerge from the shadows and grab themselves a partner.

Both women and men viewed a lack of dancing ability as a significant impediment to picking up. 'I do not go to dances because I cannot dance well,' wrote one man.[27] 'Even now at 18 I can't dance, which I consider is one of my downfalls,' confided one of Pearl Jephcott's sample, 'a very normal girl who fears that she has already imperilled her chances in the matrimonial stakes'.[28]

Bachelor adverts in the *Matrimonial Post and Fashionable Marriage Advertiser* sometimes dealt with the problem head-on by specifying 'no dancer' as a requirement of any potential partner. During the war the popularity of American servicemen was founded in part upon their generally superior prowess on the nation's dance floors. Nonetheless they also had their critics. 'There were a few Americans,' one woman remembered, 'but their style of dancing (jitter bug) and bad reputations made me steer clear of them. I was interested in males who were good dancers in the Victor Sylvester fashion.'[29] Dancing skill was clearly in the eye of the beholder and framed by cultural norms. Young British men were not unaware of the attractiveness of dancing ability to women. 'What I did notice though, was that when the record player went on at the youth club the girls liked to dance to the music of Glenn Miller, the Dorseys, Harry James etc.', recalled a Mass-Observer who grew up in Enfield.

> I also noticed that the blokes who could do a nifty foxtrot went home with the best looking birds. It was time for yours truly to invest some of his scarce cash in the local school of ballroom dancing. It worked wonders. Well I thought it did. With a little perseverance, I started with two left feet, I eventually became quite good at ballroom dancing and found that I in fact enjoyed it . . . Graduating to jive worked even more wonders.[30]

This very precise form of self-improvement apparently brought both enhanced courting success and unexpected personal pleasure.

There was not universal approval of the dance hall as a courting venue. 'Modern dance halls seem to me ideal places for strange fast young men to pick up decent girls and cause trouble,' suggested one woman in 1939.[31] Even after the Second World War negative attitudes persisted. In 1955 18-year-old Shirley Eakers married 31-year-old dance band leader Jimmy Maunder without her parents' consent. The couple had met in a dance hall four years previously. Reluctantly granting the pair permission to marry, Exeter magistrate Sir Leonard Costello opined that 'one can scarcely imagine a less suitable place for the engendering of what should be a life-long affection and devotion than a dance hall, to the strains of a noisy jazz band and the superheated atmosphere that exists in such places'.[32] Shirley's reported retort revealed a different hierarchy of venue respectability. 'Nine out of ten couples meet in dance halls today. Surely that's better than "picking up" in the street?'

For those who favoured an alternative hunting ground visits to the cinema could also be productive. The Sheffield school leavers that social anthropologist M. P. Carter talked to in the 1950s left him in no doubt that:

> The cinema is a good place for flirting... One girl explained that she and her friend were 'on the lookout' for boyfriends: the cinema was the obvious place to try, for 'if there are boys sitting behind you, they torment you and ask you if you have got any sweets. Then you get talking, and the boys ask if they can take you home.' The film show is but a backcloth to the main business of the evening.[33]

That the film being shown might not always be foremost in the mind of individual picture-goers is clear in a detailed account written by one of Mass-Observation's Bolton investigators. The report starts with a chance encounter:

> I passed the girl in Knowsley Street—She looked at me hard so I turned back and made her acquaintance. She must have walked very slowly because she was only about 3 yards ahead of me.
>
> I asked her where she was going in the rain. 'Oh! Just taking a stroll!', then she suggested we might go to the pictures.
>
> She was about 20, dressed in cloche hat and a brown tweed coat. Brown high-heel shoes.[34]

Having made a connection, the couple proceeded to the Embassy cinema together where the main feature was *Every Night at Eight*, starring George Raft and featuring the popular song *I'm in the Mood for Love*. The man clearly did not forget his ethnographic duties. He recorded in detail the audience response to each of the films shown and he also engaged the woman in a conversation about capes, which were apparently no longer in fashion—'it's all raincoats'—and veils which were still being worn. He also recorded their physical interaction in uncomfortable detail:

> When we went inside she went into the back seat [in this picture place the seats at the back are for two] Naturally I followed.
>
> She placed her umbrella under the seat—and asked me to remind her of it when the show as over.
>
> She sat quiet for ten minutes. Then I offered her a cigarette—she took off her hat, loosened her coat, took off her gloves—and took the cigarette. It was when the wild looking man came on screen that gave her an opportunity to appear afraid. She got hold of my hand—as she leaned slightly forward. I put my left arm around her—she slightly lifted her right arm—so I put my hand around her breast—I 'messed around'—all that picture—during the Raft picture when the singing of sentimental love songs [started] she let go of my hand and started to rub her hand up and down my thigh.
>
> I then began to feel the breasts of the girl with my now disengaged hand…She stopped my hand straying too far. We also did some kissing.

Despite these distractions the investigator was still able to ascertain the precise number of people in the Embassy cinema that evening. As this account demonstrates, courtship encouraged and perhaps demanded the performance of particular gender roles.

While romantic films were popular with British audiences, they were not the leading genre. More popular than love themes were drama, adventure, crime, music, and comedies.[35] Writing in 1926 early film critic Iris Barry suggested that:

> The love stuff is overdone. It's at such a pass now that you can't have a woman nestle in any man's arms without the collective audience reaching for its hat under the impression that the finale is due.

> I concur that a love interest would always be useful and necessary in seven-eighths of all films. But not *such* a love interest. Not this cheap business of just getting oneself married, not this insistence on the feminine power of attracting a man till he finds her bed and board till the end of her days without her making one effort to deserve it.[36]

Films continued to be criticized for promoting 'false' romantic values across the mid-century. Pearl Jephcott, for example, asserted that,

> There is no sort of doubt, for example, that constant film going makes girls of fourteen and fifteen think much, and seriously, of 'love'. Their conversation is full of 'husbands who don't believe in jealousy', of 'falling for someone', and of 'the boy who hadn't got a girl'. All the paraphernalia of cheap romance, of light-hearted and whirlwind matrimony and betrayals and recrimination are set before young people who will begin to feel that it is incumbent on them to be experiencing the same heartaches and thrills themselves.[37]

Indeed while films exploited the theme of love and romance, they could actively discourage attachments by offering visions of romantic behaviour which contrasted too sharply with everyday life. In their 1951 study *English Life and Leisure* Rowntree and Lavers quoted one 21-year-old shop girl who remarked: 'Marry and have kids you don't want, and live in a poky house, and not have any nice clothes? Not me! Marrying would be all right if it was the way they do it in the pictures, but real life isn't like that.'[38] An 18-year-old bank clerk observed that 'It [the cinema] has made me despise boys of about my own age, with whom I have been out. After seeing the polished lover on the screen it is rather disillusioning to be kissed by a clumsy inexperienced boy. I have tried not to feel like that about them, but I still find I would rather go out with an older man than a young boy.'[39] Even where films shaped taste, practicalities had a habit of intervening:

> My criteria for the perfect partner? As a teenager, looks were important and I followed the 'tall, dark and handsome' school of thought.

> My influences were not from literature or women's magazines but from the cinema. I imagined myself as Elizabeth Taylor in those days (complete with charcoaled-on beauty spot when I went out in the evening!!) You lost what you called street-cred if you went out with a wimp. Though any male was better than having no-one to take you to the school dances or the Saturday night square dancing.[40]

Films offered new romantic scripts alongside which ordinary people could plot their own experiences, but celluloid stories were acknowledged as being far removed from everyday life. 'There were a lot of films made about courtship where everything was lovely—flowers, dancing and really romantic with lots of lilting music and of course the hero as always good looking,' remembered one former typist. 'Well I think it made us feel a bit wistful but it was not like that. By the time we had finished work we felt more like sitting in a chair. And we often had to go straight out to a date without having time to get home to wash and change.'[41] When anthropologist Geoffrey Gorer asked his 1950s respondents, 'do you think English people fall in love in the way you see Americans doing it in the films?' only 7 per cent said yes.[42]

> Of course when the war started it all changed and our old way of life was really gone for ever. There were dances and suppers laid on all over the place, in old church halls and WI meeting rooms and you were sure of a partner and a bit of supper. Then as more and more servicemen came from other and more exotic places what great changes it brought especially when the Americans turned up from the land of milk and honey.[43]

* * *

There were undoubtedly clear continuities in courtship across the period 1920–1970. As we have seen, commercial leisure provided an important arena for meetings throughout. However, there were also profound discontinuities. The Second World War, in particular, brought important changes in patterns of courtship, as it did in so many other areas of everyday life. During these years life in industry and the services opened up new possibilities for romantic meetings away from family and community surveillance. Writing shortly after war's end, one 27-year-old newspaper reporter recalled that 'Uniforms and postings to places where they were unknown gave our lovers anonymity and lack of self-consciousness. This applied also to thousands of factory workers, who took up work in cities where they were unknown.'[44] A man writing from the vantage point of 2001 noted, 'we could still feel cupid's arrows and enjoy the company of the opposite sex and places such as the Army NAAFI Clubs, where dances, music and films occasionally were on offer for free for congenial company but for romance also. Remember perhaps upwards of 100 young people were all thrown together from all parts of the UK, in this Army/Air Force gathering.'[45] Such sociability was not, of course, everyone's wartime experience. 'I wouldn't join the Woman's Land Army just on the chance of meeting a boyfriend,' Leonora Eyles instructed one optimistic young woman. 'You have to like the life you know. It's hard work and there mightn't be a man within miles!'[46]

Prior to the war, rituals such as the evening walkabout had operated as meeting points. In Manchester the Sunday evening 'monkey walk' provided young people with an opportunity for sexual display and performance; a similar function was performed in Stoke-on-Trent by 'monkey-running'; in Preston by 'Monkey Racks' and in Swansea by the 'bunny run'.[47] In wartime the Sunday evening walk was largely untenable, replaced by other opportunities that sat more comfortably with the particular circumstances of war. This is not to say that black-out conditions brought a complete end to street-based meetings: young people adapted them to new conditions. Regional differences were significant. In Kent, for example, Mass-Observation found that girls were fearful of venturing out in the black-out, and that irregular hours of work and a heightened police presence had pushed other young people off the streets.[48] In Yorkshire, however,

> the blackened streets of wartime have undoubtedly served as an excitement and stimulus to the young people. There is the noise of the constant passage of feet, a continual chatter of voices, the high shrill outbreak of laughter from girls and young women, hoarse guffaws from youths, shouted interchange of badinage between the sexes. In this scuffling, bumping, blindfold promenade, the youths and girls go up and down, to and fro, save where groups gather in the dark porches of shop doorways. As the girls pass along, unseen hands suddenly press against intimate portions of their bodies. They giggle, squeal, indignantly protest; but they do not cease to parade up and down, savouring the thrill of the license and the excitement.[49]

As young people became more mobile—compelled by the state to relocate in order to perform war work—meetings occurred in new environments. For example, the informal prohibition on young people visiting public houses diminished in the face of loosened community surveillance, weaker local networks, and social dislocation. 'Several people comment that girls seem to regard the pub these days as a place where acquaintance can be made with men,' a Mass-Observation report noted. 'Sometimes they consider this as harmless, sometimes they dislike the idea very strongly.'[50] A member of the Women's Auxiliary Air Force described a night out with 'her' Canadian in August 1941. 'We visited two pubs. Had four drinks in each (rum and lime, 2/4 each). Finished it off with a double whiskey each.'[51] She concluded that: 'Drinking is the only thing to do for a short period out of camp with a RAF. Lincoln with its scanty entertainments is too far away for an early night, so usually the couple goes "on the beer".'[52] Those who disliked the idea of women using public houses drew upon a historic association between women, pubs, and sexual immorality whereby female drinkers were represented as either the instigators of sexual union or, if underage, the victims of seduction. One woman recorded that 'In Watford we have noticed very young girls coming into the quasi-smart pubs in groups, in order to pick up Americans. They usually order grapefruit for themselves. If they click they go on to gin and lime. The American's don't buy them many. They want to get on with what they've picked them up for.'[53] Nonetheless, in the changed circumstances of war the relationship between sex and the pub could be turned on its head: 'A few people feel that it is far better for young women to come into a pub by themselves than to hang about the streets, or, if they are married, go about with other men, while their husbands are serving.'[54] Here the pub was stripped of its sexualized meanings and approached as a leisure venue, providing a sociable counter-attraction to infidelity while husband/boyfriend was away. One working-class man suggested that it was '[B]etter that they should drink alone than go gallivanting round with other men.'[55] While dancing and cinema-going remained the pre-eminent leisure arenas for 'picking up' and more developed courtship activity across our period, during wartime the pub also functioned as a meeting place.

After the war the likelihood of meeting partners through community and family ties continued to diminish in the face of social and cultural change. Young people from more middle-class backgrounds were increasingly likely to meet partners when they left home and went to university rather than through family, church, or local societies. In 1957 sociologist Judith Hubback published a study of the lives and roles of married graduate women.[56] Her work highlighted the significance of higher education as a middle-class marriage market. 'It is sometimes remarked, perhaps rather cynically, that the university is the best possible marriage market for an intelligent girl, because there she will meet such a high concentration of her mental equals,' she reported, acknowledging that, 'of course, the university years are those during which it is perfectly natural for a girl to fall in love. It would undoubtedly be foolish of her parents to let a girl start a university course without at any rate pointing out these facts in advance.'[57] Thirty-six per cent of the *Wives Who Went to College* that she interviewed had met their husbands at university.[58] By 1965 a century high of 63 per cent of Oxford-educated women ended up married to an Oxford-educated man.[59] The rate declined in the decades that followed as national marriage rates fell.

The places where working-class youths met also shifted in the post-war years under the influence of new leisure opportunities and affluence. Young people were increasingly addressed as independent consumers of leisure, love and romance. Teen magazines such as *Valentine* (1957) and *Boyfriend* (1959) made the case particularly powerfully. Evolving consumer industries sought to direct youthful spending power into new avenues.[60] The milk bar—castigated by Richard Hoggart as 'a peculiarly thin and pallid form of dissipation'—provided one such new venue, offering a café experience specifically tailored for young people.[61] Following the end of rationing in 1954, the hitherto sedate Lyons Corner House café chain diversified into a range of youth-friendly cafes including the fast-food Wimpy Bar. 'For the customer, particularly the all-important teenager, they are quick, simple and classless,' wrote *The Observer*, in 1959. 'A Wimpy can be eaten in less than 10 minutes, leaving the rest of a lunch hour for shopping, flirting or jazz.'[62] The coffee bar was another 1950s innovation which a youthful clientele quickly adapted to their own ends; by 1963 it was the 'newest and most significant development in Bury'.[63] The 'members only' nightclubs, about which crime historian Louise Jackson has written, offered another youthful location away from parental supervision, as well as the target for police surveillance and press allegations of sexual danger.[64] In the 1960s, the pub re-established its footing within young people's leisure lives. More than half of the 17–19-year-old boys surveyed by sex researcher Michael Schofield and a little less than half of the girls had visited a pub the week before they were interviewed.[65] The erosion of sex segregation within the workforce during and after the war also ensured that working-class youths became as likely to meet future spouses in their work environment as their middle-class counterparts. The expansion of secondary schooling transformed schools into potential meeting places too. Anxieties about 'gym slip' mothers ensued. All of these changes encouraged greater youthful autonomy in the making of introductions.[66]

* * *

For those who failed to secure satisfactory introductions from the range of opportunities outlined above there were, of course, additional methods that could be employed. Lonely hearts could make recourse to a range of publications, organizations, and clubs explicitly dedicated to matchmaking and implicitly socially segregated. As we have already seen, those intent on marriage could place advertisements in publications such as the *Matrimonial Post and Fashionable Marriage Advertiser* although Leonora Eyles for one was suspicious of their use. 'I think there are better ways of getting married, my dear,' she instructed one interested correspondent, continuing, 'I am quite sure it is better to stay single than to marry someone for the sake of having "Mrs" before your name.'[67] And yet, correspondence clubs, friendship circles, and introduction agencies did not decline until well into the golden age of marriage. Clubs such as The Golden Circle Club established in 1935, the Two-ways Contact Club, the Victory Correspondence Club (founded in London in 1942) and Brighton's Happy Circle provided 'select' lists of fellow members' addresses for a fee of around a pound and claimed remarkable success.[68] As a Miss M.V.C. of London apparently attested in 1950, 'I became a member of the Victory Club about a month back, I myself have had in this short time one suggestion of marriage, and also an offer of marriage.'[69]

'The whole business of arranged marriages should be regarded as a social service,' suggested advice author M. B. Smith in 1951, who described singleness as 'a disastrous denial of a woman's natural rights to biological and psychological completion'.[70] The most widely known marriage bureau, Heather Jenner's of Bond Street, was established in 1939 and claimed to cater for a predominantly middle-class and upper-class clientele, advertising its services in theatre programmes, magazines, and newspapers. A Mass-Observation investigator who visited the bureau in 1947 described the clients as predominantly female including many nurses and teachers and 'mostly clerky types'.[71] The bureau retains a place within individual memories of the period. One man recalled his own experience: 'I read her book and was interested, so in due course went to see her (a member of her staff actually) I only had one introduction (not the one for me!) but this venture just overlapped with my getting to know my future wife so I cannot enlarge on my experiences with the bureau.'[72] Another man met four women after paying Heather Jenner £30, having decided in the mid-1950s that, 'if I wanted to find a wife I should have to adopt what was then a fairly unorthodox method'.[73] The services offered by organizations such as this were discreet. Upon payment of a fee and completion of a questionnaire, clients were matched according to general compatibility. Other clubs catered for particular sections of the population and were more explicitly socially segregated. The Catholic Introductions Bureau based in Ludgate Hill, London was, unsurprisingly, designed to introduce Catholic men and women with the aim of encouraging Catholic marriages. The Inter-Varsity Club 'advertised itself as a social club for young professional people. However, to all intents and purposes, it operated as a marriage bureau for educated and/or intelligent people. The vast majority of the members were single when they joined and tended to belong until they met, and married, someone from the club whereupon they would drift away.'[74] By the late 1960s clubs were also beginning to emerge which catered explicitly for divorced and separated people: a harbinger of things to come. These tended to adopt self-consciously optimistic names such Putney Phoenix and Richmond Renaissance.

The advent of computer dating in the mid-1960s, notably through the establishment of Dateline in 1966 by John Patterson, added another possible way of finding a partner. While its methods were rather similar to those of established agencies—clients were asked to complete a questionnaire—the computerization of romance made love newsworthy.[75] Press coverage was by turns enthusiastic—'Love by computer'—and dystopian—'Robot cupid'.[76] The *Daily Mirror* used 'the marriage selector of our times' to find a match for Princess Anne—presumably without her consent.[77] Computer dating inspired a London Weekend Television series called *The Mating Machine* which offered comedy of variable quality. One episode featured 'a girl who winds up with two very ardent "dates" after enrolling with a computer as "a giggle"'.[78] In another, 'a data dating bureau, famous for bringing unlikely couples together has even more trouble when the computer was brought in'.[79] The programme was scheduled between *Wheel of Fortune* and *The Adventures of Don Quick* in which 'a planet consists entirely of beautiful girls! Trouble is they cut men down to size.'

* * *

The ways in which couples met for the first time fed into their understandings of the nature of love. Was meeting in a dance hall intrinsically more 'romantic' than meeting through the orchestrations of a correspondence agency? Did meeting in the street mark a relationship as different from one established on the basis of family connections? So long as pragmatic deliberation played a part in affairs of the heart, engineered meetings were not necessarily less valued than more spontaneous encounters. In fact, persistent social segregation ensured that if not 'arranged' in the contemporary reading of the term, opportunities to meet members of the opposite sex continued to be limited to particular avenues—whether university, work, tennis club, or coffee bar. However higher expectations about love and personal fulfilment made possibly more efficient ways of finding a partner look calculating and cold-blooded. A hardening of attitudes towards the 'arranged marriage' in particular demonstrates the extent to which 'true love' was increasingly believed to be the basis for everyday happiness.

5
Private Spaces

> Sunday evening. I had my tea, washed and left for my girlfriend's house, in Bow. When I arrived her mother let me in and told me to take a seat in the living-room. Christine (my girl) and I watched 'Sunday Night at the London Palladium'. Afterwards we went for a walk until about 10.30 p.m. when I took her home and said 'Good night' for about 20 minutes before leaving...
>
> Friday evening. I went to call for Christine. I took her to the Mile End Odeon. I think they were two good films—to tell the truth I didn't pay much attention to them. After the films I took Christine down to Chinatown, and we had chow mein, which is very nice. I saw her home and, after saying my good nights, left for my own home. I got into bed at 11.45 p.m....
>
> Saturday evening. After tea I went round to Christine's house and watched television. I was tired out and fell asleep while we were smooching on the bed-settee.[1]

This diary account, written by an 18-year-old East Ender, describes the courtship practices of one teenage couple. The complex relationship between public and private space is clear—here located within the particular context of mid-1960s London. The use of the girlfriend's home as a venue for developing intimacy—rather than simply approval—is probably a distinctively post-war phenomenon. Teenage use of the bed-settee is most definitely so, as is television viewing and the chow mein supper. Reference to the evening walk, however, demonstrates the persistence of more traditional courtship patterns as does the broader determination to carve out moments of, and spaces for, emotional and sexual intimacy. Within a society where most young people continued to reside with their parents until their marriage day, finding the space to conduct a serious relationship was not necessarily easy. The need to avoid accusations of indecency or nuisance was an additional burden.

As part of its 1949 'Little Kinsey' investigation into British sexual attitudes, Mass-Observation asked its national panel of writers to answer a series of questions about 'love-making in public'.[2]

> How do you feel about people making love in public? How do you feel about making love in public yourself? Do you think that any changes have taken place in your attitudes towards this subject? If so what changes have taken place and why do you think they have occurred?[3]

Definitions of both 'love-making' and 'public' were left fairly open. 'Making love is a very elastic term; I here define it as including all of the normal activities of lovers towards one another short of what would provoke interference from a not excessively zealous policeman,' wrote a 55 year-old university lecturer.[4] 'Most people take "public" to mean any situation where the lovers are not completely alone and enclosed by four walls,' Mass-Observation added.[5] The subject generated strong and diverse responses rooted in opinion, feeling, and experience.

Mass-Obscrvation found that women were more likely to be opposed to public love-making than men. A sense of embarrassment, a view that physical intimacy was an inherently private activity and a belief that public affection demonstrated 'lack of breeding' were the dominant explanations for this position. 'I don't like it at all, because love-making is perhaps the most intimate and personal thing imaginable,' wrote one housewife.[6] Another claimed that 'On places like Wimbledon Common entwined couples are a bit of a nuisance—one is apt to fall over them going round the bushes. My spaniel has an embarrassing habit of standing stock still and gazing at them with wide-eyed interest; or alternatively, if they're in a prone position, rushes up and breathes heavily upon them.'[7] Men were slightly more supportive than women. Some were positively enthusiastic. 'If it was a massive orgy such as the Ancient Greeks used to go in for, I think it would be quite amusing,' suggested a young economist, continuing, 'If there were, say, a dozen couples in some warm leafy glade all intent on their own doings and not taking very much interest in anyone else then I would not mind.'[8] Nonetheless half of these—largely middle-class—men remained opposed to public displays of affection. They were certainly more likely than women to articulate their objections in moral terms. 'Any girl who allows herself to be made love to in public is not a girl with a very high moral standard. Any man making love to a girl in the same circumstances is a cad! I think the whole question is disgusting,' wrote a single male civil servant.[9]

Those who condoned love-making in public justified their position by citing the lack of alterative locations. 'Better make love in a park, with what privacy one can find, than with grinning relatives around!' wrote a sympathetic housewife.[10] Another woman acknowledged with relief the access to privacy that married life had brought her: 'I feel sympathy for those whom circumstances force into the dark doorway or the park already littered with recumbent couples and couplings, and am heartily glad that I am freed from the necessity of behaving likewise.'[11] A young unmarried man conjured up the post-war context of acute housing need in stating, 'I don't like the idea of making love in public at all but it is a question of lack of opportunity. Someday a philanthropist will start a centre of courting rooms.'[12]

The ability to court in private was framed by social class, economic circumstance and social expectation. Ingeniousness and deception could also play a role. The emergence of the motor car, for example, facilitated a measure of mobile privacy for those who could afford it; an illicit night in a holiday boarding house might offer momentary seclusion.[13] Perhaps the clearest change over the

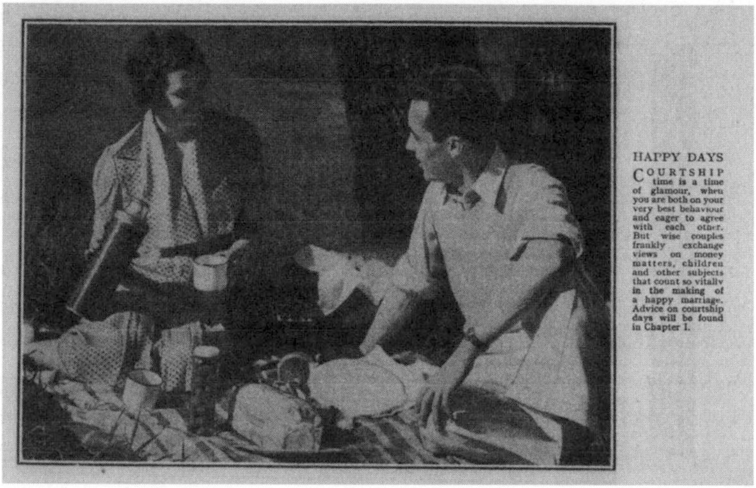

FIGURE 9 For many courting couples privacy was more difficult to come by than this idyllic image suggests.

mid-century period concerns a process whereby courting became simultaneously *less* private (moving from clearly defined experiences such as the evening walk, cinema-going, and dancing to virtually any youthful leisure activity) and *more* private (in that community and parental control declined in importance so that youthful courtship became relatively autonomous even within the parental home). Courting couples were increasingly seen in public, at their leisure, and this fuelled public discussion of youthful sexuality. Their behaviour was a lens through which generational difference could be monitored and assessed. Nonetheless young lovers increasingly carved out what cultural theorist Eva Illouz has described as 'islands of privacy' within these public spaces.[14] These were islands of emotional as well as physical privacy, reflecting understandings of love which privileged togetherness and exclusivity.

* * *

The archetypal public space with a private dimension was the cinema, which was 'always looked on as a good place for courting as it was dark, warm and comfortable'.[15] For those who could afford the price of entry, cinemas effectively offered the 'courting rooms' of our young Mass-Observer's imagination. A 1949 survey of London women found that cinema-going was by far the most popular activity amongst young courting couples—'twice as popular as any other recreation'.[16] Some cinemas were more explicit in promoting their courtship credentials than others; just as some catered for a more affluent clientele. The provision of double seats on the back row sent out a fairly clear message. Quoting Cecil Day Lewis's poem 'Newsreel' ('this loving | Darkness'), film historian Annette Kuhn draws attention to the deeply embedded link between cinema and courtship in the memories of early film goers.[17] The giving and receiving of chocolates was an additional element within this remembered association.

And yet the pursuit of private intimacy within a public leisure arena could cause tensions amongst cinema-goers as it did within other public spaces. A particularly heated *Manchester Evening News* letters page exchange on the subject on cinema etiquette concluded with a stinging attack on those courtship critics with an 'austere vision'.[18] A 33-year-old housewife in the late 1940s stated, 'I think people should please themselves as far as love-making in public is concerned, but if they want to sit cheek to cheek in the pictures I would rather they chose the back row as it is very difficult to look through or round two people glued together', whilst a nurse drew attention to the awkwardness of sitting next to an actively courting couple.[19] Tensions could emerge between courting couples. 'I have no objection to having somebody's arm around me in the pictures but kissing is definitely *out*,' commented one young woman. 'For one thing it makes you miss bits of the picture and for another it's too inclined to make a noise, and that's inexcusable!'[20] A man's response to a particular film gave an insight into his capacity for feeling and could be a way of gauging his continued suitability as

DODD
Whatever you do, don't make rustling noises with a box of chocolates during the show !

FIGURE 10 Chocolates were the obvious gift when courting in public leisure arenas.

boyfriend material. 'I don't go unless I think it is going to be a crying sort of film,' one woman admitted. 'I saw *Rebecca* three times. In *Scott of the Antarctic* I remember crying when he left his wife on the quay...I went once with a man I knew, he laughed about it, and I knew right away I wouldn't be seeing him anymore.'[21]

Beyond the cinema it is pretty clear that any leisure activity was a potential arena for courting. From the Lyons Corner tea house through to the post-war coffee bar, as each emergent leisure arena developed it was used by courting couples. Some were of more long-standing use. Municipal parks, for example, provided an expense-free location, albeit one not bereft of regulation. 'Why are the parks, the public parks, closed against the public on Sunday night, or any other night for that matter?' one *Manchester Evening News* reader demanded in 1930, identifying a clear class distinction. 'Why not give the working class lover a chance? They have no weird and wonderful parties, but most have a strict sense of decency.'[22] In 1938, Windsor magistrates investigated the town council's attempts to close 'Lovers-Lane' to the passing public. 'Occupants of houses which have been built all-round the lane, complain that they are annoyed by courting couples who throw litter over the fences into their gardens and awaken their babies by their giggling.'[23] Nonetheless the public performance of intimate attachment had a social as well as an emotional purpose: at least in the years prior to the Second World War. As one Mass-Observer put it retrospectively: 'It was almost like a ritual pre-marriage cycle that young people went through to give notice to the world at large that here was a forthcoming couple who were about to be made one.'[24]

Alongside public leisure arenas, the home also remained an important location for courtship; not least for those seeking family approval for their choice of partner. Amongst working-class families, etiquette dictated that the man should visit his girlfriend's home first and be entertained within the formal setting of the 'parlour'. Describing his courtship experiences on the eve of war, a retired decorator outlined the invitation to Sunday tea as 'a most terrifying experience':

> After being led into the houses, usually the parlour in which a fire had been set for the first time in years, you'd find all the family lined up in their Sunday best and the table laid with a dazzling white cloth. There would be matching plates and cups and saucers and a cake on a glass stand. A trifle in a glass bowl, neatly cut bread already buttered, and of course, that most essential for all significant occasions, the red salmon. Everybody would pretend to be jolly while putting you under the closest scrutiny, you wouldn't know what to say and yet no banal word uttered or nervous gesture would get you off the hook.[25]

Family endorsement diminished in importance after the war as the enhanced independence of youth described in Chapter Four changed inter-generational power dynamics. However, the need to secure parental approval did not disappear entirely. First, the law on the age of majority did not change until 1969 and so those who wished to marry young still required their parents' permission to do so. Second, the informal assent of families for individual choices still mattered in much the same way as it undoubtedly still does today. A woman born in 1931 confirmed this dynamic. 'My family had no objection to my courting but rules were strict. He had to be presented at home for the parents to look over and I had to be in by 9:30 on weeknights and 10 p.m. on Saturdays.'[26] Social researchers Young and Willmott even included a section entitled 'courting the mother-in-law' in their study of post-war London.[27] 'Any mother wants to have a look at her daughter's young man. She wants to see the goods laid out on the table,' they were informed.[28]

* * *

During wartime, love could be acutely important to individual men and women as a support in dark times. As Martin Francis puts it in his cultural history of the Royal Air Force, 'For all its agonies, love clearly offered a source of hope and comfort amidst a world marked by chaos and destruction.'[29] And yet relationships were difficult to maintain within this context. Wartime courtships were more often than not underpinned by fear, longing, and anxiety as well as a pressing desire to live in the moment. Confiding in her diary for June 1940, a young aerodynamicist recorded that she 'Travelled up to Shrewsbury with two very sleepy and two rather talkative soldiers. Jack met me, and we found that we had to feel a little unhappy, for it becomes so increasingly difficult to see each other, and the future we had planned is so impossible to think of now. However we could soon forget that and live in the present.'[30] A young Royal Air Force man described 'Hurried marriages, friends getting suddenly engaged, boys and girls trying desperately for a good time in the argument that "next week may be too late..."'.[31]

During wartime, established courtship practices were disrupted and the relationship between public and private expression was differently weighted. Within the general context of wartime dislocation, and the particular context of conscript mobility, courtship outside the orbit of parents and community became a possibility for increasing numbers of young people. 'It was extraordinary to be in a sense an adult and freed from the shackles of family,' one woman recalled.[32] Courtship etiquette therefore adapted to the exigencies of war whereby 'love-making had often to be done hurriedly on a 24-hour pass and in a district to which both were visitors'.[33] As one man recalled, 'everything altered with WW2: courtship had to be hurried as the man was likely to be drafted overseas in one of the armed services at any moment, never to come back—or to return some years later, very changed...the old fashioned courting routine had mainly disappeared.'[34] The carefully planned inter-war courtship with levels to pass through, evidence to accumulate, advice to solicit and resources to accumulate gave way to different ways of 'knowing' each other. 'I myself have always said that I should not marry and yet got married 6 months ago at the age of 21 though having no job to return to after the war and no private means,' admitted one young man.[35] The courtship patterns and romantic expectations of this generation, and of those that followed, were markedly different from those who conducted their courtships before the war.

Wartime conditions brought new places within which courting couples could carve out spaces for intimacy. The blackout was widely held to facilitate sexual encounters in public places. 'You could not expect people to put up with all the disadvantages of the black-out and not avail themselves of its advantages,' speculated a married secretary, declaring that 'One must take the smooth with the rough!'[36] Other aspects of everyday wartime life were held to offer similar opportunities. A 34-year-old food-packing manager found himself in command of a local air raid shelter. 'We are forbidden to lock the gates'—he seemed disappointed—'and in consequence I frequently have to listen to complaints from the

Shelter Warden.'[37] 'He tells me that some couples are generally to be found occupying various bunks after dark, and frequently stay there all night. Evidence is ample of their occupation and purpose in so doing.' Not everyone subscribed to a wartime discourse of moral decay, however. 'My own experience is that immoral or "fast" women are exceedingly difficult to find,' wrote one man, adding that 'the behaviour of couples establishing temporary relationships is remarkably restrained... young men are moral in practice though not in theory.'[38]

For some the pressures of war proved difficult to negotiate. The absence of boyfriends serving overseas created moral dilemmas for young women who saw no end to the conflict. 'Since my boyfriend was called up I've hardly gone out anywhere, and honestly, it's getting me down!' wrote 'Fed Up' to Jane Dawson of the *Manchester Evening News* in 1940.[39] 'I feel I'll go melancholy if I don't have some enjoyment, but a girl can't go out alone these nights. Do you think it would be very mean of me to go out with another boy who often asks me?' Dawson helpfully suggested that 'fed up' should busy herself with war work but the dilemma was a real one as the years of war stretched out over the prime of young women's lives. Anxieties amongst servicemen were not inconsiderable either. 'Here is a question that is disturbing many of us,' two air force men wrote in *Picture Post*. 'Is a serviceman (on overseas service) asking his girl too much by expecting her to remain faithful to him until he returns? There are twenty men in my section and five have been "given the boot" since arriving overseas. Thirteen of the twenty are married, so you can see for yourself the reason for asking this question.'[40] Nazi propaganda dropped on allied troops in 1944 sought to exploit such concerns through representations of British women in the arms of American servicemen.[41]

For many involved in the war, letter-writing was the only practical way of sustaining a relationship: an intensely private form of communication although one subject to military censorship. The love letter was not a wartime innovation but during this conflict it became an ordinary means of communicating extraordinary experiences. It provided a private courtship space at a time where the challenges of finding any space at all were considerable. Certainly a 1943 survey found that 'writing letters' was one of seven things people were doing more of since war had started.[42] The others were working, making new friends, staying at home, worrying about international affairs, reading newspapers, and listening to the radio. Not everyone was confident in their epistolary abilities. 'I am very worried about my writing!' one young woman confided in Leonora Eyles. 'I am in love with an officer and he has asked me to write now he has gone away. But I am afraid to let him see how bad my writing is.'[43] Such women feared the exposure of any limitations in their education. For others it was content rather than style which prompted concerns, particularly as the war dragged on. 'When our young men first went away overseas we found plenty to write about but now it is very difficult to find things to say,' one group of girls confided. 'We tell them what has happened in the office and that's all, but we are very anxious not to let them think we are cooling off.'[44] Eyles suggested a more ambitious and certainly more taxing approach: 'talk about your ideas for the future, what you think of marriage, and all the plans being made for a better world after the war.' Those in search of more detailed advice on writing could turn to Macandrew's *Courtship by Post (How to write Love Letters)* first published in 1941, but reissued until at least 1957, which helpfully offered advice, 'not only on what to write, but on what is better left unwritten'.[45]

Bill Cook and Helen Appleton were in need of no such advice. Bill was chaplain to the 6th Armoured Division whilst Helen taught at Ipswich High School. They met in a Norfolk Rectory in 1941—'our eyes met and that was it'—and married in 1946.[46] In the interim they exchanged six thousand letters by 'airmail, airgraph and seamail—written compulsively during four and a half years of separation'.[47] These were sufficiently valued to be kept as a full set. Historian of letter writing, Margaretta Jolly tells us: 'Letters are not just the means of communication but a physical token of the absent other, [which] gives them a fetishistic quality, easily recognizable by the importance of their physical aspects: the handwriting; the envelope; the way they are hoarded or tied in ribbons.'[48] A man writing in 2001 recalled that 'Life in the armed forces would have been much harder to bear without the mail call. Letters from everybody of course but particularly welcomed were love letters. It was common to stick the stamp on sideways which meant affection and even to write SWALK on the rear of the envelope (SEALED WITH A LOVING KISS). Letters were promptly replied to lest one should receive a dreaded "Dear John" letter calling off the relationship.'[49] Local historian Maureen Sutton's list of the secret codes used by her Lincolnshire interviewees across the mid-century included ITALY (I trust and love you), HOLLAND (Hoping our love lasts and never dies), BOLTOP (Better on lips than on paper), BURMA (Be undressed and ready my angel) and the significantly more blunt BYYGGI (Brace yourself, you're gonna get it).[50]

Conducting a relationship by letter took time. The more time was invested, the more the letter came to mean. A 23-year-old reporter in the Royal Engineers recorded in his diary for 1 April 1940: 'I stayed up late I remember, writing to my girl. Such letters though not properly and passionately love letters of the approved high falutin [*sic*] kind that sound ridiculous when read in court, are at least lovey and they take a long time to write. That was why diary didn't get written on Monday.'[51] A relationship developed through letter writing possessed a distinct pace, intensity, and, importantly, privacy. Some believed that an enhanced level of authenticity was reached within such relationships. Albert and Gladys Read conducted their courtship almost entirely by correspondence. 'I got to know her by letter,' Arthur later told film-maker and interviewer Tamasin Day-Lewis. 'I was able to tell her everything, including the things about me I thought a girl wouldn't like, my shyness, my glasses. Your nature comes out in your writing. We both liked cycling and music. You get to know more about a person through letters than when you meet them and they're on their best behaviour. It was the inner person I got to know.'[52] The relationship was sustained over a five-year separation. Writing a day before they were reunited in October 1945, Gladys wrote, 'I shall always love and adore you my dearest, and hope that I shall never cause you any hurt. When you come home darling never let us part. I want to be with you always for I love you, and it has been so long.'[53]

As historian Matt Houlbrook suggests, privacy is not the same as authenticity.[54] Wartime writers conjured up images and fantasies of themselves and the future through their letters. Pearl Jephcott, for one, urged a degree of caution. 'Girls spend an amazing amount of time on letter-writing, occasionally to a ghostly correspondent whom they have never seen and of whom they know nothing except what he has told them in his letters.'[55] Nonetheless within the epistolary context relationships could develop well away from the observations of family and community. 'So we separated for four years,' a retired carpenter remembered. 'It took nearly a year before her first letter reached me, it had been chasing me all over the Middle East. After a few letters over a couple of years, I wrote suggesting that we got engaged and enclosed some money in the letter for a ring... Four months later I received a letter showing the girl friend wearing the engagement ring she had chosen.'[56] This man married his girlfriend upon his return to England observing that a long-distance courtship was 'A thing to hang on to during adversity and distance. If you like, hope for the future at that time'. Love letters were not always quite so successful. 'Men and women unaccustomed to writing had sometimes to get their feelings on to paper,' observed Slater and Woodside of the couples they studied in the 1940s. 'This in itself was a source of misunderstandings. When one husband in the Middle East tried to expound his philosophy of life, his wife thought he was going mental... Letters were a thin thread, and a sense of loss of touch was universal. Delays or interruptions of delivery made this much more acute.'[57]

Beyond the apparent privacy of the love letter itself, the influence of family and community upon courtships diminished during the war. Some parents responded sympathetically to the changed context. 'Although my father was strict about my behaviour, my mother was not, possibly with the idea that as we could easily lose our lives and the future was uncertain, as much as possible should be got out of life.'[58] Nevertheless, the growing autonomy of courting couples was not permitted without a fight, or at least without a modicum of regret: 'Am I being old-fashioned in asking him to wait at least until we have met her and seen what type of girl she is?' asked one distressed mother whose son had announced his plans to marry.[59] In fact, the agony aunts were increasingly likely to side with youthful romantics against 'old-fashioned parents' in the battle for emotional autonomy. When a young woman complained about her boyfriend's mother in 1940, Eyles suggested: 'when a boy is so much at the mercy of a selfish mother as he is, the only thing to do is to try to force his hand and give him courage. Tell him you will have to give him up if he won't fix a date for the marriage.'[60] A mother considering whether to inform her daughter's fiancé of her infidelity was basically told to mind her own business: 'Her behaviour, in this instance, is a matter entirely for herself and her fiancé and if you interfere you will only make mischief.'[61]

* * *

After the war, young people were increasingly independent in their courtship behaviour. This was in part because the changes set in play by the war proved difficult to roll back and partly because of their enhanced financial status. The post-war years brought a significant increase in young people's wages with a commensurate rise in their disposable income: 'distinctive teenage spending for distinctive teenage ends in a distinctive teenage world,' as Mark Abrams put it in 1961.[62] Harry Hopkins observed that, 'Mere shillings of free spending money before the war were transformed into pounds, creating a new *jeunesse dorée* able to enjoy in these years between leaving school and marriage a freedom and an opulence which many would never know again in their lives.'[63] Courtship practices mirrored this trend towards youthful autonomy. 'Today there is a tendency for the young man to meet his girl at a friend's party, to date her at the cinema or the club and drop her off at her home,' wrote Edwards and Beyfus in their 1956 advice manual. 'And parents have got used to it. In fact, parents are growing to accept the idea that their offspring go out when they like, and few questions asked. Until one day they casually remark: "I'm going to marry John."'[64]

These advice authors undoubtedly overstated the freedom of youth, just as Abrams and Hopkins exaggerated its affluence. A Mass-Observer born as late as 1950 recalled that:

> Actually my mother seemed a bit confused about what she wanted for me. On the one hand, if there was a chance she'd be the first to suggest I buy something new or have my hair done or whatever, but the minute a male turned up on the doorstep she seemed to take on a different personality. She either interrogated them, turning them into gibbering wrecks, or was incredibly rude to them. Either way she managed to ensure that they never came near our house again.[65]

In her study of 1960s Swansea Diana Leonard noted a 'slight tendency' for middle-class and skilled working-class parents to be more 'actively interventionist' in their children's courtships and observed that a number 'warned off' particular partners.[66] 'Get that scruffy layabout off my doorstep' was the not-so-gentle nudge administered by one mother.[67]

Parental influence was not negligible—in England as well as Wales—even at the end of the 1960s. Both direct and indirect influence was brought to bear upon courting couples. A trip to the magistrate's court was the only way young couples could confound parental opposition to a proposed marriage. Moreover whilst National Service persisted for boys aged 18 and upwards, the State itself continued to actively disrupt courtship patterns. As Pearl Jephcott observed in 1954, 'The call-up was a dreadful menace to those who were accustomed to spending all their free time with their boy.'[68] Nonetheless, the maturing identity of 'youth', and emphasis upon its social and financial autonomy, led to a reduction in parental control, if not parental interference, in the everyday courtships of youth. Negotiations between parents and their children concerning the conduct of long-term courtships continued into the post-war world but they were differently weighted and the trend was towards decreasing intervention. More significantly, love itself had become a sphere for the assertion of independence: a private realm within which to fashion the self and the future.

6
Exchange and Negotiation

'May I take you home?'
'Yes.'
'May I kiss you on the doorstep?'
'No.'
'Then what's the good of taking you home?'[1]

Within the mid-twentieth century, courtship was the primary mechanism for moving from spinsterhood and bachelordom to married adulthood. Courtship could also be a space within which individuals became the men and women they wished to be or practised the roles they expected to fulfil. Couples mapped—or rejected—a shared future during a courtship; families supported—or discouraged—the plans of their children. Courtship could be a conduit for mutual transformation. But if the desires and expectations of those involved conflicted, it could also be a site of real anxiety. Tensions within courtship were most acute in relation to two intimately linked issues: money and sex. In an increasingly commodified leisure landscape, the question of who should pay for courting activity was not insignificant, although the cultural meaning of such payment probably mattered more. In an increasingly sexualized relational terrain, the question of 'how far to go' preoccupied courting couples and everyday experts. Penetrative pre-marital sex, at a time when access to reliable contraceptives was restricted, could change lives. In both areas ideas about how men and women should behave underpinned readings of, and responses to, actual everyday behaviour.

The exchange dimension to everyday courtship worked according to clear ideas about how men and women should behave. Men invested money in courtship; women invested emotion while safeguarding their sexual reputation. But the precise contours of exchange were not always transparent and it was possible to get the exchange relationship badly wrong. Those who miscalculated risked social castigation. 'Gold-diggers', for example, were held to exploit the financial dimension without emotional reciprocation. Usually represented as female, the gold-digger label was occasionally attached to a man if the relationship seemed otherwise inexplicable. 'How can I prove to them that the fact that the woman I love is wealthy hasn't influenced my feelings?', a 21-year-old man in love with a much older woman asked Evelyn Home in 1954.[2] The 'amateur'—a woman conceptualized as a sexual transgressor but not a professional prostitute—went a step further, exchanging sex for leisure treats.[3] 'The payment takes the form of a gift, or a dinner, or a motor run,' wrote Gladys Mary Hall in a 1933 study of the matter.[4] 'The episode appears less commercial and suggests more of passion and spontaneity than a similar episode with a professional prostitute, and for this reason is usually infinitely more attractive.' While women were ordinarily expected to control male desire within everyday relationships, the amateur actively exploited it for personal material gain. Both the amateur and the gold-digger transgressed the carefully constructed, yet quite fragile, framework within which modern heterosexual relationships were enacted. Each made explicit the implicit exchange upon which those relationships were founded and pointed up the ambiguous role of money and sex within the mid-century courtship.

* * *

The idea that a man should be the primary breadwinner underpinned heterosexual relations from courtship through to marriage. Men were expected to finance courtship, in part because their wages tended to be higher than women's. 'In those days the man always paid,' one woman recalled. 'It would never have occurred to me then to offer to pay. It would have been insulting to him.'[5] Another was informed by her mother that 'if a boy pays for your company, his intentions are serious'.[6] Adherence to this arrangement had cultural as well as practical significance although there were apparent contradictions in how it was practised. 'My parents had instilled in me the notion that if someone wanted to ask me out then it would be considered cheap if I paid my way until I knew them better,' explained one woman.[7] Here 'cheap' presumably means unfeminine. Men, on the whole, concurred with the arrangement. 'I never expected a girl I had a date with to go Dutch nor did I ever take out a girl who offered. I think most girls believed a man would be insulted by such an offer. Perhaps it was the kind of girl I dated but I always felt that I was favoured being allowed to take them out.'[8] As we will see, even where advice writers suggested that the arrangement be modified, they emphasized the necessity of safeguarding masculine pride. Writing in *Woman's Own* prior to the war, E. Russel Fortescue suggested that such courtesy be extended to complete strangers. When sharing a meal on a train, for example, a male companion—even if previously unknown—should be allowed to pay and the woman should settle up afterwards.[9] The performance, and witnessing, of ideal gender roles was vital regardless of actual behaviour. Women were expected to collude in a fantasy of male altruism.

Gift exchange added a further layer to courtship economics. Once again women were often—though not always—the beneficiaries. 'One way in which the girl's family judges the eligibility as well as the moral character of a prospective "in-law" is by the material pledges that he makes,' reported Pearl Jephcott in 1945.[10] A suitor's 'eligibility' and 'moral character' were demonstrated through gift giving: these two rather distinct factors were here seen as synonymous. Romantic gifts carried a range of meanings for couples, family members and those beyond. In her work on wedding presents, historian Louise Purbrick suggests that 'a gift is inevitably a social thing. What is at stake in every gift exchange is a relationship between people since the object is understood to carry some part of a person with it.'[11] Martin Francis records a precise, and touching, example of this social dynamic: 'Flyers begged their sweethearts to give them a stocking to wear as a talisman around their neck when in action, a testing request for young women faced with an acute shortage of hosiery during the war.'[12] As this example suggests, gifts did not necessarily need to cost a great deal financially to wield significance. In the post-war period the range of possible gifts expanded markedly. 'Every girl wants to go steady and your going steady ring will tell the world how you feel,' enthused a 1959 advertisement.[13] The ring itself cost 3s 9d—less than the price of two cinema tickets and a relatively small proportion of income in an era when wages were rising.[14]

Whether in the form of the going steady ring or the weekly trip to the cinema, courtship came at a price. As commercial leisure and everyday romance were increasingly entwined, courtship became an expense some men could not afford—particularly in periods of unemployment.[15] The anthropologist Geoffrey Gorer found that even amongst men in the immediate post-war years of 'full' employment 'the going out with a girl rises with income'.[16] In contrast, 'the poorest girls go out with men as much as their wealthier sisters, and indeed slightly more than most of them.' Gorer's findings help to explain why girls might see courtship as a general life cycle stage, while men were arguably more discerning. Post-war commentators consistently picked up on the financial costs of courting for young men. 'What is better, a car or a wife?' one young man asked Ferdynand Zweig. 'I was courting,' confided another, 'and should have been married by now, but instead I bought a car.' Zweig recorded that 'At first I treated it as a joke, but afterwards I heard it so many times in different versions ("I can't afford both a car and a wife, so I drifted away from my girl") that I had to regard it as a main issue for youth at present.'[17] The repetition of this statement across post-war social surveys suggests a historically distinctive way of understanding the choices available to young working-class men. Nonetheless in his study of 100 Sheffield youths who left school in 1959, M. P. Carter found that the custom of boys financing courting activity persisted:

> It was usual for boys to pay for entertainments when they took girls out—most girls did not have sufficient spending money left to pay their share, after having bought the clothes and make-up which were to catch the boys' eyes. One girl was treated to the cinema five evenings each week by her boyfriend, himself only seventeen years of age. Youths who did take girls out for the most part *expected* to pay—it was the right and done thing: 'I pay when we go out', said one youth, 'who doesn't?' One girl said that she had offered to go shares with her boyfriend, but had not pressed the point because she had 'had her head snapped off twice' for doing so. Part of the young man's pleasure was to be able to pay for the girl friend.[18]

Sheffield men clearly delighted in shouldering the costs of courtship. Carter's interviewees understood the gendered nature of wage inequality and took personal pleasure in being able to pay. This was not a perspective shared by all men. Although middle-class couples were significantly less likely to adhere to the practice than were working-class couples, opposition to the practice of paying spanned the mid-century, and traversed social classes. Where the issue was debated on the pages of popular magazines and newspapers, arguments about women's equality were never far behind. 'Girls want as much as they can get for as little as they can give. They shout for sex equality, but if they got it it would bring a rude awakening for many,' one local newspaper reader proclaimed.[19]

And yet life histories suggest that courting couples responded more flexibly to the conditions within which they found themselves. Social and economic differences between couples could be addressed through a modification in exchange practice. 'I am engaged to a girl in Worcester, a library assistant and from a definitely less wealthy household than mine,' one man told Mass-Observation in 1939.[20] 'Her father is a skilled worker at a big glove factory in W. For myself the class difference, such as there is, plays no part in this; but my fiancée herself is always very concerned that she should pay her share.' People who attended university in the post-war world remembered a more equitable financing of courtship activities related both to the semi-dependent status of the student and a certain freedom from social expectation. 'When I was at university things changed, mainly because we were freer,' one woman recalled. 'Of course there were still rules but again one could get round those if necessary. Until this time I wouldn't have expected to pay for activities, but it soon became clear that we were all on small allowances and it would have been ridiculous for the man to pay always—we would never have done anything.'[21] Whilst this woman believed that a measure of social and cultural liberty was a partial explanation for this state of affairs, economics was the real driver here. Both men and women in higher education lacked full economic independence and this led them to understand the exchange relationship differently at least for the duration of their studies.[22] During wartime limited resources placed established practices under considerable pressure too. Writing his Mass-Observation diary for November 1940, an electrician described a trip to London to visit his girlfriend. It was a rainy day and they spent rather a lot of time in cafes. Their lunch venue was the Lyons Corner House in Trafalgar Square. 'Although it was not summer we both had salad and I had a grapefruit first. We had tea to follow. My girl insisted on paying for the lunch as I had had to pay my fare up. I argued but gave in for she is obstinate and a dear.'[23]

In the aftermath of war, uncertainty concerning courtship economics grew. New strategies developed in the face of rising leisure costs and consumption opportunities. Women's wages were also increasing—although they remained dramatically lower than those of men at a time when the principle of equal pay had not yet been fully established.[24] Historian Selina Todd argues that from the 1940s working-class young women increasingly paid their own way in leisure.[25] I agree, but it wasn't always clear to the world that they were doing so. 'If a girl knows just what the expenses are to be she can give her boy her share beforehand otherwise she can settle afterwards, but she should always do this when they are by themselves and let the boy do the actual paying,' advised the *Woman's World* agony aunt in 1948.[26] A decade later etiquette experts Anne Edwards and Drusilla Beyfus argued that working girls should definitely pay for themselves. 'Once upon a time young men resented the idea of accepting money from women. These days when so many girls earn good salaries men are not noticeably averse to splitting the bill.'[27] The problem for post-war women, they averred, was in knowing precisely how to balance independence and femininity.[28] Male financial largesse was always about more than redressing the financial balance between courting couples. The act of paying modelled the version of masculinity which continued to underpin mid-century 'companionate' marriage.[29] Paying for courtship demonstrated a measure of protection and control even if the actual power dynamics of a relationship were very different. Because of this even where a woman actively limited the overall expense of a trip, and made a financial contribution herself, she was advised to do this privately. Prolific novelist and sometime etiquette expert Barbara Cartland put it particularly clearly in the early 1960s:

> On outings the girl would be wise to let her escort pay, being careful to choose inexpensive drinks and dishes, insisting that she prefers the stalls at the cinema or the gallery at the theatre. In fact she should lean over backwards not only to prove she is no gold-digger but also to avoid making her escort starve for the rest of the week, which he will do if he can—just to show off. Many a girl has spoiled what she expected to be a delightful friendship by insisting on sharing expenses or even pushing some money under or across the restaurant table. Equally, many a boy who greatly enjoyed a girl's

company had to shy off simply because he couldn't afford the more and more frequent meetings. The solution of this problem is entirely in the hands of the girl. With that frankness which is such a charming feature of the youth of today she can, after two or three outings, speak straight out, saying that although she enjoys the evenings together very much, it's unfair to go on in this way, and couldn't they come to some sensible understanding about finances? That pleasant euphemism 'Dutch treat' is a nice way of broaching the subject of sharing expenses. If the idea is grudgingly accepted, the girl should be sure to be the junior partner in the arrangement by handing over her money to her escort so that he can appear to be paying for everything. This gentle hypocrisy mollifies the masculine embarrassment.'[30]

Here we see a moral economy of courtship which adheres to the public codes of gender relations. It acknowledges the boundaries and hypocrisies of these codes, but does not overtly challenge them. The fantasy of female dependence persisted even as independence became realizable. Within this reading, courtship provided an opportunity to rehearse and perform the social relations which were expected to frame married, rather than single, life.

* * *

Amongst the materials gathered for Mass-Observation's 1949 'Little Kinsey' sex survey lies an interview with a 19-year-old from Middlesbrough. Described as a 'case history', it provides an unusually frank and richly reflexive account of the woman's early sexual experiences. At its heart lies the story of her relationship with 24-year-old merchant seaman Ted, a man she met through her work in a hotel. When she first met him, Ted was 'a perfect gentleman . . . always took me all over the place for dinner'.[31] Two months later he pressed her for sex: 'I refused at first. He asked me and I said "Nothing doing", he said "Why not?"' The couple did in fact have intercourse. She explained that:

I wouldn't have done it if I wasn't in love with him and he told me he was in love with me. I still love him though. I was sitting on the bed and he sat down beside me, he pushed me down on the bed, and put a pillow under my head, and he lay down beside me. I took my dress off, I would have got it very creased if I hadn't—nothing else. I didn't take a thing off except my shoes—I only had two more things on.

All the time I knew I shouldn't be doing it. He took most of his clothes off—and then it just happened. He used a contraceptive—I know because I refused and he said it was quite safe—there was

FIGURE 11 Established courting practices were disrupted during the Second World War.

> no danger—I agreed then. I didn't want to but I liked him and he wanted to. He said: 'You can't be in love with me unless you will do it.'

This is a complex account within which love, rather than desire, acts as an explanatory tool: 'I wouldn't have done it if I wasn't in love with him and he told me he was in love with me.'

Nonetheless in concluding her account, this young woman reflected on the tensions at the heart of her relationships with men. 'Men want to be intimate without any understandings. I couldn't be intimate with a man unless I was in love with him. Men think you are terrible if you don't want to be intimate with them—they want to know "why not" and all that sort of thing.' Crucially she observed: 'He'd always give me my own way—very good to me, but he wanted something in return.' The transactional nature of courtship was here made painfully clear.

Some men expected a sexual return on their courtship investment: '"payment" for the money he has spent'.[32] 'I have a boy-friend whom I like very much and he takes me to shows and for runs in his car,' wrote one young woman to Leonora Eyles in 1940. 'Lately he has worried me by asking me to do something wrong. I have refused to go out with him anymore but he keeps phoning. Ought I to tell my girl-friend and get her husband to talk to him?'[33] A growing post-war tendency for girls to pay their own way within courtship reflected a desire to control male expectations and behaviour. 'Then they don't expect anything of you,' Pearl Jephcott was informed.[34] In contrast, some women were undoubtedly happy to combine sexual activity with other forms of pleasure. Elizabeth Alice Clement has argued that in early twentieth-century America 'treating' created 'a moral space between prostitution and courtship' for working-class women, allowing them to 'avoid the label of prostitute but still engage in sexual exchange for material gain'.[35] Certainly within a context of expanding commercial opportunities and the world of leisure commodities, the question of payment in kind for access to sex blurred the distinctions between different categories of sexual actor—hence the moralist concern about the so-called 'amateur'. During the Second World War, the material goods gifted by North American troops were popularly believed to be a factor in encouraging sexual relations between them and local women.[36] It was not inconceivable that great dancing prowess or exceptional good looks might make a man worth paying for. A Mass-Observer stationed in Luton in 1942 recorded that 'One corporal in our section is a very good dancer and also quite a sexy chap and he has the pick of who he wants. He even tells me that one woman pays him for it. Also he says he has never had to pay for a dance, film or supper since he has been in Luton—all his women pay all his expenses.'[37]

It would be surprising if mid-century women were not as capable of sexual pleasure as were their boyfriends. Whilst sex survey authors tended towards a penetrative definition of sex in researching the topic, a wider range of sexual practice is apparent in the evidence they gathered.[38] 'Heavy petting was the general rule within the development of a relationship,' recalled a woman who married at the age of 21 in 1950. 'I was a virgin at marriage (although can admit to a few near misses with previous boyfriends before "falling in love" with my husband).'[39] Unmarried women's capacity for sexual delight terrified some social commentators. 'One of the most serious results of the new attitude of mind amongst women is the behaviour of a steadily growing class of "respectable" girls who deliberately reverse the natural order of sex life,' wrote ex-CID officer, Cecil Bishop, in 1931. 'The women belonging to this class are content no longer to be sought by men; they have themselves become the seekers. Setting no price other than a "good time" upon their favours, and putting no check to their eroticism, they constitute an element of serious unrest.'[40] Whilst inter-war efforts to dissuade the young from expressing their sexual desires focused around the motif of the amateur, the self-appointed guardians of post-war sexual morality sought to regulate *degrees* of intimate exchange, particularly through advice on sensible petting.[41] 'If a woman has had full sex experience and it suddenly ceases,' suggested Herbert Gray, 'she is often left with a very strong longing for it, and is apt to take in a hurry some other man who may not really be suited to her at all. The only wise course is not to begin sex experience until you can have it with someone with whom you can carry on freely, fully, happily and for life.'[42] Evelyn Home put it more succinctly: 'Petting need not be wrong unless it leads to the love making which belongs to marriage.'[43]

Sexual exchange of all types could be conceptualized as a gift willingly bestowed by a woman. A 23-year-old former labourer interviewed by marriage researcher Moya Woodside towards the end of the war first met his wife at Colchester barracks. Within a week of this meeting he proposed, she accepted and they had intercourse in a local park. 'He said to her: "If you're good enough to let me do it now, you're good enough to marry." It was their first experience and "both of us were frightened" but passions got the better of us.'[44] Nonetheless mid-century courtship was often portrayed—in magazine fiction, in films, within advice literature—as fundamentally conflictual. 'A kind of sexual warfare' is how historian Elizabeth Roberts puts it.[45] Within this reading, men wanted sex and women wanted commitment. Men wanted to evade commitment; women wanted to evade sex. Love was a negotiating tool to access sex; sex was a commodity exchanged for love. In effect sexual intimacy was represented as a sensitive terrain upon which immediate and long-term desires were mediated and negotiated. This representation is evident within retrospective accounts. Women Mass-Observers writing in 2001, for example, offered accounts of mid-century courtships which tended to emphasize their own sexual 'innocence'.[46] The temporal specificity of these experiences was often heightened by making explicit comparison with more recent times. As oral historian Kate Fisher notes, memories of sex are generated in dialogue with contemporary sexual discourses.[47] And yet contestation is rarely absent from these courtship accounts. 'He didn't even dare to kiss me for four months and it was longer than that before I allowed moderate necking!' one woman recalled. 'Sadly he outgrew me before I outgrew him and also, like most young men, he wanted to go further—much further!—and I wouldn't. My religious background initially held me back and also my intention of entering marriage in a virginal state.'[48]

During wartime, established codes of sexual negotiation—combative and not so combative—were destabilized.[49] 'For my own part I know that the sight of so many officers walking about in uniform... is very disturbing,' one woman told Mass-Observation echoing the Khaki Fever which had so concerned commentators during the previous conflict.[50] She explained:

> There's no doubt a uniform 'gets you', and I know jolly well that if I were to meet one sufficiently attractive and convincing, and if he could persuade me that he wanted me enough, then nothing would stop me from seeing the thing through to its natural, logical conclusion, and the effect of the uniform and the fact that the man was taking his very life in his hands the next time he went to sea would go more than half way in influencing me in my decision.[51]

Cross-cultural misunderstandings were believed to be adding to the sexual confusion. The posting of American troops raised within the formalized 'dating system', outlined by historian Beth L. Bailey, caused particular anxieties.[52] 'The phenomenon of the year in Cambridge has been the arrival of American troops,' claimed one woman in 1942. 'Largely due to lack of other entertainments or occupation their hours are spent on the streets, where their usual "hiya babe" and frequent direct passes, have to a magnified degree made the vicinity fear for its maidens. Not entirely without reason.'[53] According to sociologist Fernando Henriques, the situation was often 'absurd'. 'On the one hand English girls were outraged at what they regarded as premature attempts at seduction; on the other hand the young G.I. who found his girlfriend ready for intercourse on the first date was disgusted.'[54] As one *Woman's Own* reader put it in 1944, 'my friend and I go to dances where there are lots of very nice Americans. They see us home and want to kiss us goodnight. We told them that girls here think it cheap to kiss on such slight acquaintance, and they seemed really hurt, saying in the States boys always kissed girls goodnight. We don't want to hurt them, but what can we do?'[55]

The agony aunts discouraged romantic fraternization with foreign troops; they pointed up cultural differences in sexual attitudes and suggested that these were largely insurmountable. Leonora Eyles, for example, felt the need to offer stern words of advice to girls who fell in with European soldiers.

> Please remember that, on the Continent, relations between the sexes are rather different from here. We are much freer, and should use our freedom with dignity and self-respect. Foreigners are often puzzled by British girls because they talk about sex, and allow liberties which, on the Continent, are only allowed by paid prostitutes... That explains why girls get into trouble with foreigners. These men, accustomed to their own ways and not ours, imagine that a girl who allows liberties knows how to protect herself from the consequences.[56]

Here there is a sense that the context for complex, often implicit negotiations, had altered so dramatically that no one knew which rules to follow any more. Was sympathy for the plight of the serviceman sufficient justification for sex? 'I am friendly with a nice soldier and he keeps asking me to give way to him,' wrote one woman in 1945. 'I feel sorry for him, as he is coloured and nobody takes much notice of him, but I feel a bit scared.'[57] The reference to 'race' adds a distinctive dimension to the a well-established notion of female responsibility for male morale. Elsewhere the *Woman's Own* problem page regularly featured problems along the lines of 'I fell passionately in love with a foreign soldier and I gave way to him' which always precipitated an explanation which emphasized cultural differences in courting regimes. 'Most foreigners, divide women into two compartments; women, like their relatives, whom they respect and some-day marry; and girls who permit sexual liberties, whom they don't respect and would never dream of marrying.'[58] Indeed for Eyles, and others, the defence of British women's virtue in the face of foreign intervention became a patriotic duty. She was particularly forthright in response to a 15-year-old girl whose soldier boyfriend was particularly insistent. 'You must give him up—the man is a cad to try to work on your feelings in this way; if you do give way to him, he will soon leave you and go on to another girl. Unless you can show him that English girls are not to be brow beaten like this, and have a high sense of self-respect, you must have nothing more to do with him. Your whole life's happiness may be at stake. In any case, you know, you are far too young to be going about with a special boy.'[59]

In peacetime, patriotic duty was transformed back into mere moral duty. If men were responsible for the financing of courtship, then women were responsible for policing levels of sexual intimacy—at least until the marriage day. *Sex, Love and Society* was published in 1959 as an educational text for the young; it was described by one medical practitioner as 'readable, intelligent and very human'.[60] The book's author, psychiatrist E. R. Matthews, held uncompromising views on petting and encouraged women to police it in no uncertain terms. 'Any girl who allows a boy to indulge in passionate kissing and intimate caressing is not only running a serious risk that this will lead to such a state of sexual tension that neither of them will be able to stop short of full intercourse, but she is making herself very cheap in the boy's eyes, however much he is responsible for taking the initiative.'[61] A woman considering giving up a boy prone to taking liberties on the way back from a dance, was advised against this course of action by Leonora Eyles in 1936. 'Many boys lose their heads a little after dancing, and it is up to the girl to keep them sensible.'[62] Some developed particular strategies for repelling unwanted attention. 'I always remember a grey skirt, a right tight skirt. I couldn't get it up to go to the toilet,' one of Elizabeth

Roberts's oral history interviewees told her.[63] 'But I thought that was great because if you got a lad and he was a bit randy he had no chance of getting it up, you know. I could hardly walk in it, it was that tight. I thought I was the bees knees in it, but I felt quite safe in it.' Writing in the immediate post-war period marriage guidance expert David R. Mace acknowledged that female sexual desire could be powerful. 'I'm not forgetting that many women need sex as much as men do,' he explained, but 'the real woman wants sex in the right atmosphere... as part of an enduring comradeship.'[64] According to Mace, and indeed nearly everyone else, it was women's responsibility to create this happy circumstance. 'If women insisted that men only got sex in return for shouldering the responsibilities of providing a home and accepting the duties of parenthood, then men would have to come into line', he insisted.

The exchange value of virginity remained high across the mid-century. If the central courtship investment for men was money, for women it was sexual reputation. Sex researcher Michael Schofield found that although half the boys he surveyed in the early 1960s agreed with sex before marriage, 64 per cent of the boys nonetheless wanted to marry a woman who had not experienced sexual intercourse herself.[65] Eighty-five per cent of the women he interviewed apparently wanted to enter marriage as virgins. A sexual double standard underpinned these and other similar survey findings, with clear distinctions drawn between marriageable and non-marriageable women. 'If it was a girl I was going to marry I wouldn't have it,' one young man told a BBC interviewer in a 1964 programme called *Marriage Today*.[66] 'I think it would spoil it for when you did get married. But if it was just a girlfriend like, yes I would.' In his 1971 survey *Sex and Marriage in England Today* Geoffrey Gorer found that 46 per cent of men and 88 per cent of women reached betrothal, if not marriage itself, as 'technical virgins'.[67] 'England still appears to be a very chaste society,' he concluded, although reported levels of chastity clearly remained deeply gendered.[68] Schofield found far more support for male sexual experience before marriage than for female sexual experience. Nearly half of the women he surveyed believed that experience was advisable for boys but not for girls.[69] As late as 1959, *Woman* advised its readers to avoid even a goodnight kiss with a new boyfriend—'he'll think you are cheap'.[70] The magazine may not have been entirely wrong. It was not uncommon for young women to be castigated by the very men with whom they had sexual relations. Peter Willmott reported the views of some East End adolescents:

> The boys suggested that this more promiscuous sexual intercourse was usually with a minority of girls who, in their words, were 'easy lays', 'old slags' or 'bangers'.
>
> 'I could see straight away she was a right banger,' said a 17 year old of one girl. 'A banger's a goer—a girl who'll do anything with anyone.'
>
> 'You can always get a bit if you want it, with the girls with the big mouths. It gets around that they're that sort of girl. But that sort of thing turns you off after a while—you realize that if you can get it, so can anyone else.' (18-year-old.)[71]

The negotiation of degrees of sexual intimacy operated within a web of meaning. Couples negotiated physical desire, emotional attachment, prescriptive norms, and the fundamental messiness of human relations in a moment. But sexual activity also had a future meaning not least in its ramifications for a woman's value as a marriage partner. Consequently in the middle of our period, when 'honesty' had yet to become a central element of ideals of emotional intimacy, the massaging of sexual histories was not necessarily seen as wrong. In some cases it was positively encouraged as a reasonable response to the sexual double standard. 'Will he know?' a young woman asked Leonora Eyles, wondering whether she should tell her fiancé about a previous sexual encounter. 'There is no reason for him to know unless you tell him; a girl's past is her own business, and no man has a right to pry into it,' Eyles replied, suggesting a delicate balance of mutual delusion.[72] Honesty was definitely not the best policy. Even a woman who had previously given birth to a—subsequently adopted—baby, was urged to resist disclosing this information to the man she now loved. 'This is how to look at it; few girls have such a confession to make, but most men, if they had babies every time they made mistakes, would have to confess to this sort of past. But very few do, or, if they do, their womenfolk overlook it. I feel that we are, at this moment, what our past has made us, and if you regret past mistakes, as I know you do, it is nobody's business but your own.'[73] In this response we see Eyles encouraging a kind of self-determination, or at least granting her reader licence to control the past in order to make a better future.

Nonetheless, as this case demonstrates, risk as well as pleasure framed courtship relations across the mid-century. Losing one's head, giving in, giving way, were terms used by women to describe an act which in retrospect they constructed as a mistake—particularly if it ended in an unplanned pregnancy. Amongst men, the risk of disease remained a concern until at least the end of the Second World War; a risk made very public in the hard-hitting press and Ministry of Health campaigns.[74] It greatly concerned some people. 'My adolescence was a combination of innocence and ignorance,' recalled one man who met his wife during the war.

> I knew nothing of contraception, not that I needed such knowledge, the closest relationship with the opposite sex we found in the local cinema in blissful hours of holding hands in its cosy darkness. After many such 'dates', [you] might have progressed to some petting but by then you were considered as 'courting' (is that word used today I wonder?) and even entitled to some reward, such as a kiss or two. Never occurred to me to try for anything else. But all so wonderful. Five years of wartime service in the RAF altered all that, however. Many sexual adventures in different countries of South-East Asia were inevitably to be followed by agonising days on the watch for symptoms of disease.[75]

Fear of pregnancy was *the* key risk of sexual exchange for courting couples across our period who lacked access to reliable contraception or legal abortion. 'Before marriage I had several boy-friends but no intimate relationships—it just wasn't done in those days, and the girls were afraid of pregnancy anyway, contraception not being freely available to all then,' recalled one woman. 'My husband is the only man with whom I have had, or felt I wanted to have, a close relationship.'[76]

The spectre of unplanned pregnancy was a constant on the letters pages of *Woman's Own*. 'My parents have absolutely forbidden me to see a certain boy, but we meet in secret, because we are very fond of each other,' one reader confided before adding, 'A little while ago we lost our heads and are now terrified. What shall we do if things turn out badly? Do help us; we are so unhappy.'[77] The response was reassuring yet firm: 'You must wait, my dear, until you know definitely, and then let me know. You could go to his parents possibly for a while, or in certain cases magistrates can overrule parents about marriage. But there is probably no need for all this worry. Please don't ever do this again; it is wrong and only brings unhappiness...' Those unmarried women who did find themselves pregnant anticipated parental anger and were generally advised to contact the National Council for the Unmarried Mother and Her Child for support. Nonetheless attitudes towards pre-marital pregnancy were not uniform across or within classes.[78] In her 1958 study of working-class Ship Street in Liverpool, Madeline Kerr observed that 'The attitude to illegitimacy in this group is very different from the English middle-class one. So far as we can see little shame or guilt is felt. Parents do not turn the girl out and generally accept the baby as another member of the family.'[79] In contrast, a study by Virginia Wimperis of the same period pointed to women who were largely 'cut off from family and friends and from the neighbours who would normally lend a hand in times of trouble'.[80]

Extra-marital pregnancy changed the lives of both men and women. There was a powerful social expectation that a pregnant woman would marry the father of her child. 'I fell in love aged

19 years with my husband and became pregnant,' wrote one Mass-Observer.[81]

> By the time my parents knew and had made it plain to me that I must marry I had fallen out of love but was too scared of my mother and scandal to back out; who would help me, where could I go. There was only back street abortion available then; my husband wanted to marry me so what other option did I have. I soon discovered my husband was too fond of drink and very moody and bad tempered after several pints of beer when a wrong look or word from me could result in blows or his food thrown at me.

Sexual intercourse carried risks for men too. It might cause them to lose their shot at educationally driven social mobility or at 'real' love. The fear of being tied down prematurely permeates the Angry Young Men fiction of the period. It forms a central plot device within the film *A Kind of Loving* (1962) in which Vic Brown (played by Alan Bates) exchanges plans for travel and advancement at work for an unhappy marriage living with his mother-in-law, because his girlfriend becomes pregnant.[82] A letter to *Woman's Own* in 1950 outlined the dilemma well: 'A girl is going to have a baby, of which I am the father. Both the girl and her parents have said we must marry. However, since we have very little in common and as the affection I had for the girl has diminished, I am opposed to the idea, as I feel sure that such a marriage would be a failure. I am perfectly willing to contribute to the child's maintenance, but the girl and her people say this is not enough.'[83] Mary Grant's response was perhaps more lenient than might be expected: 'My opinion is that a man who has so little sense of responsibility would make a poor husband. I hope you realise that your passing affection has left its mark on at least two lives. Will you ask the girl to write to me, enclosing a stamped addressed envelope?'

* * *

Courting changed lives; that was its fundamental purpose. Writing in 1954 Pearl Jephcott noted the impact of courtship upon the young Nottingham women she surveyed:

> The Nottingham interviewees were in two minds about this early courting. It certainly shook some sense into some of the more scatter-brained individuals, and sometimes the girl or boyfriend was a provider of informal education in the more rigid sense of the word. Romance and love even at this teen-age could and did enrich some lives—noticeably so. But it aged others and occasionally turned a girl into a wife before she had grown to be a woman. The anxiety attached to even a temporary boy weighed certain of them down, as, for example, the girl who, for all her delight in her boy and the adult status she had acquired, nevertheless admitted that courting put years on you, 'you can't be so light-hearted like'.[84]

The dominance of marriage as both aspiration and social practice provided a powerfully persistent context for courtship across the mid-twentieth century. Heterosexual courtships provided training in the roles upon which marriage remained based. Despite shifts in women's employment opportunities and earning capacity, the etiquette of courtship was rooted in a model of economic behaviour that prescribed male breadwinning and female dependence. The sexual dynamics of courtship remained rooted in a persistent double standard.

Yet changes in the economic and social lives of young people brought about modifications in courtship behaviour. Affluence, National Service, modern employment patterns and leisure practices are just some of the factors which differentiated pre-war from post-war youth. The Second World War fundamentally destabilized the careful planning upon which courtship practices had long depended. Whilst dominant models of exchange were not so different if we compare the two periods, the terrain upon which negotiations were conducted was changing fast. In their everyday courting practice individual men and women increasingly questioned, subverted and sometimes actively rejected the economic and sexual models which their parents had taken for granted.

Part III: Commitment

I was engaged at the tender age of 17 years to a young man who had been called up to do his National Service in the Army. I had known him for several years and we had gone out together regularly. My mother and father were against this engagement really as they thought I was far too young. I know now that I was but in those days (1953) young engagements and marriages were the norm—there was nothing much else for a girl to do in those days.

(MOA, DR C1548, Summer 1990, woman born in 1936)

7
Making Commitment

Boyfriend magazine was launched in May 1959 priced at 4d.[1] Each week a celebrity 'boyfriend'—Frankie Vaughan in issue one, Cliff Richard in issue two—contributed a love story apparently drawn from 'his experience of life'. Readers were also introduced to 'the girl behind the boy'. Billy Fury was interviewed about a girlfriend who had helped him to succeed. Marty Wilde talked about his mum. Teen culture, romance, and marriage were unquestioningly entwined. Advertisements for engagement rings—'Why wait to get engaged? You can have a Cresta diamond ring now and pay later without touching your savings'—sat alongside those for record players.[2] Picture stories dwelt on the challenges of being young and in love while the Talbot Twins, Johnny and Jeannie, offered youthful advice to troubled teens negotiating romantic commitment.

'Café Congo' was *Boyfriend*'s first picture serial, spread over eight issues of the magazine. It told the story of Sue Peters, a young woman determined to transform her aunt's Oxford Tea Shoppe into a modern coffee house. When she spots an African dance mask for sale in the local market she decides to give the café an 'African' theme. The transformation costs £25 and a lot of emotional capital. Dramatic tension is provided by Sue's romantic dilemmas—chiefly her attempts to avoid entanglements with men. 'She's young and she wants to have fun and do something before she gets married,' ran the opening caption.[3] 'Her problem—how to stay single long enough to realise her ambitions.' The inevitability

FIGURE 12 Café Congo was *Boyfriend* magazine's first picture serial.

of early marriage and the limitations it could bring were brought into sharp relief. Here, Richard Hoggart's characterization of youth as a 'brief flowering period' for girls was given dramatic form.[4] Unsurprisingly, given the generally upbeat tone of *Boyfriend* magazine, the story ended happily. After being wooed by more than one man, Sue—'the sweetie from Suffolk'—agreed to marry the one who shared her enthusiasm for café culture. Marriage, it appeared, was not necessarily incompatible with youthful ambition. The pair would run the café together.

'Café Congo' illustrates one of the most distinctive characteristics of mid-century social relations: the ubiquity of marriage and its penetration of youth culture. 'Marriage has never been a more popular institution,' asserted Rachel M. Pierce in 1963.[5] Not only were more people marrying than ever before, but they were doing so at ever younger ages. A 1959 survey indicated that a quarter of working-class brides were still teenagers on their wedding day; more than three-quarters were under 25 years of age.[6] At a time when youth culture was increasingly visible, and periodically castigated, the age at marriage question generated significant debate. One, perhaps surprising, aspect of the post-war teenage revolt was an apparent enthusiasm for married adulthood. Across social groups the mid-1970s marked a break. The age at first marriage began to rise and the popularity of marriage began to diminish.

Of course neither marriage, nor heterosexuality, was a universal destination.[7] 'How am I to get my sex impulses satisfied, so as to live a full life, without having to go out to catch a man, ensnare him into marriage, and settle down to a dreary domestic life?' asked one female diarist in 1940.[8] Marriage was, nonetheless, an aspiration for most men and women in the mid-century, operating as a 'mental full stop' according to marriage researchers Slater and Woodside.[9] But what were the rituals which facilitated the making of commitment? At what point did 'going steady' become 'being engaged' and then 'becoming a spouse'? How do we account for the declining age at first marriage and what challenges did youthful marriage actually pose? Like love itself, the meaning of commitment was not historically stable. Both war and affluence had a fundamental impact upon the texture of commitment, stimulating interventions by parents, the state, professional bodies and everyday experts. Their attempts to control marital commitment amongst the young did not always meet with unqualified success.

* * *

Writing from the vantage point of 1990, one female Mass-Observer explained how mid-century commitment had become cemented around a set of highly distinctive norms.[10] Married in 1955, she had courted a number of different men before she met her husband-to-be but had not been sexually intimate with any of them. Her everyday courtship patterns mirrored those outlined in Part Two. Dance halls and the cinema provided forums for becoming better acquainted; becoming known to each other's families was also important.

> Then came the great day of the engagement, when the ring was bought and, in most cases, a period of saving began so that there was a nest-egg to put towards the future home. About a year to eighteen months after the engagement came the wedding and the couple started life together and in most cases also started their sexual relationship after marriage. I know this was true in my own case, and in the cases of my close friends. What all this meant was that there was plenty of time in which to get to know your prospective partner as a person. Getting to know them as a lover came in the comfortable surroundings of marriage, where there was plenty of time to develop the relationship and no embarrassment at being 'caught in the act' because you were in the privacy of your own home.

The purchase of the ring marked a step change in this relationship. The importance of structures which facilitated mutual knowledge before marriage is made clear in this account. The significance of home as both a physical and emotional space after the wedding day is also striking. It was a place to enjoy sex without embarrass-

BECOMING ENGAGED 155
It is one of life's great moments for any young couple when they tell their families of their engagement. Though it is often a shock—and not always a welcome one—families should try to be sympathetic and greet the new member with every kindness.

FIGURE 13 Becoming engaged was a rite of passage.

ment. The basic chronology is undoubtedly fairly typical. In the early 1950s, anthropologist Geoffrey Gorer suggested that a courtship of between 1 and 2 years followed by a short engagement of less than twelve months was the norm.[11] In the 1920s and 1930s engagements had been longer but as Margot Lawrence explained in *The Complete Guide to Wedding Etiquette*, 'Now that the majority of girls continue in paid work after their marriage, there is usually no financial reason to make a long engagement necessary.'[12] Nonetheless even before the war the perils of excessively long engagements, during which enthusiasm might diminish or sexual temptation overwhelm, were highlighted by everyday experts. 'A long engagement...almost always seems to lead to disaster,' warned Helen Worth of the short-lived *Modern Marriage* magazine.[13] 'Bad for the nerves', was Leonora Eyles's diagnosis.[14] By 1952 Gallup found only 30 per cent of the British public in favour of long engagements.[15] 'In the end the engagement just drifts into indifference or the man clears off to make a hurried, unconsidered marriage with someone else,' was Eyles's downbeat assessment.[16]

Becoming engaged was a rite of passage which brought with it both status and licence. According to Zweig, each phase in the commitment journey brought the working-class woman, in particular, additional respect: 'When she has reached the stage where she can display an engagement ring, her prestige is nearly at the peak and the ring is passed from hand to hand with words of appreciation and vicarious enjoyment of the great event.'[17] In addition to peer group acclaim, the announcement of an engagement could enhance status at home. It might, for example, bring a softening of parental control over issues such as the evening curfew. Parents who did not grant such freedoms were increasingly construed as out of touch. 'My girlfriend and I are twenty one and are engaged to be married,' one young man told Mary Grant in 1950.[18]

> The trouble is that my future father-in-law is very old-fashioned and insists that his daughter should be in by 10.15 at night, Saturday's

> and Sunday's included. This, of course, is very annoying at times, and the most annoying thing is that he will only allow her to go out on two nights during the week. The other evenings we are compelled to spend apart. If you can possibly spare a little of your limited space I should be very glad to know your view on the matter.

Grant suggested a direct confrontation: 'Either she goes out and comes in when she likes or she leaves home and goes into lodgings. I imagine that her father will give up in the face of a direct attack.' What the father of this young woman failed to recognize was that being engaged was a clear marker of maturity and so merited some increased measure of independence. Engagement itself also served an educational function as young men and women learned about themselves and each other.

The first area of training was practical. A properly conducted engagement laid down economic and social foundations for the future, but it could only do so if the parties were compatible. 'The engagement is a testing time, a trial time, a "preliminary canter", to see whether you two can run in double harness successfully,' suggested *Every Woman's Book of Love and Marriage*. 'It is not yet too late to draw back.'[19] Engagement was a time for domestic planning. 'It is wise to have the financial position made as clear as it can be before marriage,' advised Leonora Eyles.[20] Whilst the man might continue to finance shared leisure pursuits, a woman was expected to save for their future together and to accumulate items for her 'bottom drawer'. By so doing she would demonstrate the skills of housekeeping which underpinned the housewifely role. A man was expected to model his value as a husband during an engagement. 'My future husband is spending all his money on me now, instead of saving it up to buy the things we shall need when we are married,' worried Marjorie on the pages of *Modern Marriage* in 1931.[21] Young women were encouraged to uncover character flaws that might impede her potential future husband's capacity for family life. The *Every Woman's Book* was unforgiving in its approach to personal weakness:

> 'I am unhappy because my fiancé is sometimes the worse for drink,' many a girl has said. 'He has promised to give it up when we are married. Do you think I dare risk my happiness with him? I love him but I hate this weakness.' Now if this young man really cared enough for the girl to overcome this habit, he would do it during their period of courtship when his love, if anything, is at its height. If he does not do it then, the probability is that he never will.[22]

'If you don't like him now, don't marry him,' was the Rector of Aldrington's blunt advice.[23] Marriage-guidance expert David Mace proffered a whole list of questions for a bride-to-be to ask: 'Is it really *me* he cares for? Will he be just as glad to be with me when I'm not all dressed up and made-up?' and, crucially, 'Will he be a good provider? Does he handle money wisely, acting neither as a miser nor as a spendthrift?'[24] For religiously motivated writers such as these, careful preparation for marriage was not just of benefit to individual couples. It formed part of a strategy to defend matrimony itself against growing 'divorce mindedness'. Marital relations based on love and sex might be more vulnerable than those rooted in pragmatism, but with the provision of proper training the irrational world of love could be made matrimonially secure.

The other major area of marriage preparation involved bodies and sex. Engagement sanctioned new levels of intimacy. An engaged person was by definition sufficiently mature to handle some degree of physicality; the successful marriage presumed a degree of prior sexual knowledge. 'It is the engagement ring which justifies petting,' asserted one commentator—but the real question was, 'how far shall we go'.[25] Within the pages of women's magazines the negotiation of sexual intimacy in engagement was invariably fraught. 'I am engaged to be married and since our engagement my fiancé has asked me to do something which I know is wrong,' one woman told Mary Grant in 1950, 'I have refused so far, but he says it is not wrong as we are *nearly* married. I am so afraid of losing him if I do not give in.'[26] Grant's reply was characteristically firm.

FIGURE 14 Engagement was a time for identifying character flaws and personal weaknesses.

'What he asks you to do is an important part of marriage, but has no place in any association outside it. Discuss it once, agree to wait, and don't mention the subject again.' Another who had already 'done wrong' with her fiancé, feared he would leave her if she now started to refuse: 'if he loves you, he won't finish with you. It was a mistake to allow yourself to be persuaded before, but it would be madness to make a second mistake.'[27] 'You have a duty to uphold the laws of the society in which you live,' was Grant's belligerent response to a woman considering her fiancé's invitation to holiday as husband and wife.[28]

Agony aunts deployed a range of arguments in favour of engaged chastity. A favoured ploy was to use the misery of one individual to make the wait-until-marriage point. When sexually active young women wrote of sexual experiences that were unsatisfying, or even actively unpleasant, they were told that sex in marriage would be different. According to these everyday experts, sex before marriage was always likely to cause guilt and anxiety and was therefore unlikely to produce satisfaction. As late as 1970 a girl who had hitherto failed to achieve orgasm with her fiancé was assured that

> Having a climax is, for a woman, arrived at through *feelings* of being loved, secure, free from doubts and fears and willing to let herself go. Since it is naturally hard to have all these feelings outside marriage—this is biology not morals!—there's nothing wrong with you or sensible about pretending to your fiancé that your feelings are different. I can suggest some helpful books for you on the sexual side of marriage if you'd like to write to me for a list.[29]

When agony aunts felt they could no longer rely on shared moral frameworks to dissuade their readers from engaging in premarital sex, they constructed arguments based on physiology instead.

The acquisition of sexual knowledge—if not experience—was nonetheless encouraged. The damage its absence could wreak on a marriage underpinned the writings of Marie Stopes, Leonora Eyles, Rennie Macandrew, and later the National Marriage Guidance

Council. 'Ignorance is not a happy condition, my dear, and may well be dangerous as well,' Eyles told two 19-year-olds whose fiancés sometimes 'lost their heads'.[30] In 1950 Mary Grant insisted, 'it is unwise for a girl to enter upon marriage without adequate knowledge,' offering to send a list of helpful texts.[31] *The Way to Healthy Womanhood* and *The Way to Happy Marriage*, at 7½d each, were both regularly suggested to *Woman's Own* readers as helpful introductions. Some went further. Advice author Macandrew warned that 'Only by close body contact can one assess a person's generosity in the physical expression of love ... Beware of the girl who says, "I'll be all right when we're married, but please don't be passionate now." What guarantee have you that she'll not be frigid? None at all; she MAY be all right when she is past the altar; but let some other fellow prove it.'[32] In fact, Macandrew counselled at least one holiday together before marriage. According to a 1961 National Marriage Guidance Council leaflet, engagement could be a 'wonderful time for love-making'.[33] It explained that 'the joy of kissing and touching each other is part of the life of a loving marriage. If physical nearness is not a delight to an engaged couple they should hesitate and seek advice before marrying. Sometimes the tragedy of homosexuality only becomes evident when men or women find they cannot bear the embraces of the other sex.' Here, as elsewhere, a fine line was drawn. Engaged couples were encouraged to attain sufficient sexual experience to gauge the partner's capacity for response, but warned against going too far. Intercourse itself was no test of compatibility. As the *Every Woman's Book of Love and Marriage* rather mysteriously put it, 'You have not entered the inner palace of love—you are, so far, only in the courtyard surrounding the palace—and you must not anticipate the joys of the inmost palace itself.'[34]

Nonetheless, the firm promise of marriage did apparently justify sexual relations amongst a significant minority of engaged couples. The Chesser Report of 1956 found 'a fairly extensive practice of sexual intercourse during the engagement period' and this pattern persisted into the 1960s.[35] Amongst those Peter Wilmott surveyed for *Adolescent Boys of East London*, sex was more likely to occur within a committed relationship. 'I've been going out with the same girl for two years,' one 19-year-old told him.

> We're engaged now. We'd never done anything except kissing and petting until a couple of months ago, when her mum and dad went away for the week-end. We got up to some really heavy petting, and we just couldn't hold it back any more. I think it's all right to do it—to have intercourse—if you really intend to get married. Just don't take it too far, is what I think—don't knock the daylights out of it.[36]

In her study of teenage brides in the 1950s, Rachel Pierce found that the majority of pregnant brides conceived whilst engaged, suggesting that the wedding day itself had been accelerated, rather than precipitated, by the pregnancy.[37]

* * *

An engagement was a public statement of commitment. 'It is speedily borne upon both the man and the girl that what they had thought was a purely private matter, affecting only themselves, is a subject of intense concern to everyone they know,' wrote etiquette adviser Margot Lawrence in 1963.[38] According to Mace the list of interested parties included kin and employers, friends and church ministers, 'the statisticians who study the population figures, and the manufacturers of perambulators'.[39] The law also took an interest, defining the promise to marry as a legal contract. Those who broke it could, theoretically at least, find themselves on trial for breach of promise of marriage.

Historian Ginger S. Frost has shown that breach of promise suits were an important source of financial recompense for women within late nineteenth-century England.[40] They were also the subject of satirical scorn.[41] By the twentieth century breach of promise was widely viewed as a legal action out of step with modern intimacies. 'Few girls would have the brazenness to sue a man for breach of promise these days. It simply isn't done,' was Macandrew's confident assessment.[42] 'A breach of promise case would be an expensive and undignified procedure,' a post-war *Woman's Own* reader was advised.[43] Revealingly, however, the action remained a realistic proposition. Although rare, such cases were not unheard of. The idea of breach of promise, as much as its legal reality, haunted mid-century engagements. 'I was courting in 1959 and before my boyfriend went away to Liverpool University we became engaged,' confided one of local historian Maureen Sutton's Lincolnshire interviewees.[44] 'We were very young, I was seventeen. It was a lovely ring: two little diamonds and a ruby. When he was away he met someone else and broke off the engagement. My mother said I could sue him for breaking his promise to marry me, but my father said he'd no money, so keep the ring and forget about him. I married someone else years later.'

The majority of breach of promise suits were brought by women against men. The impact of a broken engagement tended to be gendered. The operation of the marriage bar, for example, could leave a fiancée unlucky enough to be jilted at the last minute with neither husband nor job.[45] If she had been assiduous in collecting for her bottom drawer, she might also find herself with unwanted household goods of which to dispose. The tendency to engage in sexual intimacy once a promise of marriage had been made added a reputational dimension. Because of their engagement, a court was told in 1958, Alicia Whittle had allowed her boyfriend to 'seduce her'. 'Love-making took place "quite often" in Jimmy's room at the University, and in "a remarkable old car"—a former London taxi bought for £30.'[46] Breach of promise was not infrequently used to secure financial recompense for a woman left pregnant. 'He promised her a ring—and gave her a baby,' observed Mr Justice Cassels in awarding £750 damages to 22-year-old Valerie Slater in 1958.[47] Her former fiancé married someone else just two weeks after the judgement.[48] Suits were also brought against those who proposed when they were already married to someone else.

SMALL-ADVERTISEMENTS DEPT
ENGAGEMENTS
"Congratulations, sir, and as Miss Bute is such a good customer for this column, we're giving you a reduced price."

FIGURE 15 Despite this cartoonist's suggestion, a broken engagement tended to have more serious consequences for a woman than a man.

The sums awarded in damages varied according to the financial circumstances of those involved. In March 1930, for example, a Miss Eva Phillips of Whitechapel was awarded £25;[49] in December 1931 Miss Alice Constance Matthews, a professional dancer, was awarded £750;[50] a year later Miss Ursula Winifred Rolls received the sum of £5,000 from the defendant Mr George Sinclair Fletcher after he had broken off their engagement and publicly alleged that he was not the father of her child.[51] In the post-war years damages continued to be paid. Nurse Edith Manley received £3,289—£500 of which was for her 'lacerated feelings'—after a commercial traveller 'mesmerized', defrauded, and then jilted her.[52]

In addition to offering the individual financial compensation for their troubles, breach of promise cases also operated as a forum for the articulation of courtship rules and etiquette; an opportunity for the courts to remind the public how commitment was supposed to work. Mr Justice Hawke felt the need to remind people that just because a wedding date had not been set did not mean that an engagement was not official.[53] Presiding over the case of Miss Ivy May Holton of Streatham—whose fiancé cancelled their marriage by telegram an hour before the ceremony—Mr Under-Sheriff Burchill advised: 'His conduct has been very blackguardly and hopelessly cruel.'[54] Breach of promise suits also shed light on the conventions of letter writing; not least because love letters were often the star exhibit. A travelling engineer had cause to regret the intensity of his love letters when they were presented as evidence in a 1937 suit. 'My darling Wife-To-Be,' he had written, 'My heart would break, my darling, for I love you so much, even if I didn't get your precious letters regularly.... Your happiness means everything to me.'[55] The end of this relationship cost him £150 in damages.

Opponents of breach of promise employed diverse arguments. Some suggested that it reinforced gender inequality; others that it encouraged gold-digging or that it made affairs public that ought to remain private.[56] Essentially, though, the debate hinged on ideas about love. In 1936 the *Daily Mirror* dedicated one of its 'dog-fight' debates to the question 'Should breach of promise be scrapped?'[57] Writing under the heading, 'you can't put a price on love', Gordon Glover took the romantic route. 'In these often disgusting affairs we are treated to the not very pretty sight of people unashamedly profiting by the loss of what they are pleased to call "love". What it should truly be called is hard to say, but love it certainly is not.' 'It is a man's responsibility to propose marriage only to the woman he knows he loves,' wrote Edward Armstrong in response. 'If he asks her to join her life with his without looking first into his own heart and hers, he is not just making a casual mistake—he is proving himself a cad and a fool.'

After the war opposition to breach of promise suits hardened. Legal aid was not available for the pursuit of such cases, so the cost alone was often prohibitive. Responding in 1945 to a man's reluctance to end an engagement because of what his fiancée might do, Mary Grant was reassuring. 'She can try, but it is an expensive business. Also it is pretty much recognised that such a vindictive thing rather spoils a girl's chance of marriage to someone else. I really think you should stick to your intention and risk what she may do; I am sorry for her but her present attitude is so undignified that it rather takes away one's sympathy.'[58] Nonetheless the threat still had power. 'Since I have become engaged my fiancé has turned possessive and domineering, so much so that I want to break off the engagement because I couldn't stand such behaviour for the rest of my life,' wrote 'worried' of Weston-Super-Mare. 'He now threatens me with a breach of promise action unless I promise to marry him. Can he do this, or is he trying to frighten me?'[59]

There were periodic attempts to abolish breach of promise throughout the twentieth century. By the 1960s pressure came from groups such as the Married Women's Association and campaigning agony aunts such as Marjorie Proops.[60] The law on breach of promise sat uneasily with the enhanced status of matrimonial love. What price could be put on falling out of love? In recommending abolition in 1969, the Law Commission argued that marriage should be based on affection rather than legal compulsion. Abolition of breach of promise reflected a changing statutory environment which saw the state withdrawing from the etiquette of private life. One of the last cases to be widely reported before abolition came into effect was that of footballer George Best and Eva Haraldsted. They reached an out of court settlement of £500.[61]

* * *

In July 1941, a Mass-Observation investigator who served in the Women's Auxiliary Air Force moved station. Her new base was Digby in Lincolnshire, home to an increasing number of Canadian units. Her first report from Digby focused on questions of sexual morality and suggested dramatic changes in the nature of commitment.

> Conventions of marriage and engagement are thrown to the wind. This was so among the men of Preston, but not among the women. Here, the married women flirt with young pilots, engaged women go gay while their fiancés are away—'And who can blame them?' one Canadian asked me—'You can't expect a woman to sit around and mope all day.'
>
> One Canadian told me of a man who was discharged for committing bigamy (or is it termed polygamy) four times. He was sacked and imprisoned. The 'crime' was discerned when the various wives applied for money allotments and were told that one wife was already drawing it. Bigamy is evidently quite the thing among the Canadians.
>
> There are a great many hasty marriages—cases of a girl who marries an airman in a mad moment, lives separately but sleeps with him every night, then he's posted, and she may never see him again. Without hesitation I can say that most of the RAF/WAAF marriages I've come into contact with are failures. The couple are carried away on the spur of the moment. They have no money, no prospect of married life. And many a more serious attachment is broken up by this sort of infatuation.[62]

What is so clear about this report is the fracturing of the careful economic, as well as emotional, planning which a formal engagement was supposed to involve. During wartime, the tempo of courtship accelerated and people committed without necessarily 'knowing' each other. The difficulties of assessing authentic emotional attachment are also clear in this account and we will return to wartime bigamy in Chapter Eight. This WAAF observer had no alternative but to judge wartime courtship practices by a set of inter-war standards; at the time of writing she did not know that post-war affluence would re-cast such standards.

During wartime established matrimonial rituals, and the steadying influence of material consideration, dissipated. 'I am struck by the rather unusual nature of the marriages i.e. between students in very poor circumstances,' one young flyer noted of his immediate circle.[63] He had himself married '6 months ago at the age of 21 though having no job to return to after the war and no private means'. For men—and women—such as these, wartime brought a distinct type of maturity. This was a maturity rooted in experience rather than age and given poetic form in John Pudney's much quoted 1941 poem 'For Johnny'.[64] During wartime people had to grow up fast and they became consequential more quickly. There was a dramatic increase in the general marriage rate at the beginning of the war, reaching an all-century high point in 1940.[65] Although the rate fell sharply between 1941 and 1943, there was another significant increase thereafter. 'My own marriage is directly due to the war', one woman wrote in 1940, continuing,

> I met my husband in September when we were working at the same post, and we became publicly engaged in December. I doubt very much whether we should have become married so quickly if it were not that all the pressure and the dread of being called up have influenced us strongly. I know of three other couples who have been engaged for some time and who might have drifted on for some time yet, but who have definitely been driven by war pressure into marrying.[66]

In 1945 the organization concluded that one in ten war marriages had been contracted directly because of the war context.[67]

A 23-year-old who had married at the age of 20 explained her motivation: 'Well, the war and the excitement and the blitz—feeling you might be gone tomorrow.'[68] An 18-year-old who had married two years previously explained that, 'the main reason was he was going abroad and I wanted him to know he'd have someone to come back to.'[69]

In December 1942 Mass-Observation asked its volunteer panel to report on sex in war, specifying that they should attend to 'changes in the atmosphere and speed of engagements' amongst other issues.[70] Those who responded were convinced that very real change was afoot: hasty engagements and even hastier marriages were all identified with greater or lesser degrees of anxiety. According to an Edgbaston man:

> The increased importance of personal relationships has also increased the sex interest by way of love-making, engagements and marriages. With the bombing, the realisation came to many that material ties such as personal belongings, jobs and spare time occupations, were of such a fragile nature that the only worth-while ties were those of friendship and of love. The increased call-up has now taken over from the bombing as the main cause of this. A consequence of this is that the period of 'walking out', being engaged and making the actual preparations for marriage have been startlingly shortened. I know of several wartime marriages caused by this desire for haste.[71]

A steelworker living in Ayrshire went as far as to suggest 'there's no engagement period now. Its quick meetings, quick marriages. Girls are marrying younger than they were 18, 19, 20s the usual. People say "its silly", or "there to quick" [*sic*] or "what like will it be after the war" but they seem pleased just the same and not against it.'[72] The deliberate planning phase represented by an interwar engagement was replaced by the very reverse during the war: hasty, unplanned and highly emotional encounters simultaneously framed by love and fear of loss. 'We thought we might both be killed, or one of us would be, so we were determined to be married first,' was how one woman put it.[73]

Some argued that such speed made for poor judgement. 'All this emphasis on sex and romance encourages girls to get engaged before they have a reasonable chance to get to know their prospective husbands and vice versa,' opined social researcher Pearl Jephcott.[74] In this reading, successful commitment necessitated pragmatic calculation and an accumulation of knowledge that took time to acquire. And yet whilst hasty marriages could symbolize the triumph of love in the face of adversity, they could also stem from more practical concerns. As we saw in Chapter Two, a determination to secure a separation allowance or to avoid the call-up might frame wartime commitment.

Not everyone believed that wartime was a good time to marry however. A 22-year-old serviceman provided Mass-Observation with a careful summation of his unit's discussion of the marriage question:

Pro

1. The need to have the pleasures of marriage while there is still a chance before the wartime risks of overseas exile or death intervene.
2. The need to live life normally in spite of the war
3. The mutual support given by husband and wife in difficult times.

Con

1. The essential impermanence of all wartime arrangements.
2. The unnatural married life that war imposes. The long separations and the hectic unnatural times together.
3. The great changes that wartime experience causes in husband and wife. These imperil a marriage particularly during wartime separation.
4. Wartime financial worries. The threat of post war slump.

5. Loss of independence for young men. They have grown up in war, and do not wish to come out of it burdened by responsibility, when they are eager to gain the experience of which the war has deprived them.[75]

For this thoughtful young man, the negatives outweighed the positives. The everyday experience of war made others suspicious of deep emotional ties. As a Mass-Observer explained:

> I find outside threats to one's emotional life still the most incalculable and difficult element of living in wartime. The only answer, for any composure at all, seems to be to admit that control is out of one's hands. Honesty, generosity, good management, intelligence, and capacity for love, are no longer sufficient to attain good things. A torpedo destroys an irreplaceable love, a cancelled leave aborts a set marriage date, or a Service man's mind is so uncertain of its future he cannot in fairness to himself or another undertake a tie of permanence. Conclusion: the only thing to do so long as the war continues is to live for the present only, and evade ties so deep that their destruction would destroy as well one's stability. Not a healthy nor a happy 'Feeling' to face 1943 with, but the result of three years war living and allowing of a quieter outlook than has been the case up till now.[76]

Here the loss of the capacity to plan, brought about by war, underlines the pointlessness of adherence to pre-war mechanisms for the making of commitment.

Divorce statistics suggest that wartime marriages were, in fact, considerably more vulnerable to dissolution than those contracted before the war. Wartime marriages were four times more likely to end in the divorce courts than those contracted in the mid-1930s.[77] These figures are not unproblematic, but a legacy of marital fragility framed the commitment debate for the next twenty years. In this, as in so many other areas of English life, the Second World War cast a long shadow.

* * *

After the war, attention shifted from the too-hasty to the too-early marriage. As the popularity of marriage grew, people committed to each other at a progressively younger age. The most immediate question is, of course, why? Historians have pointed to broad changes in the sex ratio as a partial explanation. A decline in male migration, for example, helped to resolve the so-called 'surplus women problem'.[78] By 1962, the men's magazine *Parade* warned its—presumably concerned—readers that 'Britain faces a girl shortage'.[79] 'Girls are getting scarce, the outlook for men is alarming,' it proclaimed. However, the declining age at first marriage must also be located within a material context. The willingness to marry for love *above all else* was strongly linked to economic security. Economic factors also influenced the speed with which marriage was possible. Quite simply, young people's rising employment opportunities and earnings 'eroded the financial need for long courtships'.[80] Contemporaries suggested that high levels of employment, particularly opportunities for married women to continue to work *after* marriage; access to family planning; the welfare state and the attractions of post-war homes, may also have been factors making earlier marriage more feasible and desirable.[81] Sociologist Ferdynand Zweig suggested that the provision of family allowances for married National Servicemen may have acted as an additional incentive. 'I married before National Service to save money,' one man told him. 'My wife lived with her parents doing a full-time job and getting, during the two years of my service, £2 19s 0d a week as well as her pay. That was put away with part of her wages and from this we bought a house.'[82]

Zweig's evidence suggests that the increasing popularity of early marriage could rest upon careful consideration of the material benefits of matrimony, be it access to benefits, housing or tax breaks. As we have seen, even in wartime, quick marriages could arise from pragmatic motivations. A lack of financial alternatives could also be a factor. Social historian Selina Todd suggests that despite the 'rosy image' of youthful independence in this decade, 'for most working-class people, marriage remained the most viable and attractive financial and emotional opportunity for independence and status'.[83] By 1971, women married for the first time at an average age of 22; amongst men it was 24: the press decried a rising tide of 'gym slip mothers'. Young marriages became big business. Even a product as apparently unromantic as milk was sold to teenage girls as a guarantor of marriage proposals—it was, apparently, 'the beauty pinta'.[84] 'Is this too soon for girls to wed?' asked the *Manchester Evening News*.[85] 'Girls believe that if they are not married by the time they are 19 they are on the shelf,' admitted marriage guidance counsellor Rose Hacker in 1960.[86] Teenage spouses' marriage vows were assumed to be more fragile than most; the 1956 Royal Commission on Marriage and Divorce identified 'a tendency to take the duties and responsibilities of marriage less seriously than formerly'.[87] In fact, as Griselda Rowntree demonstrated, young brides and grooms were 'by no means predominantly forced into marriage by pregnancy' and had 'a fairly good chance of success'.[88]

The age at marriage question was, of course, inherently linked to wider discussion surrounding the identity and status of youth within post-war social democracy. The Crowther Report of 1959, for example, argued that educational provision for 15 to 18-year-olds should accommodate the trend to early marriage.[89] 'The prospect of courtship and marriage should rightly influence the education of the adolescent girl,' it asserted. Women educationalists protested: the president of the National Union of Women Teachers described the findings as 'disturbing'.[90] The state increasingly mediated between youthful autonomy and parental authority. If parents did not grant the permission those under 21 needed in order to marry, an application to the magistrate's courts invariably did the trick. 'I think if a boy can show he can provide adequately—support a family...or if they're in the family way—that definitely influences the magistrates to give permission,' Diana Leonard was told in the late 1960s.[91] Parental authority over their child's matrimonial affairs thus slipped away. When 19-year-old Janet Weavers was given permission to marry Cecil, a fisherman, on 14 February 1958 the magistrate reportedly chuckled, 'I suppose I played the part of Cupid today. Appropriate isn't it?'[92] Press coverage of court decisions like this undoubtedly contributed to perceptions of youthful autonomy. In such circumstances pregnancy on the part of the bride to be might help the process along and demonstrated a strategic response to attempts at parental control: 'not really an accident. [We] knew they wouldn't say yes otherwise,' one couple stated in court.[93]

Elopement was another option. In Scotland, until 1940, marriage at 16 was permitted without parental consent and by means of a simple declaration in front of two witnesses.[94] While residence in Scotland was demanded for 21 days before the wedding, the difference in the law offered the possibility of a legal wedding without parental approval.[95] Prior to the Marriage (Scotland) Act of 1939 irregular marriages conducted by the Gretna Green 'blacksmith priest' were particularly newsworthy. In June 1930 Labour MP, and future director of publications for the British Union of Fascists, John Beckett, was photographed with his wife 'joining hands over the blacksmith's anvil at their marriage at Gretna Green'.[96] Richard Rennison—the blacksmith who presided over 5,000 marriages—was forthright on the matter. 'I do not disapprove of runaway marriages, because I know that they invariably turn out successfully. My own marriage has been a great success, although I married my wife only five weeks after I had met her,' he told the press.[97]

Gretna Green, or rather the *idea* of Gretna Green, holds a particular place within the story of twentieth-century love, and not just for young people. In a Gretna retrospective it was claimed that Rennison had once married an 81-year-old man and 79-year-old woman.[98] However, it was those English youths who ran away to marry in Scotland in order to circumvent the need for parental approval at home who captured the imagination. Gretna Green stories appeared in the press throughout the mid-century. Sometimes these were reported in approving tones, as testament to the

FIGURE 16 The trend towards younger marriages was exploited to advertise the most unlikely of products.

power of love: 'We're glad we did it,' reported two couples, a year after marrying at Gretna.[99] Mr de Courtney wrote to the *Daily Mirror* in 1950 to defend his own decision. 'My wife and I were married at Gretna by Richard Rennison the blacksmith, in November 1929. We are deeply in love with one another still and despite our trials and difficulties we are still happy only in each other's company.'[100] At other times the stories framed the pursuit of love more explicitly as a generational challenge to old-fashioned emotional codes. 'Father forbade me from marrying,' one 19-year-old admitted in 1939, 'His idea was that I should have girl-friends, but a different one week by week. However I have been in love with Olga since we met two years ago, and felt determined to marry her.'[101] Within this story the son draws a distinct line between his own ability to commit wholeheartedly and his father's sense of appropriate masculine behaviour. For some young men the desire to circumvent parental authority was given an additional urgency given their imminent conscription into National Service.[102]

More often than not, however, Gretna Green stories were reported as grand capers within which runaway brides headed north by a variety of means, fathers followed in hot pursuit, future mothers-in-law colluded with young lovers and there were occasional outbreaks of violence.[103] Sheenagh Parsons, 16, was apparently confronted by her police constable father in a Gretna Green café, who 'after a struggle in which tables were overturned, bundled her into his car'.[104] On the whole, however, the weddings were reported in good humour. The stories themselves were testament to young peoples' tenacity and powers of evasion. Beryl Banfield, a 17-year-old typist, married Bristol grocer Horace Paget at Gretna in 1938. 'Why are you all dressed up?' her mother had asked her. 'Oh well, it's spring Mother,' she had replied as if on her way to the office. In fact she was en route to the express train to Carlisle.[105] Sometimes newspaper coverage was just plain salacious. The *Mirror* dedicated three pages on consecutive days to the 1958 saga of Ted Hope, a 19-year-old salesman from Gillingham, who had run away to Gretna with one sister but ended up deciding to marry the other.[106]

* * *

Twenty-year-old Ronald William Peters married Florence Wilkinson, a munitions worker, in May 1943. His father had objected, suggesting the boy was not yet ready to commit himself to matrimony. Magistrate Gervais Rentoul disagreed. 'He is a man—for he is doing a man's job.' Peters was a fitter in the Fleet Air Arm.[107] Three decades on his age, as well as his experience, would have denoted his adulthood. Mr Justice Latey's Committee on the Age of Majority sat between 1965 and 1967, appointed to consider the desirability of changing the age of full legal capacity. The question of youthful marriage was assessed alongside a range of other contractual matters. Nonetheless, for this committee marriage was the most important issue: 'make the wrong contract and you suffer for a year or two, and perhaps make an adult trader miserable for a few months; make a wrong marriage and you may suffer for life and spoil the lives of your children after you.'[108] The Committee explored proposals for compulsory betrothal—to 'give the couple time to get the moonshine out of their eyes and save up for a few down payments'—but rejected the proposal as unworkable.[109] Its report—accessibly written by journalist and committee member Katharine Whitehorn—provided a resounding defence of young people's capacity to make marital commitment autonomously from the age of 18:

> We have concluded on every ground that it is not wise to demand parental consent to marriage past the age of 18. We can only end by saying that this is not because we think parents should never discourage their children's marriages but because this is not the way to do it; not because we think well of marriages made in defiance; not because the family is too weak to use this weapon but because it is strong enough to do without it. It is because good parents know that

> the way to help their sons and daughters of any age is to hold tight with looser hands that we recommend removing the knuckle-duster of the law.[110]

The change was implemented under the Family Law Reform Act of 1969, taking its place alongside the significant law reforms on abortion, homosexuality, and marriage which emerged under the second Wilson government.[111] Debates on the making of commitment had played a crucial role in driving this legislative milestone.

What went unquestioned in such debates was the popularity and inevitability of marriage. 'Everybody seems to sooner or later. All my brothers and sisters are married. It seems the most natural thing to do. You have your fling, then settle down,' one 17-year-old had told Peter Wilmott earlier in the decade. A 19-year-old had confessed that, 'There's not much else to do after you stop being a teenager. You've got to have a change some time—I more or less just go out drinking now. I don't want to go on doing that.'[112] Marriage was a boundary marker. It signified the end of teenage life. Matrimony made different demands and necessitated new ways of being. For these men, then, marriage was a key feature of the cultural life cycle and was crucial to their developing sense of self. And yet the twenty years that followed were to witness the rapid unravelling of this model. Why? The final chapter of *The English in Love* suggests that it was mid-century love, rather than late-century sex, that lay at the heart of this dramatic social change.

8

Happy Ever After?

In March 1956 the Royal Commission on Marriage and Divorce published its long-awaited report.[1] During its deliberations it had taken oral evidence from forty-eight witnesses, selected for interview on the basis of expertise or position. We have encountered a number of these already in this book. David Mace had given evidence on day 19, Eliot Slater and Moya Woodside on day 16, and Marie Stopes on the 32nd day. Evidence from sixty-seven organizations had also been heard. A diverse range of groups were represented, from the National Marriage Guidance Society to the Fabian Society; the Women's Cooperative Guild to the Federation of British Detectives. All had an interest in the marriage question. Ordinary individuals also attempted to make their mark by writing privately to the Commission; it is not clear how seriously their evidence was taken:

> The letters, which we found very helpful, generally contained accounts of the personal histories of the individuals concerned, and against that background the writers argued for or against various changes in the law. It would have been impracticable to ask all these correspondents to amplify their statements by oral evidence and in most cases we considered it unnecessary to do so. The facts were set out clearly, and the reasons for the suggestions made were based on the human experience of the writers and needed no further elucidation.[2]

The Report's conclusions undoubtedly disappointed many of these individuals. Rather than calling for a clear change in the law on divorce, the commission was split on its desirability. Hopes that legislative change would quickly follow publication of the report were therefore dashed. A *Daily Mirror* editorial on the matter was scathing. What was needed was 'an ordinary commission of ordinary folk reporting on married life as they see it, and live it,' it concluded.[3]

Whilst members of the Royal Commission on Marriage and Divorce disagreed on the question of divorce law reform, they did hold similar views on the importance of matrimony. 'It is obvious that life-long marriage is the basis of a secure and stable family life and that to ensure their well-being children must have that background,' their report stated.[4] Like many other mid-century people, they believed marriage to be the foundation of modern civil society, as well as the basis for personal contentment. 'Marriage is essential for a full and happy life,' an RAF officer had told Mass-Observation a decade earlier; 'It's a natural state for all men and women to be in,' suggested a policeman's wife.[5] *Picture Post* dedicated an entire special issue to marriage in 1954. 'We, who have produced this paper are ourselves halves of many marriages, trying to make our marriages work,' the editorial announced.[6] And yet, as *Picture Post* hinted, marriage had come under considerable pressure in the immediate aftermath of war. Spiralling divorce rates went hand in hand with the demobilization and reassimilation of service personnel into family life.[7] Some identified a 'marriage crisis', in the face of massive social, economic and cultural change.[8] 'Marriages today are at risk to a greater extent than formerly,' proclaimed the Royal Commission Report, suggesting that a tendency to make greater demands of the institution was at least partly to blame.[9] Slater and Woodside were more optimistic, although their analysis was not dissimilar.

> We are coming to expect more and more of our marriages. The economic emancipation of women, a rise in the standard of living,

> the decreased pressure to take the first comer regardless of his suitability, and the growing cult of the 'personality', all help to make the choice more difficult, and the chances of what is *felt* to be a failure greater. We are more inclined now than we used to be to demand a capacity for response between the partners, to look for intellectual and temperamental compatibility, as well as purely material welfare, in addition to the ordinary social and parental satisfactions. The more we demand in these respects, the more frequently, perhaps, we shall have to count our failures, but also the higher may be our level of achievement. The tendency to require more from marriage may well lead to better relationships in the long run. Those attitudes which we call romantic do not only have a value as a psychological experience in life, but they contain the kernel out of which may grow a better order of things. To come to maturity, they need perspective, cleansing from the colourwash of glamour, and a firm basis on what scientific study shows to be the pre-determinants of an equable affection.[10]

The risk that accompanied heightened expectations, chiefly the possibility of far greater disappointment, was clear to these authors. Ultimately, however, they proffered an upbeat assessment. By applying rational scientific planning to emotional life something better could be secured. Love and marriage became the bearer of post-war hopes for a rationally planned, efficient and hopeful future. Moving from prescription to practice, however, it is clear that ordinary people experienced love in a wide variety of ways, sometimes within the institution of marriage, sometimes outside of it. Love and commitment took disparate forms.

* * *

Twentieth-century people, like those of earlier periods, married for a variety of reasons and harboured diverse expectations when they did so. Marriage promised to fulfil a range of needs—a desire for sexual or emotional intimacy was not always the most important of these. Across much of the period between the 1920s and the 1960s, home was central to visions of matrimony. Mavis Knight of

Campbell Bunk, Islington, married Willie Knowles in 1936. When asked why she married, she replied, 'the home, having the home. And having each other, I suppose as well. You didn't realise that part until you were together. To get a home you had to have each other didn't you?'[11] Another working-class woman who married in the 1930s told Mass-Observation that she did so '[t]o get out of my mum's house more than anything. My mum and dad were always squabbling; he's fond of his pint, and he used to have more than was good for him, and that used to set them off. I wanted to get married and have a home of my own and a bit of peace.'[12]

The quest for security and self-determination underpinned marital choices for many people. 'Most normal working-class citizens want from their house an expression of independence, autonomy, control of life,' suggested one wartime report.[13] Richard Hoggart put it well: 'Where almost everything else is ruled from outside, is chancy and likely to knock you down when you least expect it, the home is yours and real.'[14] As historian Judy Giles has shown, the 'sustaining dream' of attaining a 'home of one's own' through marriage was widely shared, becoming a reality for increasing numbers of middle-class and increasingly working-class families prior to the war.[15] Four million new homes were built during the inter-war period, of which 1.5 million were state-aided: the post-war Labour government presided over the building of 900,000 new houses and by 1957 2.5 million flats and homes had been constructed, the majority by local authorities.[16]

Within this context, having a family was another significant motivation to marry—'"It's what you get married for"; "children make a marriage".'[17] Slater and Woodside found that children 'are popularly thought to be essential and, linked with the idea of home, the *purpose* of marriage'.[18] Caring for the family, through gendered role execution, was a key matrimonial characteristic. 'He'll be a lucky man who marries you,' was the response of one advertising father when his daughter served up a tin of John West tinned salmon.[19] Being a good husband and father was rooted in good breadwinning; being a good wife and mother was rooted in good housekeeping. In a wartime magistrate's court, a young husband explained that he had left his young working wife of just nine months because she 'had not made a proper home for him'.[20] A particular bone of contention seemed to be the regularity with which she served him fish and chips: the relationship between this and her status as a full-time worker had not, apparently, occurred to the man. Other qualities were nonetheless also valued in a spouse. 'If men only knew why women loved them!' the *Manchester Evening News* asserted on the back of a 1935 reader-driven feature entitled 'I'm glad I married'. 'It is not for heroism, looks, or luxury. In nine cases out of ten, it is because they are "kind".... Just a good fire and a smiling face to welcome him is all most men want out of life.'[21]

During wartime, home became a source of national strength; something to fight for and a symbol of the future. 'A happy home and family life is the bulwark of a Nation' and 'a refuge, a haven, a place of peace', according to wartime Mass-Observers.[22] Yet the actual circumstances of war complicated the relationship between matrimony and family-building.

'My boy and I are being married on his next leave, but, as we have no money saved and I am in a big war job, I must not have babies yet,' declared one *Woman's Own* reader.[23] 'Birth control is quite simple,' reassured Leonora Eyles, 'but do make up your mind to save every penny for your home so that you can have babies while you are both young. It is so much happier for you and for them.' A Mass-Observer recorded that 'most of the people who get married now make no attempt to start a home. The most that can be attempted where both are engaged in civil work is to procure a transfer so that both can find work in the same town or city and then try and find a couple of furnished rooms.'[24] A survey of eight London boroughs and Gloucester towards the end of the war found that 56 per cent of couples who had been married for less

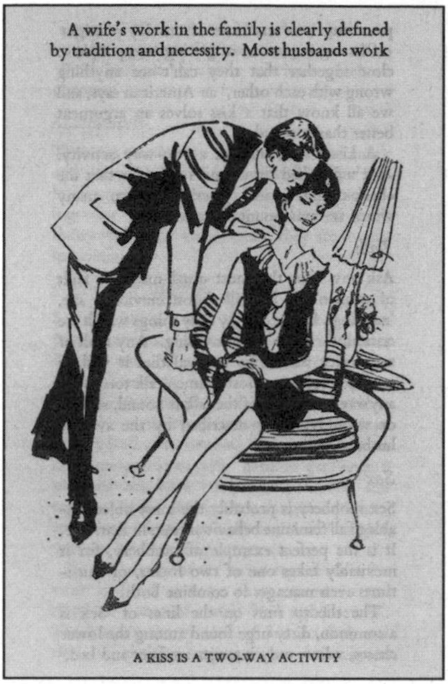

A wife's work in the family is clearly defined
by tradition and necessity. Most husbands work
A KISS IS A TWO-WAY ACTIVITY

FIGURE 17 The importance of sexual compatibility grew alongside the increasing importance of romantic love.

than five years were living with relatives or otherwise sharing their accommodation. Another 38 per cent lived in a flat, maisonette or self-contained part of a house. Only 6 per cent had a whole house to themselves.[25]

Perhaps it is not surprising then that home-making loomed large in marital aspirations. 'Marriage and home are synonymous in many people's minds, and the equation of the two is a characteristic feature of our sample,' reported Slater and Woodside, 'at this social level, practical advantages are given a higher ranking than temperamental compatibilities. Marriage is less *to* someone than *for* something.'[26] For the young women surveyed by Pearl Jephcott in 1945, this pragmatic sense of purpose was moulded by experience:

> The intelligent girls realize how much the badly planned, over-packed home has added to their mother's work, which, in the

mining families, is normally heavy. The girls know at first-hand how difficult it is to bring up children satisfactorily under such conditions. They realize what extra effort an additional child causes and what difficulties even minor illnesses may add. They have seen and shared these burdens for all their eighteen years and they do not intend, if they can avoid it, to have a similar life for themselves.[27]

A powerful sense of generational change is here apparent. For such women post-war home-making, through marriage, had a historically distinct meaning, offering something other than the maternal drudgery of their mother's lives.

Of course expectation did not always match practice, here as elsewhere in post-war matrimony. A housing shortage brought very precise difficulties for the Attlee government as well as newly married couples. A widely expressed desire to re-establish marital and family life in the years after war, seen most clearly in the post-war baby-boom, in reality saw countless young couples compelled to live with their parents or other relatives in houses that were inadequate to start with. Social investigators Rowntree and Lavers recorded the case of:

Miss R., aged about 20 or rather more, is engaged and shortly to be married. She comes from a bad home—drunken parents, large family and a good deal of privation when dinner money is spent on beer and horses. Nevertheless, Miss R. is clean and well turned out. She is looking forward to a home of her own but will start married life in two rooms of her mother-in-law's house. Of her future mother-in-law, Miss R. says, 'She is more of a mother to me than my Mum has ever been.'[28]

Sociologist Rachel Pierce noted the 'disturbing finding' that only a quarter of 1950s married couples was able to begin married life living independently.[29] Young and Willmott found that in Bethnal Green 'few couples have much choice at the start of their marriage. They have to find space under a roof belonging to someone else, and, since there is little enough of that, they have to put up with what they can get. So it is not surprising that many couples begin their married life in the parental home.'[30] In fact nearly half of the couples they surveyed in the mid-1950s lived with parents immediately after marriage. Nonetheless the fantasy of a 'home of your own' was strongly held by all married couples: 'for most people anything else is second best.'[31] As late as 1962 the National Marriage Guidance Council felt it necessary to promote the virtues of temporary accommodation for young married couples. 'Perhaps houses and flats are particularly hard to come by in your neighbourhood but at the same time you are determined to have a home of your own, right from the beginning. Many people nowadays find that the only way of achieving this is by renting or buying a caravan.'[32]

Home was an essential component of married life across our period. The importance of sexual compatibility grew alongside the increasing importance of romantic love. As we have already seen in Chapter Two, a disentangling of sex from reproduction facilitated the reframing of married sex as a form of mutual pleasure. Here advice literature led the way. Dr Francis Upton's advice to honeymooners on the pages of *Modern Marriage*, for example, was potentially chastening. 'True marriage is an affair of mutual love and passion, a glad response to each caress. Can you imagine how humiliating it must be to a sensitive man when he comes to woo his bride to find his love and passion received with coldness and aversion.'[33] Sex was not, of course, necessarily something that women wished to evade and men wished to impose. A desire for sexual pleasure is evident in a minority of the letters sent to Marie Stopes in the aftermath of the publication of *Married Love*. 'A mother of four outlined the difficulties she encountered in moderating her desire for sex: 'my husband tells me to control and hold myself in check, well I can, but we do without kisses, and oh, lots of other things that help to make life pleasant, then I get depressed, my husband gets ill tempered, we quarrel, make it up and afterwards I am in torment.'[34] Nonetheless as this letter powerfully indicates there were opportunity costs attached to sexual pleasure without reliable ways of preventing conception. Within this context, sex was not necessarily the linchpin of married life.[35] Even in the early 1950s anthropologist Geoffrey Gorer discovered that spousal qualities such as 'sense of humour, fairness, faithfulness, moral qualities, personal qualities, intelligence, [being] economical and being a good cook' were held to be more important than sex.[36] When Gorer returned to the subject in 1969, he found a change in the ranking of spousal qualities amongst his sample. Psychological aspects were ranked more highly than before, as were 'understanding, love and affection, patience, equanimity, shared responsibilities and interests and, emphatically for the husbands, being a good mother'.[37] A key finding was 'the virtual disappearance of material circumstances as essential to a happy marriage... relative prosperity is, as it were, almost *taken for granted*'.[38] Gorer suggested that husbands and wives now expected to like one another.[39] Sexual compatibility was, apparently, assumed.[40]

Within this post-war context, husbands and wives were conceptualized as inhabiting emotionally and sexually exclusive worlds: investments outside of the central family relationship were increasingly questioned. As a woman who married in 1950 aged 20 retrospectively acknowledged, 'Having such a close relationship does "stunt" other relationships, especially with the opposite sex. I have been very friendly with other men, but knew I could never become intimate at the risk of my marriage.'[41] By way of contrast, early twentieth-century commentators had not been so afraid to recommend emotional and spatial independence. Stopes, for example, had suggested separate bedrooms because 'everyday association in the commonplace daily necessities tends to reduce the keen pleasure each takes in the other.'[42] Twin beds were sold as fashionable items for modern couples suggesting 'a *relative* autonomy, an interdependence premised on a proximate but separable relation with the other element of the pair'.[43] Neither arrangement was accessible to most ordinary people, but the importance of maintaining separate interests once married was widely emphasized. 'No one should belong completely to another, spiritually speaking,' argued activist and author Edith Lyttelton in the pages of the *Daily Mirror*. 'Complete fusion is not only impossible but a wrong ideal.'[44]

> If a pair of trees are planted too close to each other what happens? Neither grows to its full roundness, both become one-sided, for the branches which touch and interlace rub and fret and finally deform the shape of the trees.
>
> It is just the same with two friends or two lovers; each must have space to grow and expand, though they flourish under the same sky, are fed by the same rains and feel their leaves stirred by the same mysterious winds and airs. Their unity does not lie in the nearness of their stems and branches but in the atmosphere by which they live.[45]

Maintaining separate interests and a degree of emotional distance was the basic tenor of marital advice inter-war style. Even separate holidays were not a problem. 'The independence of each must be guaranteed,' Edward Griffith advised in 1935.[46] Rennie Macandrew was a little more direct: 'A woman may love her husband with all her heart, but even love needs an occasional rest.'[47] As we will see shortly, as the costs of the expectation of emotional togetherness became apparent, everyday experts returned to these earlier prescriptions with renewed enthusiasm.

* * *

A model of matrimony which placed love and sex—as well as continued prosperity—at its heart was a fragile model. A growing emphasis upon the relational aspects of marriage could conflict with its institutional basis. As a number of commentators have argued, romantic love, held by post-war marriage reformers to be the 'moral cement of personal relationships', provided an unstable basis upon which to build actual marriages.[48] Love had the potential to destabilize, not least because people could fall out of love as readily as they could fall in love. Tensions, contradictions, and ultimately discontents accompanied the rising status of love. Where love tied partners to each other, what, other than the divorce laws, would keep them together if that emotion dwindled to nothing? Love, in fact, had a habit of escaping the bounds of marriage. Claims to an emotional authenticity that only the lover could judge provided powerful self-justification for transgression as well as commitment. If good sex was a way of demonstrating marital love, could a marriage survive bad sex? The everyday experts were equivocal on this point. The National Marriage Guidance Council, for example, suggested that, 'Intercourse should be enjoyed as the physical expression of the whole of the love of husband and wife for each other, and when it is so enjoyed it adds immeasurable enrichment to the marriage and to the personalities of each partner.'[49] A lack of good sex might lead to affairs and bitterness in addition, presumably, to an underdeveloped personality. And yet the National Marriage Guidance Council was aware that this ideal was not always attained in practice and therefore presented conflicting views on the subject. Disappointed wives, for example, should 'remember that the sex relationship is only one side of married life and that even if all treatment to improve this fails, they still have the deep and lasting delight of love and companionship which is one of the most enduring joys of happy marriage'.[50] On the one hand love and sex were so closely interwoven within mid-century marriage as to be indistinguishable. On the other, good sex was simply one part of marriage; its absence was not a licence to move on. This contradiction was to prove problematic.[51] The challenge which faced the everyday experts was a difficult one: to promote the self-consciously modern view of marriage as a relationship rooted in love rather than duty, and to contain love and sex within the institution of matrimony.

Given this context the 1940s and 1950s could not possibly be an unproblematic age of marital harmony. In fact, it was a period of some instability as higher expectations bred greater disappointments.[52] Increasingly it seemed that being a good wage-earner or a good housekeeper was no longer enough to fulfil the marriage contract, but the sustainability of love-based lifelong commitment was the subject of anxiety even as it apparently triumphed as a model. In 1953, the Bishop of Sheffield pondered the emotional turn which marriages seemed to be taking:

> The new conception of marriage turns away from the idea of marriage as a social institution, to the constitution of marriage... as a freely entered and freely maintained personal relationship worked out by the persons concerned... is this change pure gain for the community or is it likely to increase the sum total of human happiness? The greater emotional tension that it involves and the degree of compatibility and identity of interest which it demands, and also of privacy and physical propinquity, makes the risk of failure far greater. One might ask... what is the long-term reaction of all this on the adventurous spirit of a seafaring nation?'[53]

The Royal Commission on Marriage and Divorce identified a number of factors making for marital instability: the decreasing age at marriage, a shortage of suitable housing, the changing status of women, a growth of individualism, and 'an undue emphasis on the overriding importance of a satisfactory sex relationship'.[54] In evidence submitted to the Commission, Moya Woodside offered a clear assessment of contemporaneous marital aspirations—and their possible effect:

> Marriage and a home of one's own are still the desired and predominant goals. But expectations are higher: the more thoughtful young men and women today see marriage as a partnership and a sharing of aims and activities in every sphere of life. Their sex relationship is intended to be satisfying to both. They set an increased rating on the needs and welfare of children, and the small *planned* family is a general ideal. If they are disappointed, they are less willing to go on with a hopeless or even unsatisfactory mating than were their parents.[55]

In the 1960s BBC television dedicated a number of documentary series to the topic of marriage. 'With improved living standards people generally expect more all round,' stated *Marriage Today*, 'including from each other.'[56] The notion that expectations were out of sync with real life underlined expert contributions to this six-part series. Echoing the warnings of inter-war commentators, Psychologist Peter Fletcher advised: 'it's a completely false concept of human nature to imagine that a husband can be all to his wife or a wife to her husband. It just isn't possible because no single human being has the qualities that are necessary to enable another human being to enrich his experience sufficiently to make life feel worthwhile.' Writer and critic Marghanita Laski suggested: 'people have to adjust from the romantic view of marriage whereby I am served by the other person to a deeper love in which you are the server.'[57] For Eustace Chesser blame lay at the door of commercial interests who used romantic love to sell goods. 'If we believe that marriage should be built on this flimsy foundation then we must not be surprised if it frequently breaks down.'

* * *

Olivia Crockett was amongst those who wrote regular diary entries for Mass Observation in the early years of the Second World War.[58] Born in 1912, she lived in London throughout the war working as a civil servant. She never married, but conducted a long-term relationship with Bill Hole, referred to as 'Man' in her war diary. Mr Hole was married to someone else. Like many other Mass-Observation diarists, Olivia's unfolding relationship with the organization facilitated the disclosure of emotional details that are often absent from other types of historical source. These include accounts of snatched time with her married lover—'Man came home with me this afternoon... two hours of the most heavenly love making we've had in all our eleven years... '—and the changing status of the affair as Bill at one stage left his wife only to return to her two weeks later.[59]

By 1940 the affair was already a decade old. 'Am still beatifically in love, still with insurmountable odds against marrying,' she confided on 29 July 1940.[60] The diary records her frustration with the relationship, her 'terrifying ache for children', and in mid-1941 his final break with his wife and her agreement to sue for divorce.[61]

> See the man every day and all every evening and weekend. Have been served with divorce notice. Arranged to meet solicitor's clerk at the flat of Peg, who lives near his office, to keep expenses down. Was not so unpleasant a ten minutes as we had feared. Have seen notice in local paper of Charles Madge's divorce. Felt a fellow feeling wondrous kind, and envied him, being through with it. Stayed the night at Peg's, and committed the offence for which we are indicted, very happily.[62]

The divorce was in fact thrown out on grounds of suspected collusion leaving much immediate unhappiness and a debt of £80. Nonetheless the couple continued their relationship, living together throughout the 1950s and retiring together to Dorset in the 1960s where she changed her surname to Mrs Hole by deed poll.[63] They did not, in the end, have children.

As this story demonstrates, obtaining a divorce in mid-century Britain was not easy. Within the adversarial system that existed until 1969, a divorce was likely to be refused if the court suspected spouses to be working together in order to end a marriage. Effectively, the more both parties wished to be released; the less likely it was that they would succeed. Collusion was one of a series of bars: a mechanism designed to deter divorce by mutual agreement. In an age when love was increasingly central to marital dreams, its absence did not legitimize divorce. Unsurprisingly within this context divorce was more widely debated than ever before. The royal crises of 1936 and 1955 provided a sharply public focus for what was more generally a private drama. Anthony Eden, Prime Minister when Margaret made the split with Townsend, was the country's first divorced prime minister.

Public attitudes to divorce were mixed. On the cusp of the legislative change of 1937—the Herbert Act which extended the grounds for divorce beyond adultery to include desertion, cruelty, and insanity—pollsters found 58 per cent in favour of easier divorce.[64] 'I would not be too condemning on husbands and wives who leave one another,' wrote one woman just before the war, 'only those who have been tempted know what it is.'[65] When Mass-Observation asked a random street sample for their views on the topic as part of its 'Little Kinsey' survey, they found a marked disjuncture between people's perception of the law and the actual law. While one in three were opposed to divorce—often on religious grounds—others 'spontaneously and specifically insist that divorce is all right if husband and wife do not get on together'.[66] 'If they're not happy it's no use living together, life is too short,' stated a 45-year-old woman, 'You don't know when you marry what they are like.'[67] 60 per cent of those polled by Gallup in 1951 felt that divorce should be possible after seven years' separation—something MP Eirene White had proposed that year.[68] By 1956, that number had increased to 72 per cent.[69]

During the 1960s the pressure for reform became overwhelming. Placing romantic love so firmly at the centre of modern marriage ultimately made the existing divorce laws unsustainable. If love was the key to personal fulfilment, then why should anyone be condemned to life in a loveless, 'empty shell' marriage, it was argued. The right to love lay at the heart of the divorce law reform movement. Both *Putting Asunder*—the Church of England's thoughts on divorce law reform—and *The Field of Choice*—the Law Commission's report on reform of the grounds of divorce—rejected exclusive reliance upon matrimonial offence within the divorce courts and accepted notions of irretrievable breakdown as grounds for divorce when they were published in 1966.[70] By 1968, 70 per cent of those polled by Gallup believed a husband and wife who had lived apart for two years and agreed on a divorce should be able to access one—one of the five grounds for divorce available today.

In 1968, only 10 per cent of those asked believed a child was better off living with unhappily married parents than with one divorced parent.[71] A whole raft of BBC television programmes subjected modern marriage and divorce to forensic examination. *Panorama*, for example, interviewed a private detective whose job was to visit the guilty party and extract a confession: 'nine times out of ten, people are waiting for you to come as they want the matter finished with,' he claimed.[72]

The television programmes of the 1960s drew upon the kinds of experts who had been interviewed by the Royal Commission on Marriage and Divorce in the early 1950s. They also featured the views and experiences of ordinary people. *Panorama* interviewed a woman who had been living with a man legally separated from his wife—but not divorced—for 27 years: 'I think that for anyone to be in love all these years, it can't be wrong.' A 76-year-old man, who had lived with his 73-year-old lover for 33 years, had continued to pay maintenance to his legal wife throughout.[73] Ted and Joan, interviewed for a 1966 edition of the current affairs programme *Man Alive* entitled 'Living in Sin?', lived with the child from their own relationship and those from their respective marriages.[74] 'It's down to earth living,' Ted explained, making a claim for the authenticity of their emotional attachment to each other and the everyday nature of their living practices. 'You've got to make a life for yourself,' he continued, 'at the moment we're not divorced, rather than wait and let the children grow up and let our own lives run to waste we've started now.' Ted and Joan refused to have their life together stymied by the divorce laws. Instead they exercised real agency to carve out a life, not as they pleased, but as best they could under the difficult circumstances in which they found themselves.

'It seems beyond doubt', *Panorama* had concluded, 'that the present laws do create misery and confusion.' The experiences of Ted and Joan, as well as Olivia Crockett and Bill Hole, would seem to support this assessment. These were people who ultimately exhibited a huge attachment to the idea of marriage, rather than a determination to transgress social codes. In the end both couples lived together but at no little cost. Although she became 'Mrs Hole', Olivia Crockett had missed many happy years with Bill and of course had no children. Reform of the divorce laws, when it did come, drew attention to the enthusiasm of such couples for matrimonial commitment. Reform was promoted on the grounds that it would make people more marriage-minded, rather than less, and would protect the family rather than threaten it. People should be permitted to leave unhappy marriages in order to make new happier marriages. The Divorce Law Reform Act of 1969 became effective from 1 January 1971 allowing for irretrievable breakdown, after a period of separation, as possible grounds for divorce. The *Daily Mirror*'s 1956 assertion that 'People should be held together in marriage by happiness, not bound together in misery', seemed to have found legislative expression.[75]

* * *

When Mass-Observation researchers investigated *Britain and Her Birth Rate* towards the end of the Second World War, they defined one in ten of the marriages they surveyed as unsuccessful.[76]

> Some of the breakdowns have resulted in separations, but by no means all. A woman married at 18, now 27, for example. She says: 'It wasn't love. I made a mistake. I was wrong.' About the disadvantages of married life: 'Yes, plenty. For one thing you're tied too much. I like dancing and enjoying myself, and my husband likes sitting at home.' Asked whether she and her husband agree about family-planning: 'He don't talk much—he just says hello and goodnight.' And after the interview: 'It wasn't till the lodger came along that I knew I was so discontented. He's just the same type as I am—he likes laughing, he likes a joke and he likes going to dances. Oh, the capers I've been at and the lies I've told my husband. The truth is I married him to spite his mother—and now I wish she'd kept him. But he's a gloomy man with never a laugh in him—just sits by the fire and says nothing. There's a girl writes to him. She's welcome to

> him for all I care—and yet he won't let me go to a dance if he can stop me.'[77]

If it was the function of mid-century marriage to act as a container for love and desire then it did not always succeed in this endeavour. In the everyday practices of a not insignificant proportion of the married population the principle of lifelong monogamy was broken, sometimes once, sometimes with regularity. Amongst the post-war Mass-Observation volunteer panel, one man in four and one woman in five admitted to breaking their wedding vows.[78] By 1954 Lord Denning apparently believed that a position had been reached 'where adultery, or infidelity or misconduct, as soft-spoken folk called it, was considered to be a matter of little moment'.[79] The Archbishop of Canterbury spoke of a 'tide of adultery' and asked whether it had 'become such a public menace that the time has come when it ought to be made a criminal offence?'[80]

Whether or not adultery constituted a public menace, it was certainly testament to the destabilizing power of love. 'We know we really love each other, that's all that really matters,' Trevor Howard's Alex Harvey tells Celia Johnson's Laura Jesson towards the end of their *Brief Encounter*.[81] Her response, 'it isn't all that matters—other things matter—self-respect and decency', is a pivotal moment in the narrative. In the outstanding 1957 film *Woman in a Dressing Gown*, the young woman with whom her husband has been conducting an affair tells Yvonne Mitchell's Amy, 'I love him.'[82] Amy's reply—'Love him. You want to sleep with him that's what you want. Love—you don't know the meaning of the word'—tells us much about the instability of the emotion. For Amy, love is about 'knowing a man inside out and then loving him', an accumulation of knowledge over time. Being *in* love is a very different thing.

Expert attitudes towards everyday adultery differed depending upon whether the transgressor was male or female, revealing an impregnable sexual double standard. In the early mid-century, wives were discouraged from viewing a husband's infidelity as a marriage breaker. Instead they were advised to forgive, forget, and crucially to take responsibility. 'Have you tried to find out if there was anything in you that caused him to be unfaithful? Forgive him—but be honest with yourself and see if you were at all to blame,' Leonora Eyles told one poor woman.[83] A *Tribune* reader who asked Eyles for her advice about a husband who had fallen in love with his wartime landlady was urged to be patient. 'Do nothing in a hurry; a lonely man, uprooted from home, ill and sentimental can easily get into this state through propinquity and gratitude. Set your teeth and put up with it for another six months at least. It is going to be almost unbearable to do this but it may mean his coming back in the end.'[84] Eyles's advice was founded upon emotional and practical grounds: 'Apart from the fact that you and the children need him, and that a man can't just walk out on his responsibilities, a working man can't afford divorce unless one of the women is at least self-supporting. His wages won't run to two homes and I believe, if you can be patient and understanding, he will get over his attraction in time and the home and all it means will call him.' 'What can one do with a husband who flirts?' *Modern Marriage* reader Josephine asked the Heart-to-Heart bureau in 1931. 'He will outgrow this habit, as children outgrow teething troubles,' was Helen Worth's reassuring response.[85]

Adulteresses were dealt with more sharply. First they were admonished to end the affair with immediate effect. Second they were instructed to resist the 'morbid honesty' of a confession—particularly during the war. A 'lonely wife' who found herself pregnant whilst her husband was a prisoner of war received short shrift from Leonora Eyles: 'it isn't easy to be sympathetic to you.'[86] 'I beg you not to tell him yet; it would knock him out to know what you have done whilst he has been making rosy dreams of getting back to you.' Even a woman who feared she had contracted venereal disease through extra marital sex was advised, 'don't make your husband suffer too by telling him about your disloyalty. He can't know *unless* you tell him.'[87] Dishonesty was aggressively advanced as a legitimate strategy in defence of matrimony. Single women involved with married men were construed as either 'foolish', or 'shockingly dishonourable'.[88] 'I am nearly seventeen, and am great friends with a young married couple,' confided one *Woman's Own* reader in 1936.[89] 'The husband has begun to make love to me, and I must confess I love him. What shall I do? Does it matter as long as the wife does not know?' 'It matters quite a lot!' replied Leonora Eyles unequivocally.

> The wife is your friend and you are behaving very badly to her. The very best thing you can do is to stop going to the house until you have got over this infatuation, and can trust yourself with the husband. It is quite easy to tell the wife some reason why you do not go so often. Please think seriously about this, as you may be the cause of untold suffering later on. I'm sure you wouldn't like to think that your friend's married life had been smashed up through your foolishness.

Often the veracity of feeling was disputed. 'Probably you don't love him at all, you are just in love with romance and the idea of doing something wrong,' another woman was informed.[90] Many failed to heed the warning. The dilemmas of single women ensnared in relationships with married men were a regular feature of mid-century magazines and featured in other advice literature too. According to M. B. Smith, for example, 'Monogamous marriage is a cultural expectancy in our society, and is deep rooted in the traditional pattern of Western civilisation, and the girl who chooses to challenge it... is still up against a sense of sin and of guilt which is damaging to the whole personality, and at the extreme leads to suicide, premature death, or manic-depressive neurosis.'[91] Rather than suffer this dire fate, such women were instructed to give up the relationship and never to believe the promises of men. 'He is talking nonsense about divorcing her. Stop seeing him,' was the rather blunt reply offered to one hopeful young woman.[92]

The pressure of war placed English marriages under particular strain. Eyles identified a 'sort of epidemic' of wartime adultery.[93]

A married man, working in a Royal Ordnance Factory reported in 1942 that:

> The R.O.F. where I am employed is fairly rife with irregular associations and the local term 'budgerigar' or 'budgie' has become a widely used euphemism for 'mistress'. Irregular association between married men and single girls or with girls whose husbands are away is widespread amongst operatives and junior supervisory grades. Pregnancy (obviously out of wedlock) is fairly frequent. I am not sure of the reason for this general laxity and am not aware whether it is peculiar to R.O.F.s (I know it existed in Woolwich) or to any rapidly grown industrial concern. Reasons may lie with the transfer of men here away from their wives, high wages and consequent fairly heavy drinking, a general moral slackening in war-time or an exaggeration of South Wales' Valleys morality where a high incidence of illegitimacy (and abortion) is normal.[94]

Slater and Woodside found that men were, more often than not, minded to confess their infidelities to their wives. 'These women were not deeply concerned, and felt for the most part that the circumstances of war exonerated the husband. One wife said she would overlook what happened abroad but not in England.'[95] Husbands tended to be more upset about their wives' affairs and their responses varied widely: 'anxiety, suspiciousness, compulsive worrying on the one side . . . understanding and reasonableness on the other.'[96] The case of one 26-year-old provided a good example of the latter response:

> Bertram W. (98c), twenty-six, says the six years of his marriage have been happy—'she'd go out of her way to do anything for me'. It was an American airman, and his mother told him about it. 'She was weak'; he was away so long, but all the same 'a woman shouldn't give in'. Yet he can understand that 'Americans have feelings just like other people'. He waited and didn't say anything, and let her tell him. It's all over now and he won't ever bring it up against her.[97]

In 1949, Mass-Observation asked both its panel of correspondents and a street sample their opinions on the question, 'how do you feel about the idea of sex relations between people who are not married to one another?' Although respondents held strong views on the matter, with few positively welcoming such behaviour, the responses are remarkable for their unwillingness to make judgements without an understanding of individual circumstance. For some love acted as a key justification for extra-marital sex, particularly amongst the young. An assistant drainage officer aged 28 observed: 'It's up to them. I don't think it matters whether one is married or not. The parties however should *feel* that they are in love. One should not regard the marriage licence as a copulation certificate.'[98] Another married man stated, 'If people love each other and wish to copulate and for one reason or another are not married I see no reason why they should not. I disagree with copulation without love.'[99] What is perhaps most surprising about these responses is people's reluctance to judge. Whilst cultural authorities suggested a clear set of norms, these could be resisted. Instead, when asked, individuals asserted their own capacity for discrimination, bringing their own authority and expertise to bear. Contingency was important, individuality was central, but a significant factor for consideration was also emotional authenticity.

Mass-Observation concluded: 'neither Panel nor street opinions of marriage often mention the need for complete sexual fidelity.'[100] Certainly the centrality of sexual fidelity to marriage relations in the immediate post-war years can be questioned. In his research for *Exploring English Character* Geoffrey Gorer found that infidelity was rarely perceived to be the worst crime that a spouse could commit: only a minority of his sample believed that infidelity should automatically end a marriage.[101] Significantly, he noted, 'the interesting correlation that those who consider sexual love "very important" in marriage are much more likely to consider terminating the marriage if the spouse is discovered to be unfaithful than those who consider it "fairly important".'[102] As marriage became less an institution founded upon role performance and more a relationship of emotional and sexual companionship, infidelity wielded a fatal power. 'To so many people adultery strikes at the very heart of married life,' stated Labour MP Alec Jones in presenting the Divorce Law Reform Bill to parliament.[103] Gorer's 1969 cohort put much greater emphasis upon infidelity and jealousy as factors making for marital failure than had his previous cohort.[104] Sexual fidelity was much more central to ideas of married happiness, although when Gorer mapped individual attitudes on to actual behaviour he found that, 'frequently there was little consistency between their views and their admissions.'[105] As contemporary sociologists Richards and Elliott have argued, whilst post-war attitudes towards extra-marital sex softened with increased incidences; attitudes towards extra-marital affairs became harsher even as they apparently became more common.[106]

* * *

The hardening of attitudes towards adultery reflected a growing sense that married love should be founded upon absolute honesty. However, not all mid-century adultery was rooted in day-to-day duplicity. The nature of the divorce laws encouraged others to openly 'live in sin' with a partner who was not legally their spouse. In 1949 *Picture Post* received a letter from one such 'unmarried husband'.[107]

> This is a plea for the many thousands of men and women who are living respectably with the partners of their choice but who are prevented by the marriage laws, the high cost of divorce, or the obstinacy of a disgruntled ex-wife or husband, from legalising their union. It is also an appeal for children of such unions.
>
> Not all persons who are unfaithful to their marriage-vows are abandoned profligates. Drunken and brutal husbands, nagging or sluttish wives, these and a thousand other causes may render life with a legal partner a hell on earth. Must the victims of unhappy marriages condemn themselves to lifelong loneliness when they may find happiness with someone better able to partner them?

> Such irregular unions are often happier than legal ones. Yet in the eyes of the law, men and women who are thus situated rank as little more than members of the oldest profession on the planet.

Across the mid-century individual men and women, like 'unmarried husband', found ways of subverting social and legal restrictions on their behaviour in order to create their own forms of commitment and build emotional intimacies on their own terms and within their own framework of respectability. By attending to these everyday dramas we can access ordinary people's attempts to reconcile mutuality with individualism, self-sacrifice with self-fulfilment, and duty with love.

Long-term 'irregular' relationships were not, of course, an innovation of the twentieth century. Historian Ginger S. Frost has examined nineteenth-century cohabitation, describing an England where ideas about matrimony could be extremely flexible and where both emotion and pragmatism informed decisions to live together unmarried.[108] Joanna Klein's careful analysis of English police personnel records has illuminated the strategies by which individuals confounded legal definitions of marriage in the first part of the twentieth century:

> Some formed new relationships while still living with their spouses, some abandoned their spouses, some lived as if married to new unofficial spouses and some married bigamous spouses. Some couples progressed from one type of arrangement to another. These irregular affiliations did not indicate a rejection of marriage but rather attempts to find a marriage that worked for them regardless of its lack of legal sanction.[109]

During wartime the language of irregular commitment was apparently in common usage. 'When I was young—and I think until after the last war—we should never in our family have dreamt of mentioning people who were "living in sin"; now we can refer to "unofficial marriages" without blame or embarrassment,' suggested one Mass-Observer.[110] Rowntree and Lavers exempted 'unmarried wives' from their consideration of sexual promiscuity because 'whatever the moral and legal positions, they have—largely through the necessity of providing for them during the war—gained recognition of their status amounting to a degree of respectability'.[111] By the 1960s the rights and wrongs of 'living in sin' attracted the attention of BBC television. BBC2's *Marriage Today* documentary series interviewed a series of young students at Sussex University with attitudes 'as self-consciously modern as their architecture'.[112] They were not enthusiastic supporters of marriage. 'I think marriage today is obsolent [*sic*]. At one time it was a useful way of preserving society in an insecure society. I think that with the growth of such things as the welfare state, also with the decline of traditional moral values, marriage is becoming an increasingly unworkable concept,' one young man opined. Another bluntly stated that 'marriage has no future.' Although such views were not the norm the *Man Alive* series did manage to find two young cohabiting couples to interview for a 'Living in Sin?' documentary in 1966. On the same programme, *Daily Mirror* agony aunt Marjorie Proops maintained that women within such relationships 'would much prefer to be married'.[113]

Those inhabiting irregular unions employed a range of methods, informal and formal, to carve out lives of everyday respectability. Moving district was one such method—employed as we have already seen by Olivia Cockett and Bill Hole. Another was the practice of changing one's name by deed poll. 14,038 British subjects changed their surname in this manner between 1920 and 1939, although probably not all for this reason.[114] The practice seems to have spread during the Second World War as a response to the bureaucratization of everyday life; the awarding, as in the previous conflict, of servicemens' allowances to unmarried 'wives'; and a Home Service broadcast entitled 'changing your name' which had suggested that 'to the couple who are not married it means avoiding the embarrassment of ration books made out in the same address but in different names'.[115] By 1947 it 'was undoubtedly becoming a common practice' though never actually quantified.[116] The so-called 'illegal "wife"' attracted the attention of the Church of England in the 1940s—the Church's Moral Welfare Council prepared a detailed report on the subject—and of the London Housewives' Association a decade later.[117] Both pressed the Lord Chancellor for legislation on the matter. Both failed to secure the result that they hoped for.[118]

The practice of name changing was contentious. It also demonstrates that ordinary individuals were willing to subvert available legal processes in an attempt to achieve social legitimation for established relationships. Just four years before the Divorce Law Reform Act of 1969 *Woman's Own* agony aunt, Evelyn Home, received the following reader letter:

> Two problems—first, could I divorce my husband for cruelty after not seeing him for seven years? I only lived with him a month, then he injured me so terribly I was in hospital for a time and never went back to him. He is away at sea a lot; I don't know where he is and don't really want him to know where I am. Second is it all right to change my name by deed poll, so that people will think I am married to the man I now love and live with? He will marry me any time, and has been kind and good to me and our baby daughter. But meanwhile it is awkward being called by my own name; I'd like to be known as his wife, because I truly feel that I am. Both his family and mine know the full truth about our relationship.[119]

The primacy of feeling over legality is striking here—as is the support of both families. While Evelyn Home warned that divorce might not be straightforward, nor was she overtly condemnatory. Rather she suggested, with no hint of irony, that 'what you most need is advice from an expert.'

Although controversial, name changing was perfectly legal. Bigamy was not. A felony under the 1828 Offences Against the Persons Act, there were on average ninety-eight trials a year in England and Wales for the offence between 1857 and 1904, a figure which fails to capture the scale of the problem.[120] Ginger Frost suggests that only one in five nineteenth-century bigamists were actually prosecuted.[121]

The attitudes of the courts and community towards bigamy were complex, but 'all were convinced that happy bigamous marriages were preferable to miserable legal ones'.[122] In effect bigamy provided a practical—if illegal—way of circumventing the divorce laws and providing for a marriage of choice. Within the nineteenth-century court cases Frost examined, bigamy was held to be more acceptable if the first spouse had reneged on the marriage contract by failing to fulfil their gendered role, or by committing sexual misconduct, or an act of violence.

The criminal statistics for twentieth-century bigamy are particularly sensitive to war and its immediate aftermath. At the beginning of the century, the annual average number of cases was 112. By 1920–4 the figure stood at 506.[123] Thereafter the figures declined until the Second World War sparked another significant increase, reaching a century high of 986 cases in 1943.[124] Mr Justice Hallett sought to explain this marked increase: 'Men are living away from their own homes and their wives, getting into relations with other young women and in some cases proceeding to go through marriage ceremonies with those other young women. I understand the temptations and difficulties. The fact remains that in any civilized state, as I see it, bigamy must be a serious offence.'[125] The annual average remained relatively high through 1945–9 at 657, declining to 240 in 1950–4 and ninety-three in the period 1960–4.[126] In 1968, a year before Divorce Law Reform finally succeeded, just fifty-eight individuals were prosecuted for the crime.[127] Although women as well as men were prosecuted for bigamy, men tended to dominate the statistics.

Accounts of bigamy trials suggest a wide range of motivations for the crime including theft, deception, fear, and weakness. Love was also a frequently cited factor in the decision to marry bigamously and could play a significant role within the accused's defence. Reuben Dight believed himself legally married to 29-year-old Phyllis Levey until she confessed the bigamy and they informed the police. The court heard that she had left her legal husband because of his violence against her and had fallen in love with Dight. 'She has done me no harm. I love her and I want her back. If it is possible to get a divorce I wish to marry her legally.'[128] An unsatisfactory first marriage might encourage judicial leniency when sentencing. Edward Gregory, for example, was dealt with leniently at the West Riding Assizes in 1942 because Mr Justice Birkett took his 'loveless marriage' and 'good character' into account.[129] Judges did not always exercise such sensitivity, however. ATS woman Gladys Morrisson's appearance at the Yorkshire Assizes coincided with Mr Justice Croon-Johnson railing against 'far too much bigamy among women in the West Riding of Yorkshire'.[130] When the court was told of her unhappy marriage the judge retorted 'Is this an appeal that I should make women the spoilt darlings of the law?' and sentenced her to six months' imprisonment.[131]

Nonetheless it seems clear that bigamy cases persisted into the twentieth century because individuals *felt* married to people they were not legally bound to. Within this context the authenticity of their own feeling was given higher status and authority than any sense of marriage as a legally binding contract. The act of bigamy was, within this context, a claim for the respectability which married love bestowed: for such individuals it was the legal marriage which lacked authenticity. It seems that the courts themselves sometimes shared this idea. What we see goes beyond individual acts of law breaking, suggesting a systematic recognition that the divorce laws were problematic. Within this context the legal significance of bigamy was markedly unstable. In 1937, John Smith, described by his wife as a 'fine man', was advised by Mr Justice Goddard: 'Divorce your wife and marry the woman with whom you have been living.' Smith reportedly told the *Daily Mirror* after his immediate release, 'We have always wanted to put things right and become man and wife.'[132] This emphasis upon putting things right was reiterated by *Daily Mirror* reporter Noel Whitcomb, who investigated the wartime increase in bigamy cases in early 1945. 'The vast majority of these bigamy cases—cruel and wicked as they are—are committed not by criminals, but by ordinary people who have drifted apart through war conditions from their legal partners. Respectability is the keynote of their "crime"—however muddled and untrue the idea of respectability may be, Marriage is respectable.'[133]

In September 1942, *Picture Post* published a detailed account from a serving soldier.[134] The man had signed up in January 1940 as a cook in the Royal Army Service Corps and had married after a brief courtship later that year. The marriage had not been a success. Upon being posted to Northern Ireland he had met another woman, 'the only girl in the world who ever could have mattered'. As he told it, 'At first I was content to have her friendship, and thanked Providence for it, but this soon ripened into a love I had never known nor ever dreamed possible.' When she fell pregnant and asked him to marry her he consented, notwithstanding his actual marital status.

When the bigamy was discovered, the soldier went to trial.

> I was sentenced to nine months' hard labour, despite the fact that I produced a letter in court from my legal wife, wishing myself, the bigamous wife and baby, good luck and every happiness. I offered a statement in which I apologised for the trouble I had caused the authorities, but saying I was sorry for what I had done, as all parties concerned were satisfied, and, as soon as possible, we should straighten the tangle out and everybody be happy.

Upon release he fell ill and was unable to resume his RASC duties. The army refused to pay his legal wife the serviceman's allowance, so instead the Army Council sent her a stoppage out of his wages. His new wife and child received nothing. 'In writing this,' he concluded, 'I have tried to be brief and clear, but I could not include really the half of the heart-break and suffering that two people have been through because they fell in love.' The response from *Picture Post*'s readers was overwhelmingly supportive. Of thirteen responses to his letter only three condemned his actions. Whilst the context of war and his status as a soldier are significant here, his expression of true love seems also to have provided justification for his actions. And yet this did not help in the eyes of the state. Within the context of mid-century laws on commitment a hasty—but ill-advised—wedding could have life-changing consequences. Laws could be subverted but only up to a point. The golden age of marriage had its casualties as well as its survivors.

Epilogue

On Valentine's Day 1938, Dorothy Dix of the *Daily Mirror* 'Love Bureau' addressed the problems of a 20-year-old married mother of one.[1] 'Troubled' had married three years earlier but now worried that she had made a mistake. 'My husband is as good a man as anyone could find. He is kind and affectionate, very thrifty and provides generously for me. But I am dissatisfied and don't know what to do. I don't even know whether I love my husband or not. I think I don't because I get no thrill from being with him or from his caresses,' she confided. Dix had little sympathy. 'A lot of girls make this same mistake. They think that marriage is going to be sentiment and romance and a perpetual petting party, and that they will live in a state of thrills. They are disgruntled and disappointed when they find that marriage is work, responsibility and self-sacrifice, doing their duty and being taken for granted.' The young woman's dilemma had its roots in the instability of mid-century matrimonial expectation. While her husband exhibited one set of spousal virtues, she aspired to another. As we have seen, it was ultimately her approach which triumphed. Although duty and self-sacrifice remained central to the practice of parenthood, they declined in matrimonial importance. Instead, self-expression and the quest for fulfilment emerged as key aspirations for the modern self.

As new understandings of love and partnership developed, tensions and contradictions emerged. A shifting emotional context undermined established notions of planning and commitment. Wartime conditions, in particular, set off profound shock waves producing lasting changes in affective relations. The institution of formal marriage could not always contain the understandings of love and partnership that took hold in the 1940s and 1950s. New emotional frameworks could actively conflict with established notions of monogamous heterosexuality. Couples were increasingly unwilling to put up with 'loveless' relationships and found ways to remedy or circumvent them. 'People will not tolerate the mediocre marriage that our grandparents would have endured almost without comment,' wrote Joseph Bradshaw of the National Marriage Guidance Council. 'At the same time that marriage has become more difficult, therefore, there tends to be ever more opportunity to abdicate from its responsibilities.'[2] Individual relationships were subject to heightened levels of scrutiny. 'How do you treat your wife?' asked the *Daily Mirror* in 1956.[3] Not particularly well according to some discontented correspondents. 'I never get taken out. My husband never buys me anything. I never had a honeymoon and he has never taken me on a holiday. He goes out every night and he has never bought a thing for the house. He is a nasty, arrogant, bombastic, vicious bully, selfish to the core,' wrote a Harrogate woman. In 1955, *Picture Post* posed the question, 'Does your husband really love you?' and offered a quick quiz to help its readers find out.[4] It was difficult to authenticate love in the post-war world.

There were, of course, many who sat outside of dominant mores and values, contesting or subverting structures and prescriptions. Mass-Observation, for example, was 'continually impressed by the discrepancy between what is supposed to happen and what does happen, between the law and the fact, the institution and the individual, what people say they do and what they actually do, what leaders think people want and what people do want'.[5] There were undoubtedly many women and men who loved passionately well before the Second World War, just as there were many in the years that followed who loved more pragmatically. Everyday love was complicated, always operating in a number of registers. Courtship, for example, could be a period of high romance and mutual discovery. Or it might be something more mundane. 'What does the word courtship mean to me? Well I think not very much except in films like those in my youth of Jeanette Macdonald and Nelson Eddy,' asserted one Mass-Observer in 2001.

> I think courtship means something very polite and formal whereas as working girls we mostly got somebody of similar ilk where we spent a certain amount of time lurking on badly lit corners and usually on about the second meeting we found we had nothing in common and it fizzled out. I don't remember a single person of my acquaintance being courted with flowers or chocolates. I think we would have felt uneasy if they had done so—where would they have got the money from![6]

Nonetheless a distinctive set of social interactions framed heterosexual love across mid-century England. Those who lived through the period frequently positioned themselves within a distinctive historical era on the basis of their experience of affective relations. 'My parents disapproved of too much freedom between the sexes . . . I accept companionate marriage, sex novels, frequent divorces etc. tolerantly as part of life today,' wrote a Mass-Observer in 1939 adding, 'It is no good being shocked at anything as it will probably be quite an ordinary custom tomorrow.'[7] For this woman, and many others, a feeling of being part of a distinctive historical cohort was rooted in sexual and emotional practice. 'I think courting has changed dramatically over the last 30 years,' wrote a woman in 2001. Another explained that

> In years gone by, right up to the sixties I would say, 'courting' was something that took place in a series. Courting was something you did up to getting engaged. Being engaged meant you were going to get married. Sex figured possibly in the 'courting' phase or maybe you waited until being engaged. Or perhaps you might even have

> waited until you were married. But now sex comes much earlier on. Living together, even in the sixties, generally meant you were going to get married. But not now. Even being engaged doesn't seem to mean you're going to get married. So there doesn't seem to be much room for the courting phase does there.[8]

The implications of new understandings of the relationship between love and partnership unfolded generationally. The teenagers of the 1950s were parents in the late 1960s and 1970s and were possibly less antagonistic to the apparently more liberal arrangements of their own children than their own parents had been.

Certainly the social relations that framed mid-century love were reconstituted in the period after 1970. Marriage remained incredibly popular at the beginning of that decade. It had penetrated teenage culture and was a key aspect of youthful identity. Most people expected to marry and they generally wished to do so early in life. In 1972 the General Marriage Rate for England and Wales was nearly as high as the century-long peak achieved in the early years of the Second World War.[9] And yet love and marriage were about to change once again, heralding the rapid decomposition of short-lived mid-century ideals. The liberation movements of the 1970s, changing contraceptive practices, increased socio-economic insecurity, structural workplace shifts and the legislative actions of the state undoubtedly played a role. So too did everyday understandings of the nature and significance of love. Existing social structures were difficult to sustain in the face of emotional revolution. In the years that followed the marriage rate plummeted. By 2009 it had fallen to the lowest level since calculations began in 1862. This is not to say that people no longer committed to long-term relationships, but love and marriage were no longer so inextricably linked. As heterosexual love escaped the confines of matrimony, legal commitment moved beyond the realm of heterosexuality. The Civil Partnership Act became effective early in the twenty-first century providing legal recognition for same-sex relationships. By the end of 2010, 46,622 partnerships had been formed in the United Kingdom.[10] In 2012 the Coalition government announced plans to legislate for same-sex marriage in England and Wales. The age at which heterosexuals married increased significantly when compared to mid-century figures. In 1970 the average age at first marriage for men and women was 24 and 22 respectively. By 2012 it had risen by eight years for both. The association between married life and youth was significantly weakened. Within this context, sex unaccompanied by either love or commitment became a commonplace for women, as well as for men. The sexual double standard nonetheless persisted.

Seventy years earlier love, sex, and commitment had been entangled in a complex web of meaning with public and private significance. 'Love in its highest sense is not made up of sex, nor is sex love. The two are entwined together in an unbreakable thread,' Edward Griffith had suggested. 'Sex can ennoble a marriage; it can likewise debase it.'[11] When Mass-Observation diarist number 5165 married in December 1940 he was just 21. We last encountered him at the beginning of this book as he enjoyed Christmas Day with his wife. The couple had spent the evening prior to their wedding day listening to the sounds of war. 'We didn't go to shelter. Being together it didn't really matter, the awful thing is if it happens to only one.'[12] In March 1942 he submitted the final instalment of his wartime diary. His views on the war effort were entangled with his feelings about married life. For this man, writing in the dark days of 1942, the distinction between public life and private life was blurred. On the night of Sunday 1 March the couple stayed at home. In his account of that evening, his need for private emotional intimacy connected with a sense of public duty in a way that sharply illuminates a particular historical moment.

> All evening we were alone again, right from 6 o'clock. It was so pleasant to be alone, and talk about things that really concerned us. We had a bath and went to bed early, so that tomorrow getting up at

6 won't seem a hardship. It is pleasant to be able to spend days at home, so much more than to be lost in some outstation right out of the way, isolated in the bloody army, far away from the war, useless in every point of view. At home I can talk with ——, think things out that are really worth while, and feel active, feel the want to do things, to fight the war, and to fight for our lives. This is so rare a feeling in the army, where almost every single thought is divorced from action, and when every active thought is of going home.[13]

Endnotes

A Note on Sources

1. On the development of social scientific methods of investigating ordinary life see Mike Savage, *Identities and Social Change in Britain since 1940* (Oxford: Oxford University Press, 2010).
2. For more on Mass-Observation's history see James Hinton, *The Mass Observers: A History, 1937–1949* (Oxford: Oxford University Press, 2013); Nick Hubble, *Mass Observation and Everyday Life: Culture, History, Theory* (Basingstoke: Palgrave Macmillan, 2005); Tony Kushner, *We Europeans? Mass-Observation, 'Race', and British Identity in Twentieth-century Britain* (London: Ashgate, 2004); Dorothy Sheridan, Brian Street, and David Bloome, *Writing Ourselves. Mass-Observation and Literary Practices* (Cresskill: Hampton Press, 2000).
3. Charles Madge and Tom Harrisson, *Mass-Observation* (London: Frederick Muller, 1937), 10.
4. On the intellectual climate within which Mass-Observation emerged see Hubble, *Mass-Observation and Everyday Life*.
5. *The New Statesman and Nation*, 30 January 1937, 155.
6. Mass Observation Archive (hereafter MOA), Day Survey (hereafter DS) 81, 'Why I write for Mass Observation', October 1937.
7. MOA, File Report (hereafter FR) A26, 'They speak for themselves. A radio enquiry into Mass Observation with Tom Harrisson and Charles Madge', 1 June 1939, 2.
8. Dorothy Sheridan, 'Anticipating history: historical consciousness and the "documentary impulse"', paper presented at *The Second World War: Popular Culture and Cultural Memory Conference*, July 2011.
9. Mass-Observation, *First Year's Work, 1937–38* (London: Lindsay Drummond, 1938), 66.

10. MOA, Worktown Collection (hereafter WC), box 60, Book drafts on Blackpool, 60-F, sex, 27. On the class and gender assumptions that informed some of Mass-Observation's work in Bolton see Peter Gurney, '"Intersex" and "Dirty Girls": Mass-Observation and Working-class Sexuality in England in the 1930s', *Journal of the History of Sexuality*, 8:2 (1997), 256–90.
11. MOA, WC, box 48, Leisure activities, fairs, and dance halls, 48-C, dance halls and dances, 'St Peters and St Paul's dance', 3.
12. An edited version of the report was published by Liz Stanley as *Sex Surveyed, 1949–1994. From Mass-Observation's 'Little Kinsey' to the National Survey and the Hite Reports* (London: Taylor and Francis, 1995). On the contemporaneous response to Little Kinsey see Adrian Bingham, 'The "K-Bomb": Social Surveys, the Popular Press and British Sexual Culture in the 1940s and 1950s', *Journal of British Studies*, 50:1 (2011), 156–79.
13. Richard Broad and Suzie Fleming (eds), *Nella Last's War: The Second World War Diaries of 'Housewife 49'* (London: Profile, 2006); Patricia Malcolmson and Robert Malcolmson (eds), *Nella Last's Peace: the Post-War Diaries of Housewife 49* (London: Profile, 2008); Patricia Malcolmson and Robert Malcolmson (eds), *Nella Last in the 1950s: Further Diaries of Housewife 49* (London: Profile, 2010).
14. On the relationship between popular culture and individual memory see Penny Summerfield, 'Culture and Composure: Creating Narratives of the Gendered Self in Oral History Interviews', *Cultural and Social History*, 1:1 (2004), 65–93.
15. MOA, Diarist number (hereafter D) 5165, December 1940.
16. Mass-Observation, *The Press and Its Readers. A Mass-Observation Survey* (London: Art & Technics, 1949), 8.

Introduction

1. *The Times*, 1 November 1955, 8.
2. *Daily Express*, 1 November 1955, 4.
3. *Daily Express*, 1 November 1955, 4.
4. MOA, Directive Replies (hereafter DR), November 1955, newspaper cutting included in submission.
5. George Horace Gallup, *Gallup International Public Opinion Polls: Great Britain, 1937–1975*. 2 vols. (London: Random House, 1976), 349.

6. *Daily Mirror*, 17 July 1953, 1.
7. MOA, DR unnumbered, November 1955. Wartime Mass-Observers are allocated an identifying number by the Mass Observation Archive. Those who started writing in the post-war period do not currently have such a number.
8. MOA, DR unnumbered, November 1955.
9. MOA, DR unnumbered, November 1955.
10. MOA, DR unnumbered, November 1955.
11. *The Times*, 19 October 1949, 2.
12. MOA, DR unnumbered, November 1955.
13. Alfred Thompson Denning, *The Equality of Women: A lecture delivered at the Annual Conference of the National Marriage Guidance Council* (London: National Marriage Guidance Council, 1950), 14.
14. Kenneth Plummer, *Telling Sexual Stories: Power, Change, and Social Worlds* (London: Routledge 1995), 145. Anthony Giddens, *The Transformation of Intimacy: Sexuality, Love and Eroticism in Modern Societies* (Cambridge: Cambridge University Press, 1992). A number of other sociologists have investigated the impact of this trend upon our intimate lives. See for example Ulrich Beck and Elizabeth Beck-Gersheim, *The Normal Chaos of Love* (Cambridge: Polity, 1995); Jeffrey Weeks, *The World We Have Won. The Remaking of Erotic and Intimate Life* (London: Routledge, 2007). For a pessimistic view of intimacy in the 'modern liquid world' see Zygmunt Bauman, *Liquid Love. On the Fragility of Human Bonds* (Cambridge: Polity, 2003). Feminist sociologists have, not unreasonably, suggested that in a society where women still shoulder the majority of responsibility for child rearing, the pursuit of happiness is not always an issue for the individual alone. See for example, Mary Evans, *Love. An Unromantic Discussion* (Cambridge: Polity, 2003); Wendy Langford, *Revolutions of the Heart: Gender, Power and the Delusions of Love* (London: Routledge, 1999); Carol Smart, *Personal Life* (Cambridge: Polity, 2007).
15. Pat Thane, 'Family Life and "Normality" in Post-War British Culture', in Richard Bessel and Dirk Schumann (eds), *Life after Death. Approaches to a Cultural and Social History of Europe During the 1940s and 1950s* (Cambridge: Cambridge University Press, 2003), 198.
16. David Coleman and John Salt, *The British Population. Patterns, Trends, and Processes* (Oxford: Oxford University Press 1992), 185.

17. The proportion of married women participating in the labour market increased from 10 per cent in 1931 to 21.7 per cent in 1951, 29.4 per cent in 1961 and to 42 per cent in 1971. Duncan Gallie, 'The Labour Force', in A. H. Halsey and Josephine Webb (eds), *Twentieth-Century British Social Trends* (Basingstoke: Macmillan, 2000), 281–323, 292.
18. Coleman and Salt, *The British Population*, 182.
19. In the period 1931 to 1935 the first marriage rate per 1,000 single women aged over 15 was 57.3 and for men it was 62.6; by 1936 to 1940 it was 73.3 and 78.7 respectively and by 1966 to 1970 it was 94.2 for women and 82.1 for men. In 1981 to 1985 it dropped to 59.9 for women and 48.1 for men. David Coleman, 'Population and Family', in A. H. Halsey and Josephine Webb (eds), *Twentieth-Century British Social Trends* (Basingstoke: Macmillan, 2000), 56–7.
20. B. R. Mitchell, *British Historical Statistics* (Cambridge: Cambridge University Press, 1987), 75–6.
21. Jane Lewis, *The End of Marriage? Individualism and Intimate Relations* (Cheltenham: Edward Elgar, 2001), 30.
22. Rachel M. Pierce, 'Marriage in the Fifties', *The Sociological Review*, NS 11:2 (March 1963), 215–40, 220.
23. Coleman and Salt, *The British Population*, 190.
24. Agnus Pearl Jephcott, *Girls Growing Up* (London: Faber & Faber, 1942), 135. Jephcott researched the experiences of 152 elementary-school-educated 'working girls' between September 1941 and March 1942.
25. Coleman and Salt, *The British Population*, 191.
26. Michael Anderson, 'The social implications of demographic change', in F. M. L. Thompson (ed.), *The Cambridge Social History of Britain 1750–1950*: Volume 2, *People and their Environment* (Cambridge: Cambridge University Press, 1990), 1–70, 67.
27. *Woman's Own*, 18 May 1950, 37.
28. For a survey see Susan J. Matt, 'Current Emotion Research in History: Or, Doing History from the Inside Out', *Emotion Review*, 3:1 (2011), 117–24.
29. Barbara H. Rosenwein, 'Writing Without Fear about Early Medieval Emotions', *Early Medieval Europe*, 10: 2 (2001), 229–34, 231.
30. For a comparative account of Western emotionology see Cas Wouters, *Sex and Manners. Female Emancipation in the West, 1890–2000* (London: Sage, 2004).

31. The work of Peter Stearns, William Reddy, and Barbara Rosenwein has been particularly influential. Recent works on the modern British context include Martin Francis's study of masculine emotional culture, 'Tears, Tantrums, and Bared Teeth: The Emotional Economy of Three Conservative Prime Ministers, 1951–1963', *Journal of British Studies*, 41:3 (2002), 354–87 and Michael Roper's methodological intervention, 'Slipping out of View: Subjectivity and Emotion in Gender History', *History Workshop Journal*, 59 (2005), 57–72.
32. Linda A. Pollock, 'Anger and the Negotiation of Relationships in Early Modern England', *The Historical Journal*, 47:3 (2004), 567–90; William M. Reddy, *The Navigation of Feeling. A Framework for the History of Emotions* (Cambridge: Cambridge University Press, 2001); Richard Bessel, 'Hatred after War. Emotion and the Postwar History of East Germany', *History and Memory*, 17:1/2 (2005), 195–216.
33. See e.g. Barbara H. Rosenwein (ed.), *Anger's Past. The Social Uses of an Emotion in the Middle Ages* (New York: Cornell University Press, 1998) and her more recent *Emotional Communities in the Early Middle Ages* (London: Cornell University Press, 2006); Joanna Bourke, 'Fear and Anxiety: Writing about Emotion in Modern History', *History Workshop Journal*, 55 (2003), 111–33 and *Fear: A Cultural History* (London: Virago, 2006).
34. For nineteenth-century middle-class America see Karen Lystra, *Searching the Heart. Women, Men and Romantic Love in Nineteenth-Century America* (Oxford: Oxford University Press, 1989). On the Soviet Union see Deborah A. Field, *Private Life and Communist Morality in Khrushchev's Russia* (London: Peter Lang, 2007); on the GDR see Josie McLellan, *Love in the Time of Communism. Intimacy and Sexuality in the GDR* (Cambridge: Cambridge University Press, 2011).
35. Stephen Brooke, *Sexual Politics. Sexuality, Family Planning and the British Left, from the 1880s to the Present Day* (Oxford: Oxford University Press, 2011); Martin Francis, *The Flyer. British Culture and the Royal Air Force 1939–1945* (Oxford: Oxford University Press, 2008); Simon Szreter and Kate Fisher, *Sex Before the Sexual Revolution. Intimate Life in England 1918–1963* (Cambridge: Cambridge University Press, 2010).
36. Luisa Passerini, *Europe in Love. Love in Europe. Imagination and Politics in Britain between the Wars* (London: I. B. Tauris, 1999); Marcus Collins,

Modern Love. An Intimate History of Men and Women in Twentieth-Century Britain (London: Atlantic, 2003); Simon May, *Love. A History* (New Haven and London: Yale University Press, 2011); Lisa Appignanesi, *All About Love. Anatomy of an Unruly Emotion* (London: Virago, 2011).

37. Collins, *Modern Love*, 4
38. Of course literary, philosophical, and sociological explorations of love abound. See e.g. Roland Barthes, *A Lover's Discourse. Fragments* (London: Vintage, 2002); Julia Kristeva, *Tales of Love* (New York: Columbia University Press, 1987); Lynne Pearce and Jackie Stacey (eds), *Romance Revisited* (London: Lawrence & Wishart, 1995).
39. G. R. Elton, *Return to Essentials: Some Reflections on the Present State of Historical Study* (Cambridge: Cambridge University Press, 1991), 117–18.
40. Historians have long debated the impact of the war on British society but the view that it acted as the 'hinge' on which the twentieth century turned has recently been re-asserted by historian Geoffrey G. Field in *Blood, Sweat and Toil. Remaking the Working Class 1939–1945* (Oxford: Oxford University Press, 2011). Historians of gender have pointed to the transformative significance of participation in the war effort on individual women even where overarching structures exhibit continuity of subjugation. See Penny Summerfield and Nicole Crockett, '"You weren't taught that with the welding": Lessons in Sexuality in the Second World War', *Women's History Review*, 1:3 (1992), 435–54; Penny Summerfield, *Reconstructing Women's Wartime Lives. Discourse and Subjectivity in Oral Histories of the Second World War* (Manchester: Manchester University Press, 1998).
41. Richard Hoggart, *A Sort of Clowning. Life and Times 1940–1959* (Oxford: Oxford University Press, 1990), 60.
42. Dorothy Sheridan (ed.), *Wartime Women. A Mass-Observation Anthology, 1937–45* (London: Heinemann, 1990), 226.
43. MOA, DR 3401, August 1943.
44. David R. Mace, 'What Britain is Doing', *Marriage and Family Living*, 10:1 (Winter 1948), 6.
45. Francis, *The Flyer*, 84.
46. Katharine Whitehorn, *Selective Memory* (London: Virago, 2007), 44.
47. Gillian Swanson, *Drunk with the Glitter. Space, Consumption and Sexual Instability in Modern Urban Culture* (Abingdon: Routledge, 2007); Frank Mort,

Capital Affairs. London and the Making of the Permissive Society (New Haven and London: Yale University Press, 2010).

48. Adrian Bingham, *Family Newspapers? Sex, Private Life and the British Popular Press 1918–1978* (Oxford: Oxford University Press, 2009), 97.
49. Mace, 'What Britain is Doing', 6.
50. Edward Shorter, *The Making of the Modern Family* (London: Collins, 1976); Lawrence Stone, *The Family, Sex and Marriage in England, 1500–1800* (London: Weidenfeld & Nicolson, 1977); Amy Louise Erickson, *Women and Property in Early Modern England* (London: Routledge, 1993), 6–7.
51. See John Burnett, David Vincent, and David Mayall (eds), *The Autobiography of the Working Class: An Annotated Critical Bibliography*: Vol. 1, *1790–1900* (Brighton: Harvester Press, 1984).
52. William Smith, 'The Memoir of William Smith', as quoted in John Burnett, *Destiny Obscure. Autobiographies of Childhood, Education and Family from the 1820s to the 1920s* (London: Allen Lane, 1982), 253.
53. Samuel Bamford, *Early Days* (London: Simpkin, Marshall & Co., 1849), 169.
54. Liz Stanley (ed.), *The Diaries of Hannah Cullwick, Victorian Maidservant* (London: Virago, 1984), 253.
55. Bamford, *Early Days*, 171.
56. Ginger S. Frost, *Living in Sin. Cohabiting as Husband and Wife in Nineteenth-Century England* (Manchester: Manchester University Press, 2008), 1.
57. See e.g. the debate between Steven King, John R. Gillis, and Richard Wall in *International Review of Social History*, 44:1 (1999), 23–76.
58. Burnett, *Destiny Obscure*, 253.
59. Thomas Carter, *Memoirs of a Working Man* (London: 1845), 206.
60. David Vincent, *Bread, Knowledge and Freedom. A Study of Nineteenth-Century Working Class Autobiography* (London: Europa, 1981), 60.
61. National Marriage Guidance Council, *Sex Difficulties in the Wife* (London: National Marriage Guidance Council, 1953), 9.
62. For a comprehensive history of the National Marriage Guidance Council see Jane Lewis, David Clark, and David Morgan, *Whom God Hath Joined Together. The Work of Marriage Guidance* (London: Routledge, 1992). See also Marcus Collins's excellent discussion of the marriage reform movement and marriage guidance in action in Collins, *Modern Love*, 90–133.

63. *Manchester Evening News*, 3 April 1930, 3.
64. Wouters, *Sex and Manners*; Matthew Thomson, *Psychological Subjects: Identity, Culture and Health in Twentieth-Century Britain* (Oxford: Blackwell, 2006).
65. http://www.britishpathe.com/record.php?id=75152
66. MOA, FR 3110A, 'Little Kinsey', 3.
67. *Picture Post*, 15 September 1951, 36, 37, 40, 43.
68. *Picture Post*, 6 October 1951, 10.
69. On the history of the problem page see Robin Kent, *Aunt Agony Advises. Problem Pages through the Ages* (London: W. H. Allen, 1979). For a recent overview of the evolution of the newspaper problem column see Adrian Bingham, 'Newspaper Problem Pages and British Sexual Culture since 1918', *Media History*, 18:1 (2012), 51–63.
70. For more on Eyles see Maroula Joannou, *'Ladies, Please Don't Smash These Windows'. Women's Writing, Feminist Consciousness and Social Change 1918–38* (Oxford: Berg, 1995).
71. On the use of problem pages as historical sources see Penny Morris, 'From Private to Public: Alba de Céspedes' Agony Column in 1950s Italy', *Modern Italy*, 9:1 (2004), 11–20.
72. Rennie Macandrew, *Friendship, Love Affairs and Marriage: An Explanation of Men to Women and Women to Men* (London: Wales Publishing Co., 1939), 7–8. 'Rennie Macandrew' was the pseudonym of Andrew George Elliot. On the interactivity of self-help literature see Matthew Thomson, 'Psychology and the "Consciousness of Modernity" in Early Twentieth Century Britain', in M. J. Daunton and Bernhad Rieger (eds), *Meanings of Modernity: Britain from the Late-Victorian Era to World War II* (Oxford: Berg, 2001), 99.
73. *Woman's Own*, 11 May 1940, 50.
74. MOA, FR 3110A, 'Little Kinsey', 19.
75. Beth L. Bailey, *Front Porch to Back Seat. Courtship in Twentieth-Century America* (Baltimore: Johns Hopkins University Press, 1988), 6.
76. Karl Marx and Frederick Engels, *Collected Works*: Volume 11, *1851*–53 (London: Lawrence and Wishart, 1979), 99–197, 103.

Chapter 1

1. *The Matrimonial Post and Fashionable Marriage Advertiser*, February 1931, 1. In 1944 George Orwell described the *Post* as an 'entirely above-board' publication which 'checks up carefully on its advertisers'. George Orwell, 'As I Please', *Tribune*, 26 May 1944.

2. 'Lonely hearts' publications were well established by the start of our period, having previously been prone to periodic press and occasionally legal investigation. Harry G. Cocks, '"Sporty" Girls and "Artistic" Boys: Friendship, Illicit Sex and the British "Companionship" Advertisement, 1913–1928', *Journal of the History of Sexuality*, 11:3 (2002), 457–82, 475. As Cocks demonstrates, companionship advertisements and correspondence clubs were used to make homosexual as well as heterosexual contacts, 481.
3. *The Matrimonial Post*, January 1930, 6.
4. *The Matrimonial Post*, January 1922, 1.
5. *The Matrimonial Post*, January 1955, 3.
6. On the shift from self-control to self-expression—a shift which he dates from the late 1950s—see Francis, 'Tears, Tantrums and Bared Teeth', 380–2.
7. Charles Davey, *Teenage Morals* (London: Councils and Education Press, 1961), 18.
8. Revd Herbert Gray, 'Preparation for Marriage', in Sybil Neville-Rolfe (ed.), *Sex in Social Life* (London, George Allen & Unwin, 1949), 288–319, 300.
9. R. Edynbry, *Real Life Problems and Their Solution* (London: Odhams, 1938), 132.
10. Matt Houlbrook, '"A Pin to See the Peepshow": Culture, Fiction, and Selfhood in Edith Thompson's Letters, 1921–1922', *Past and Present*, 207:1 (2010), 215–49.
11. *Modern Marriage*, April 1937.
12. *Woman*, 8 July 1939, 7.
13. *Daily Mirror*, 21 November 1938, 8.
14. Pearl Jephcott, *Rising Twenty: Notes on Some Ordinary Girls* (London: Faber & Faber, 1948), 94.
15. *Mothers' Union News*, March 1961, 6. Quoted in Cordelia Moyse, *A History of the Mothers' Union: Women, Anglicanism and Globalisation, 1876–2008* (Woodbridge: Boydell & Brewer, 2009), 196.
16. Brooke, *Sexual Politics*, 65–91.
17. Brooke, *Sexual Politics*, 86.
18. MOA, DR C2570, Summer 2001, woman born in 1921.
19. Although the idea of chemical attraction—'chemistry'—was established as a way of describing an instinctual personal connection by the

early twentieth century, the precise term 'sexual chemistry' came into common usage in the latter part of the century.

20. MOA, DR B1771, Summer 2001, woman born in 1936.
21. MOA, DR W571, Summer 2001, woman born in 1937.
22. MOA, DR T1843, Summer 2001, woman born in 1949.
23. Jane Lewis, 'Public Institution and Private Relationship. Marriage and Marriage Guidance, 1920–1968', *Twentieth Century British History*, 1:3 (1990), 233–63, 244.
24. Macandrew, *Friendship, Love Affairs and Marriage*, 49.
25. Eliot Slater and Moya Woodside, *Patterns of Marriage. A Study of Marriage Relationships in the Urban Working Classes* (London: Cassell, 1951), 99, 96.
26. *Daily Mirror*, 9 June 1958, 1.
27. MOA, DR H1543, Summer 2001, man born in 1930.
28. MOA, DR P1637, Summer 2001, woman born in 1930.
29. MOA, DR H2639, Summer 2001, woman born in 1940.
30. MOA, DR T2003, Summer 2001, woman born in 1949.
31. MOA, DR W2588, Summer 2001, woman born in 1923.
32. Slater and Woodside, *Patterns of Marriage*, 101.
33. Slater and Woodside, *Patterns of Marriage*, 101.
34. MOA, DR A1706, Summer 2001, woman born in 1946.
35. Edynbry, *Real Life Problems and Their Solution*, 141.
36. *Boyfriend*, 9 February 1963, 27.
37. Geoffrey Gorer, *Exploring English Character* (London: Cresset Press, 1955), 120.
38. Geoffrey Gorer, *Sex and Marriage in England Today. A Study of the Views and Experiences of the Under 45s* (London: Nelson, 1971), 25–6. This study was based on interviews with approximately 1,000 men and 1,000 women conducted in April and May 1969. The research was sponsored by *The Sunday Times*.
39. Lee Comer, *Wedlocked Women* (Leeds: Feminist Books, 1974), 219.
40. *Woman's Own*, 6 October 1934, 22.
41. Gorer, *Sex and Marriage in England Today*, 26.
42. Catherine Cubitt, 'The History of Emotions: a Debate', *Early Medieval Europe*, 10:2 (2001), 225–7, 226.
43. Penny Tinkler, *Constructing Girlhood. Popular Magazines for Girls Growing Up in England 1920–1950* (London: Taylor and Francis, 1995), 145.

44. Macandrew, *Friendship, Love Affairs and Marriage,* 53–4.
45. Macandrew, *Friendship, Love Affairs and Marriage,* 58.
46. Macandrew, *Friendship, Love Affairs and Marriage,* 58.
47. *Modern Marriage,* June 1931, 92.
48. B. M. Spinley, *The Deprived and the Privileged. Personality and Development in English Society* (London: Routledge, 1953), 87.
49. Selina Todd and Hilary Young, 'Baby-boomers to "Beanstalkers" Making the Modern Teenager in Post-War Britain', *Cultural and Social History,* 9:3 (2012), 451–67, 464.
50. MOA, DR C108, Summer 2001, woman born in 1936.
51. MOA, DR B1898, Summer 2001, woman born in 1931.
52. MOA, DR S2246, Summer 2001, man born in 1923.
53. MOA, DR S2083, Summer 2001, man born in 1930.
54. MOA, DR D996, Summer 2001, woman born in 1927. On the transcendent power of love within interwar politics see Brooke, *Sexual Politics,* 91.
55. MOA, DR G2043, Summer 1990, woman born in 1940.
56. MOA, DR A883, Summer 2001, man born in 1933.
57. MOA, DR B1442, Spring 2008, man born in 1923.
58. MOA, DR B1442, Summer 2000, man born in 1923.
59. MOA, DR H260, Summer 1990, woman born in 1930.

Chapter 2

1. Anon., *Every Woman's Book of Love and Marriage and Family Life* (London: Amalgamated Press, 1937), 4.
2. Anon., *Every Woman's Book of Love and Marriage and Family Life,* 4.
3. Anon., *Every Woman's Book of Love and Marriage and Family Life,* 4.
4. MOA, DR H1543, Summer 2001, man born in 1930.
5. *Woman's Own,* 6 January 1940, 3.
6. *Woman's Own,* 15 June 1950, 37.
7. *Daily Mirror,* 21 October 1947, 2.
8. Gray, 'Preparation for Marriage', 291.
9. David R. Mace, *Marriage Crisis* (London: Delisle, 1948), 66.
10. *Woman's Own,* 20 April 1945, 18.
11. *Woman's Own,* 24 March 1944, 18.
12. *Woman's Own,* 21 July 1955, 57.

13. Percy Hugh Beverley Lyon, *Happy Ever After?* (London: Marriage Guidance Council, 1949), 25.
14. *Woman's Own*, 1 June 1950, 45.
15. *Woman's Own*, 27 January 1940, 15.
16. *Woman's Own*, 8 January 1943, 22.
17. *Woman's Own*, 3 February 1940, 36.
18. MOA, Topic Collection (hereafter TC) 32, Women in Wartime, 1939–45, 32/3/E, WAAF: reports from an observer 1941–42, 'The Great Digby man-chase', 6.
19. *Woman's Own*, 11 September 1942, 18.
20. *Woman's Own*, 24 September 1943, 22.
21. *Woman's Own*, 20 April 1940, 54.
22. Peter Bailey, 'Jazz at the Spirella: Coming of Age in Coventry in the 1950s', in Becky Conekin, Frank Mort, and Chris Waters (eds), *Moments of Modernity. Reconstructing Britain 1945–1964* (London: River Oram Press, 1999), 22–40, 35.
23. MOA, DR B1533, Summer 1990, woman born in 1926.
24. Lewis, 'Public Institution and Private Relationship', 238–9.
25. For extensive analysis of the period's sex manual authors see Hera Cook, *The Long Sexual Revolution. English Women, Sex, and Contraception 1800–1975* (Oxford: Oxford University Press, 2004), 241–354. On the reception of Stopes's ideas about female sexual pleasure see Ellen Holtzman, 'The Pursuit of Married Love: Women's Attitudes toward Sexuality and Marriage in Great Britain, 1918–1939', *Journal of Social History*, 16:2 (1982), 39–51.
26. Elizabeth Roberts, *A Woman's Place: An Oral History of Working-class Women, 1890–1940* (Oxford: Wiley, 1984) and *Women and Families: An Oral History, 1940–1970* (Oxford: Wiley, 1995); Natalie Higgins, 'The Changing Expectations and Realities of Marriage in the English Working Class, 1920–1960', unpublished D.Phil. thesis, Cambridge, 2002.
27. Janet Finch and Penny Summerfield, 'Social Reconstruction and the Emergence of Companionate Marriage, 1945–59', in David Clark (ed.), *Marriage, Domestic Life and Social Change. Writings for Jacqueline Burgoyne (1944–88)* (London: Routledge, 1991), 7–32.
28. Marie C. Stopes, *Mother England. A Contemporary History Self-Written by those who have had no Historian* (London: J. Bale & Co., 1929). For an

important and nuanced account of what the Stopes letters reveal about male sexuality see Lesley A. Hall, *Hidden Anxieties. Male Sexuality 1900–1950* (Cambridge: Polity, 1991).

29. Stopes, *Mother England*, 74.
30. Stopes, *Mother England*, 129.
31. Simon Szreter and Kate Fisher, '"We weren't the sort that wanted intimacy every night": Birth Control and Abstinence in England, *c.* 1930–60', *The History of the Family*, 15 (2010), 139–60.
32. Stanley, *Sex Surveyed 1949–1994*, 150.
33. *The Times*, 7 November 1960, 17.
34. Annette Ballinger, 'The Guilt of the Innocent and the Innocence of the Guilty: The Cases of Marie Fahmy and Ruth Ellis', in Alice Myers and Sarah Wight (eds), *No Angels. Women who Commit Violence* (London: Pandora, 1996), 1–28, 17.
35. National Marriage Guidance Council, *Sex Difficulties in the Wife*, 1.
36. Gray, 'Preparation for Marriage', 303.
37. Gray, 'Preparation for Marriage', 304.
38. de Beauvoir, *The Second Sex,* 653; Shulamith Firestone, *The Dialectic of Sex* (1970, London: Women's Press, 1979), 121.
39. Jephcott, *Rising Twenty*, 80.
40. National Marriage Guidance Council, *16. For All Young Adults* (London: NMGC, 1964), 9.
41. Michael Schofield, *The Sexual Behaviour of Young People* (London: Longmans, 1965), 163. Schofield's study was based on 1,873 interviews with youths aged between 15 and 19.
42. *Woman's Own*, 31 July 1965, 57.
43. Christine Grandy, 'Paying for Love: Women's Work and Love in Popular Film in Interwar Britain', *Journal of the History of Sexuality*, 19:3 (2010), 483–507, 487.
44. Grandy, 'Paying for Love', 500.
45. Judy Giles, '"You meet 'em and that's it": Working Class Women's Refusal of Romance between the Wars in Britain', in Pearce and Stacey (eds), *Romance Revisited*, 283–4.
46. *Woman's Own*, 21 April 1934, 64.
47. *Woman's Own*, 12 March 1943, 22.

48. On young women's lives in the 1920s and 1930s see Sally Alexander, 'Becoming a Woman in the 1920s and 1930s', in Sally Alexander, *Becoming a Woman and Other Essays in Nineteenth and Twentieth Century Feminist History* (London: Virago, 1994); Selina Todd, *Young Women, Work, and Family in England, 1918–1950* (Oxford: Oxford University Press, 2005); Kathy Milcoy, 'Image and Reality: Working-Class Teenage Girls' Leisure in Bermondsey during the Interwar Years', D.Phil. Thesis, University of Sussex, 2000; Jerry White, *The Worst Street in North London. Campbell Bunk, Islington, Between the Wars* (London: Routledge & Kegan Paul, 1986).
49. *Miss Modern*, June 1934, 66.
50. *Woman's Own*, 24 February 1940, 46.
51. MOA, DR 3176, December 1942, man born in 1921.
52. MOA, DR 2539, December 1942, man born in 1901.
53. Slater and Woodside, *Patterns of Marriage*, 220.
54. Gorer, *Exploring English Character*, 83.
55. Gorer, *Exploring English Character*, 83.
56. Ferdynand Zweig, *Women's Life and Labour* (London: Gollancz 1952), 122.
57. John Braine, *Room at the Top* (London: Eyre & Spottiswoode, 1957).
58. *Daily Mail*, 29 May 1967, 9.
59. E. Grebenik and Griselda Rowntree, 'Factors Associated with the Age at Marriage in Britain', *Proceedings of the Royal Society of London, Series B, Biological Sciences*, 159:974 (1963), 178–202, 190.
60. Diane Leonard, *Sex and Generation. A Study of Courtship and Weddings* (London: Tavistock, 1980), 113 n. 18.
61. Moya Woodside, 'Courtship and Mating in an Urban Community', *Eugenics Review*, 38 (1946), 29–39, 30.
62. MOA, DR M1544, Summer 2001, man born in 1934.
63. *Woman's Own*, 21 July 1944, 18.
64. *Woman's Own*, 6 October 1934, 816.
65. MOA, DR 1662, June 1939, woman born in 1917.

Chapter 3

1. MOA, Directive, September 1943.
2. MOA, DR 2512, September 1943.
3. Anon., *Every Woman's Luck Book* (London: Amalgamated Press, 1935).

4. Anon., *Every Woman's Luck Book.*
5. MOA, FR 2404, 'The Bernstein Film Questionnaire, 1946/7', 2.
6. Richard Hoggart, *The Uses of Literacy: Aspects of Working-Class Life with Special Reference to Publications and Entertainments* (London: Chatto, 1957), 213.
7. Macandrew, *Friendship, Love Affairs and Marriage*, 129–37.
8. MOA, TC32, 'Women in wartime, 1939–45', 32/3/E, 'WAAF: Reports from an observer 1941–2. The great Digby man-chase', 28 December 1941, 2.
9. MOA, TC32, 'Women in wartime, 1939–45', 32/3/E, 28 December 1941, 2–3.
10. Gray, 'Preparation for Marriage', 291.
11. *Woman's Own*, 2 May 1936, 148.
12. Coleman and Salt, *The British Population*, 182.
13. *Woman's Own*, 3 May 1936, 264.
14. Gray, 'Preparation for Marriage', 293.
15. Michael Anderson, 'The Emergence of the Modern Life Cycle in Britain', *Social History*, 10:1 (1985), 69–87, 69.
16. Anderson, 'The Emergence of the Modern Life Cycle in Britain', 70, 86.
17. *The Matrimonial Post*, January 1922, 1.
18. *The Matrimonial Post*, May 1943, 3.
19. *The Matrimonial Post*, January 1922, 3.
20. *The Matrimonial Post*, January 1955, 3.
21. Gray, 'Preparation for Marriage', 296.
22. B. Seebohm Rowntree and G. R. Lavers, *English Life and Leisure. A Social Study* (London: Longmans, 1951), 27. This study was based on indirect interviews with 975 people. From amongst these, 220 case histories 'carefully selected as being typical of the whole were presented'.
23. MOA, DR G226, Summer 2001, woman born in 1941.
24. MOA, DR A883, Summer 2001, man born in 1933.
25. Callum G. Brown, *Religion and Society in Twentieth-Century Britain* (Harlow: Pearson Longman, 2006), 187, 246.
26. Gallup, *Gallup International Public Opinion Polls: Great Britain, 1937–1975*, 994.
27. Gallup, *Gallup International Public Opinion Polls: Great Britain, 1937–1975*, 1276.

28. Jephcott, *Rising Twenty*, 78.
29. MOA, DR S521, Summer 2001, woman born in 1913.
30. See e.g. Edith Maud Hull's 1919 novel *The Sheik* and the 1921 silent film version starring Rudolph Valentino.
31. *Modern Marriage*, April 1931, 100.
32. *Woman's Own*, 14 July 1944, 18.
33. *Woman's Own*, 11 August 1944, 18.
34. Marilyn Lake, 'The Desire for a Yank: Sexual Relations between Australian Women and American Servicemen during World War II', *Journal of the History of Sexuality*, 2:4 (1991), 621–33, 629.
35. David Reynolds, *Rich Relations. The American Occupation of Britain, 1942–1945* (London: Phoenix, 2000), 266.
36. Leanne McCormick, '"One Yank and They're Off": Interaction between US Troops and Northern Irish Women, 1942–1945', *Journal of the History of Sexuality*, 15:2 (2006), 228–57, 232.
37. *Woman's Own*, 1 September 1944, 22; M. Page Baldwin, 'Subject to Empire: Married Women and the British Nationality and Status of Aliens Act', *Journal of British Studies*, 40:4 (2001), 522–56, 522. British men did not, of course, lose their subject status if they married a foreigner.
38. Jerzy Zubrzycki, *Polish Immigrants in Britain. A Study of Adjustment* (The Hague: Martinus Nijhoft, 1956), 158.
39. McCormick, '"One Yank and They're Off"', 257.
40. Reynolds, *Rich Relations*, 421.
41. Reynolds, *Rich Relations*, 421.
42. Press cutting provided by Don McKay.
43. Stuart Hall, 'Reconstruction Work: Images of Postwar Black Settlement', in James Proctor (ed.), *Writing Black Britain 1948–1998* (Manchester: Manchester University Press, 2000), 92.
44. Lucy Bland, 'White Women and Men of Colour: Miscegenation Fears in Britain after the Great War', *Gender and History*, 17:1 (2005), 29–61, 33. On the 1930s, see Bill Schwarz, 'Black Metropolis, White England', in Mica Nava and Alun O'Shea (eds), *Modern Times: Reflections on a Century of English Modernity* (London: Routledge, 1996), 176–207. See also the work of Laura Tabili on this topic, particularly her essay, 'Women "of a Very Low Type": Crossing Racial Boundaries in Imperial Britain', in

Laura L. Frader and Sonya O. Rose (eds), *Gender and Class in Modern Europe* (New York: Cornell University Press, 1996), 165–90.

45. Kushner, *We Europeans?*, 117–18.
46. Gray, 'Preparation for Marriage', 294.
47. Gray, 'Preparation for Marriage', 295.
48. Sonya O. Rose, *Which People's War? National Identity and Citizenship in Wartime Britain 1939–1945* (Oxford: Oxford University Press, 2003), 79.
49. Chris Waters, '"Dark Strangers in our Midst": Discourses of Race and Nation in Britain, 1947–1963', *Journal of British Studies*, 36:2 (1997), 207–38, 229.
50. *Sunday Pictorial*, 6 September 1942, 3.
51. *Woman's Own*, 16 February 1945, 22.
52. *Woman's Own*, 12 November 1943, 18.
53. *Woman's Own*, 14 January 1944, 22.
54. Royal Commission on Population, *Report* (London: HMSO, 1949), 124.
55. *Picture Post*, 30 October 1954, 21–3.
56. On mid-century conceptions of black masculinity see Marcus Collins, 'Pride and Prejudice: West Indian Men in Mid-twentieth Century Britain', *Journal of British Studies*, 40:3 (2001), 391–418.
57. *The Times*, 30 September 1958, 6.
58. Gallup, *Gallup International Public Opinion Polls: Great Britain, 1937–1975*, 478.
59. Gallup, *Gallup International Public Opinion Polls: Great Britain, 1937–1975*, 994.
60. Clifford S. Hill, *How Colour Prejudiced is Britain?* (London: Victor Gollancz, 1965), 38.
61. Hill, *How Colour Prejudiced is Britain?*, 209.
62. Amrit Wilson, *Finding a Voice. Asian Women in Britain* (London: Virago, 1978), 112.
63. Wilson, *Finding a Voice*, 113.
64. Sydney F. Collins, 'The Social Position of White and "Half Caste" Women in Coloured Groupings in Britain', *American Sociological Review*, 16:6 (1951), 796–802, 798.
65. *The Guardian*, 13 March 1964, 10.
66. *Millions Like Us* (Frank Lauder and Sidney Gilliat, 1943).
67. Edynbry, *Real Life Problems and their Solution*, 144.
68. Edward F. Griffith, *Modern Marriage and Birth Control* (London: Victor Gollancz, 1937), 55.

69. Annette Kuhn, *Family Secrets: Acts of Memory and Imagination* (London: Verso, 1995), 98.
70. Andy Wood, 'Fear, Hatred and the Hidden Injuries of Class in Early Modern England', *Journal of Social History*, 39:3 (2006), 803–26, 819.
71. 'Taste is a match-maker, it marries colours and also people, who make "well-matched couples", initially in regard to taste.' Pierre Bourdieu, *Distinction. A Social Critique of the Judgement of Taste* (London: Routledge, 2000), 243.
72. Paul Johnson and Steph Lawler, 'Coming Home to Love and Class', *Sociological Research Online*, 10:3 (2005), 1.
73. MOA, DR G1041, Summer 2001, woman born in 1925.
74. MOA, Directive, June 1939. For an analysis of the whole directive see James Hinton, 'The "Class" Complex': Mass-Observation and Cultural Distinction in pre-war Britain', *Past and Present*, 199:1 (2008), 207–36.
75. MOA, DR 1466, June 1939, man born in 1887.
76. MOA, DR 1028, June 1939, woman born in 1919.
77. MOA, DR 1234, June 1939, man born in 1906; MOA, DR 1458, June 1939, woman born in 1918.
78. MOA, DR 2181, June 1939, woman (date of birth not given).
79. MOA, DR 2085, June 1939, man born in 1918.
80. MOA, DR 2057, June 1939, man born in 1911.
81. MOA, DR 1334, June 1939, man born in 1910.
82. MOA, DR 1631, June 1939, man born in 1912.
83. MOA, DR 2145, June 1939, man born in 1915.
84. MOA, DR 1441, June 1939, man born in 1917.
85. MOA, DR 1490, June 1939, woman born in 1914.
86. MOA, DR 1040, June 1939, woman born in 1916.
87. MOA, DR 1016, June 1939, woman born in 1887.
88. MOA, DR 1035, June 1939, woman born in 1889.
89. MOA, DR 2045, June 1939, woman born in 1895.
90. MOA, DR 1021, June 1939, man born in 1914.
91. MOA, DR 1095, June 1939, man born in 1876.
92. MOA, DR B1898, Summer 2001, woman born in 1931.
93. Johnson and Lawler, 'Coming Home to Love and Class', paragraph 7.1.

94. Daniel Bertaux and Paul Thompson (eds), *Pathways to Social Class. A Qualitative Approach to Social Mobility* (Oxford: Oxford University, 1997), 25.
95. MOA, DR H260, Summer 2001, woman born in 1930.
96. MOA, DR W571, Summer 2001, woman born in 1937.
97. Todd, *Young Women, Work, and Family in England 1918–1950*, 95–101.
98. Carol Dyhouse, 'Graduates, Mothers and Graduate Mothers: Family Investment in Higher Education in Twentieth Century England', *Gender and Education*, 14:4 (2002), 325–36.
99. *The Matrimonial Post*, January 1930, 1–8.
100. *The Matrimonial Post*, August 1942, 2.
101. *The Matrimonial Post*, June 1947, 6.
102. Mike Savage, 'Working-Class Identities in the 1960s. Revisiting the Affluent Worker Study', *Sociology*, 39:5 (2005), 929–46, 938.
103. *Manchester Evening News*, 10 April 1950, 2.
104. *Manchester Evening News*, 13 April 1950, 2.
105. *Manchester Evening News*, 13 April 1950, 2.
106. Zweig, *Women's Life and Labour*, 124.
107. MOA, DR H2637, Summer 2001, woman born in 1939.
108. Robert Anderson, *British Universities. Past and Present* (London: Hambleton Continuum, 2006), 131.
109. MOA, DR W1893, Summer 2001, man born in 1924, married in 1950.
110. *Woman's Own*, 3 September 1958, 77.
111. *Woman's Own*, 19 January 1950, 34.
112. Ferdynand Zweig, *The Student in the Age of Anxiety. A Survey of Oxford and Manchester Students* (London: Heinemann, 1963). The study grew out of a *Daily Herald* request for an investigation into final year university student's problems. Zweig combined interviews and observations with miscellany such as student magazines. Zweig randomly chose 205 students from Oxford and Manchester for his focus, stating that 'it was intended to give preference to men rather than to women, to arts students rather than science students . . . and to concentrate only on older students, excluding students in their first and second year', p. xii.
113. Zweig, *The Student in the Age of Anxiety*, 67.
114. Zweig, *The Student in the Age of Anxiety*, 68.

115. Zweig, *The Student in the Age of Anxiety*, 69.
116. Zweig, *The Student in the Age of Anxiety*, 207.
117. MOA, DR B1989, Summer 2001, man born in 1927.

Chapter 4

1. Thelma Veness, *School Leavers. Their Aspirations and Expectations* (London, Methuen & Co, 1962), 26.
2. Veness, *School Leavers*, 31.
3. Veness, *School Leavers*, 33.
4. Patrick Hamilton, *The Gorse Trilogy* (1951, London: Black Spring Press, 2007), 42.
5. Gorer, for example, lists a wide range of meeting places in his study *Sex and Marriage in England Today*, 20–2. For an account of the left as an arena for romantic encounters see Stef Pixner, 'The Oyster and the Shadow', in Liz Heron (ed.), *Truth, Dare or Promise. Girls Growing Up in the Fifties* (London, Virago, 1985), 79–102.
6. Kathleen Dayus, *Omnibus* (London: Virago, 1994), 312–13.
7. Maureen Sutton, *We Didn't Know Aught. A Study of Sexuality, Superstition and Death in Women's Lves in Lincolnshire during the 1930s, '40s and '50s* (Lincolnshire: Paul Watkins, 1992), 35.
8. MOA, DR B1220, Summer 1990.
9. Slater and Woodside, *Patterns of Marriage*, 94.
10. Eva Illouz, *Consuming the Romantic Utopia* (Berkeley: University of California Press, 1997), 37.
11. Pearl Jephcott, *Some Young People* (London: George Allen & Unwin, 1954), 66.
12. Willard Waller, 'The Rating and Dating Complex', *American Sociological Review*, 2:5 (October 1937), 727–34, 728.
13. Robert Roberts, *The Classic Slum. Salford Life in the First Quarter of the Century* (Manchester 1971, London: Penguin, 1990), 232.
14. Gary Cross (ed.), *Worktowners at Blackpool. Mass-Observation and Popular Leisure in the 1930s* (London: Routledge, 1990), 168.
15. Age Concern Manchester, *Life in Manchester* (Manchester: Age Concern Manchester, 1986), 32.
16. Pierce, 'Marriage in the Fifties', *The Sociological Review*, 219.
17. MOA, DR 1206, July 1939, woman born in 1903.

18. Matt Houlbrook, *Queer London. Perils and Pleasures in the Sexual Metropolis, 1918–1957* (Chicago: University of Chicago Press, 2005), 72–3.
19. MOA, DR 1055, January 1939, woman born in 1904.
20. MOA, WC, Box 60, Book drafts on Blackpool, 60-D, 'Dancing', 1.
21. MOA, DR 1051, January 1939.
22. James J. Nott, *Music For the People. Popular Music and Dance in Interwar Britain* (Oxford: Oxford University Press, 2002), 212–13.
23. MOA, FR 295, 'Memo on Jazz, Bolton', 25 July 1940, 2.
24. Roberts, *The Classic Slum*, 233.
25. MOA, DR 1019, January 1939.
26. MOA, FR 11A, 'Jazz and dancing', November 1939, 12.
27. MOA, DR 1123, January 1939.
28. Jephcott, *Rising Twenty*, 67.
29. MOA, D E174, Summer 2001, woman born in 1924.
30. MOA, DR H1543, Summer 2001, man born in 1930.
31. MOA, DR 1016, July 1939, woman born in 1887.
32. *Daily Mirror*, 25 January 1955, 3.
33. Carter, *Education, Employment and Leisure*, 156.
34. MOA, WC, Box 36, Cinema Observations, 36-C, 'Outing with a girl stranger observer account', 19 April 1938.
35. MOA, FR 2464, *The Bernstein Film Questionnaire 1946–7*, 5.
36. Iris Barry, *Let's Go to the Movies* (New York: Payson & Clarke, 1926), 64.
37. Jephcott, *Girls Growing Up*, 119.
38. Rowntree and Lavers, *English Life and Leisure*, 249.
39. Rowntree and Lavers, *English Life and Leisure*, 50.
40. MOA, DR G226, Summer 2001, woman born in 1941.
41. MOA, DR C2570, Summer 2001, woman born in 1921.
42. Gorer, *Exploring English Character*, 84.
43. MOA, DR C2570, Summer 2001, woman born in 1921.
44. MOA, FR 3086, 'Love Making in Public', February 1949, 11.
45. MOA, DR L1504, Summer 2001, man born in 1926.
46. *Woman's Own*, 24 February 1940, 46.
47. On the Manchester and Salford monkey parade see Andrew Davies, *Leisure, Gender and Poverty. Working-class Culture in Salford and Manchester 1900–1939* (Buckingham: Open University Press, 1992), 102–8. On the 'bunny run' see Colin Rosser and Christopher Harris, *The Family and*

Social Change. A Study of Family and Kinship in a South Wales Town (London: Routledge & Kegan Paul, 1965), 341. On the Preston 'Monkey Racks' see Derek Thompson, 'Courtship and Marriage in Preston', *Oral History*, 3:2 (1975), 39–44, 42.

48. MOA, FR 64, *US*, 29 March 1940, 80.
49. MOA, FR 64, *US*, 29 March 1940, 80.
50. MOA, FR 1611, 'Women in Pubs', February 1943, 10.
51. MOA, TC 32, Box 3, 32/3/E, 'Reasons why girls prefer Canadians', 2 August, 1941.
52. MOA, TC 32, Box 3, 32/3/E, 'Beer and Spirits', 23 August, 1941.
53. MOA, DR 3099, May 1943, woman born in 1907.
54. MOA, FR 1611, 3.
55. MOA, FR 1611, 3.
56. Judith Hubback, *Wives Who Went to College* (London: Heinemann, 1957).
57. Hubback, *Wives Who Went to College*, 25.
58. Hubback, *Wives Who Went to College*, 25.
59. Janet Howarth, 'Women', in T. H. Aston and Brian Howard Harrison (eds), *The History of the University of Oxford*: Vol. 8, *The Twentieth Century* (Oxford, Clarendon Press, 1994), 353–4.
60. Bill Osgerby, *Youth in Britain Since 1945* (Oxford: Blackwell, 1998), 38.
61. Hoggart, *The Uses of Literacy*, 248.
62. *The Observer*, 8 November 1959, 3.
63. Cyril S. Smith, *Young People at Leisure. A Report on Bury* (Manchester: University of Manchester, 1966), 21.
64. Louise Jackson, 'The Coffee Club Menace: Policing Youth, Leisure and Sexuality in Post-war Manchester', *Cultural and Social History*, 5:3 (2008), 289–308.
65. Schofield, *The Sexual Behaviour of Young People*, 175.
66. Todd, *Young Women*, 154–6. On more recent trends in meeting places see Richard Lampard, 'Couples' Places of Meeting in Late 20th Century Britain: Class, Continuity and Change', *European Sociological Review*, 23:2 (2007), 357–72.
67. *Woman's Own*, 20 January 1940, 38.
68. MOA, TC 12, Sexual Behaviour 1939–50, 12/16/E, '"Lonely hearts" and friendship clubs'.

69. MOA, TC 12, Sexual Behaviour 1939–50, 12/16/E, '"Lonely hearts" and friendship clubs'.
70. M. B. Smith, *The Single Woman of Today. Her Problems and Adjustment* (London: Watts & Co., 1951), 57, vii.
71. MOA, TC 3, Family Planning, 1944–49, 3/3/F, 'Report on a visit to a Marriage Bureau'.
72. MOA DR G2180, Summer 1990, man born in 1919.
73. MOA, DR B2240, Summer 2001, man born in 1921.
74. MOA, DR B2490, Summer 1990, man born in 1951.
75. Bob Mullan, *The Mating Trade* (London: Routledge, 1984), 63.
76. *News of the World*, 1 December 1968, 13.
77. *Daily Mirror*, 17 August 1970, 7.
78. *Daily Mirror*, 1 August 1970, 9.
79. *Daily Mirror*, 20 November 1970, 16.

Chapter 5

1. Peter Willmott, *Adolescent Boys of East London* (1966, London: Pelican 1969), 50.
2. MOA, FR 3086.
3. MOA, Directive, September 1948.
4. MOA, FR 3086, 1.
5. MOA, FR 3086, 2.
6. MOA, FR 3086, 5.
7. MOA, FR 3086, 6.
8. MOA, FR 3086, 4.
9. MOA, FR 3086, 1.
10. MOA, FR 3086, 5.
11. MOA, FR 3086, 8.
12. MOA, FR 3086, 9.
13. On the car see Sean O'Connell, *The Car in British Society. Class, Gender and Motoring, 1896–1939* (Manchester: Manchester University Press, 1998). On holiday-making see John K. Walton, *The British Seaside. Holidays and Resorts in the Twentieth Century* (Manchester: Manchester University Press, 2000).
14. Illouz, *Consuming the Romantic Utopia*, 56. In her study of courtship conventions in twentieth-century America, Beth L. Bailey also points to

the ways in which 'courtship became more and more a private act conducted in a public world'. Bailey, *From the Front Porch to the Back Seat*, 3.

15. MOA, DR C2654, Summer 2001, woman born in 1941.
16. MOA, FR 3150, 'A report on teen-age girls', August 1949, 12.
17. Annette Kuhn, *Dreaming of Fred and Ginger. Cinema and Cultural Memory* (New York: New York University Press, 2002), 139–41.
18. *Manchester Evening News*, 16 April 1930, 6.
19. MOA, FR 3086, 9.
20. MOA, FR 3086, 9.
21. Sue Harper and Vincent Porter, 'Weeping in the Cinema in 1950. A Reassessment of Mass-Observation material', MOA, Occasional Paper No. 3 (Sussex: Mass Observation Archive, 1995), 6.
22. *Manchester Evening News*, 19 January 1930, 8.
23. *Daily Mirror*, 7 September 1938, 6.
24. MOA, DR T2459, Summer 2001, man born in 1915.
25. MOA, DR R1418, Summer 2001, man born in 1922.
26. MOA, DR B1898, Summer 2001, woman born in 1931.
27. Michael Young and Peter Willmott, *Family and Kinship in East London* (1957; London: Penguin, 1962), 70–3.
28. Young and Willmott, *Family and Kinship in East London*, 70.
29. Francis, *The Flyer*, 69.
30. MOA, D 5239, woman born in 1917, 14 June 1940.
31. MOA, FR 64, *US 9*, 29 March 1940, 77.
32. MOA, DR L1504, Summer 2001, man born in 1926.
33. MOA, FR 3086, 11.
34. MOA, DR W1382, Summer 2001, man born in 1924.
35. MOA, DR 2979, December 1942, man born in 1921.
36. MOA, DR 3323, December 1942, woman born in 1899.
37. MOA, DR 2684, December 1942, man born in 1908.
38. MOA, DR 2979, December 1942, man born in 1921.
39. *Manchester Evening News*, 12 January 1940, 4.
40. *Picture Post*, 2 October 1943, 3.
41. Dagmar Herzog, *Sexuality in Europe. A Twentieth-Century History* (Cambridge: Cambridge University Press, 2011), 90.
42. MOA, FR 1632, 'Some notes on the use of leisure', March 1943, 1.
43. *Woman's Own*, 2 April 1943, 18.

44. *Woman's Own*, 14 January 1944, 22.
45. MOA, TC 12, Box 16, advertising and publications, 12/16/B, 'contraceptive and surgical products'.
46. Helen and Bill Cook, *Khaki Parish. Our War. Our Love 1940–1946* (London: Hodder & Stoughton, 1988), 30.
47. Helen and Bill Cook, *Khaki Parish*, 15.
48. Margaretta Jolly, 'Love Letters Versus Letters Carved in Stone: Gender, Memory and the "Forces Sweethearts" Exhibition', in Martin Evans and Ken Lunn (eds), *War and Memory in the Twentieth Century* (Oxford: Berg, 1997), 279–92, 115.
49. MOA, DR S2246, Summer 2001, man born in 1923.
50. All quoted in Sutton, *We Didn't Know Aught*, 42.
51. MOA, D 5010, man born in 1917, 1 April 1940.
52. Tamasin Day-Lewis (ed.), *Last Letters Home* (London: Pan, 1995), 145–8.
53. Day-Lewis, *Last Letters Home*, 167.
54. Houlbrook, 'A Pin to see the Peepshow', 226.
55. Jephcott, *Rising Twenty*, 67.
56. MOA, DR T2741, Summer 2001, man born in 1921.
57. Slater and Woodside, *Patterns of Marriage*, 128–9.
58. MOA, DR K310, Summer 2001, woman born in 1928.
59. *Woman's Own*, 16 March 1945, 22.
60. *Woman's Own*, 2 March 1940, 42.
61. *Woman's Own*, 24 February 1940, 46.
62. Osgerby, *Youth in Britain since 1945*, 22; Mark Abrams, *Teenage Consumer Spending in 1959 (Part II), Middle Class and Working Class Boys and Girls* (London: London Press Exchange, 1961), 5. Average teenage spending money was estimated at between £2–£5 a week, compared to an average wage of 26s. a week for boys and 18s. 6d. for girls in 1938. Harry Hopkins, *The New Look. A Social History of the Forties and Fifties in Britain* (London: Secker and Warburg, 1963), 424.
63. Hopkins, *The New Look*, 424.
64. Anne Edwards and Drusilla Beyfus, *Lady Behave. A Guide to Modern Manners* (London: Cassell and Company, 1956), 239.
65. MOA, DR W1813, Summer 2001, woman born in 1950.
66. Leonard, *Sex and Generation*, 93.

67. Leonard, *Sex and Generation*, 94.
68. Jephcott, *Some Young People*, 67.

Chapter 6

1. MOA, FR 229, 'Joke Report', June 1940, 27. Joke from an unnamed BBC radio programme.
2. *Woman*, 15 May 1954, 51.
3. For more on the amateur see Lucy Bland and Frank Mort, 'Look out for the "Good Time" Girl: Dangerous Sexualities as a Threat to National Health', in Formations Editorial Collective (eds), *Formations of Nation and People* (London: Routledge & Kegan Paul, 1984), 131–51.
4. Gladys Mary Hall, *Prostitution: A Survey and a Challenge* (London: Williams & Norgate, 1933), 30.
5. MOA, DR Z53, Summer 2001, woman born in 1926.
6. MOA, DR H260, Summer 2001, woman born in 1930.
7. MOA, DR M1979, Summer 2001, woman born in 1938.
8. MOA, DR H1543, Summer 2001, man born in 1930.
9. *Woman's Own*, 2 May 1936, 125.
10. Jephcott, *Rising Twenty*, 74.
11. Louise Purbrick, *The Wedding Present. Domestic Life Beyond Consumption* (Aldershot: Ashgate, 2007).
12. Francis, *The Flyer*, 72.
13. *Boyfriend*, 16 May 1959, 15.
14. Average wages rates for boys aged under 21 at the beginning of 1960 were approximately £6 3s. per week. For girls under 18 the figure was £2 4s 3d. Department of Employment and Productivity, *British Labour Statistics. Historical Abstracts 1886–1968* (London: HMSO, 1971), Table 49. For a detailed discussion of wage rates and income see Ian Gazeley, 'Income and Living Standards, 1870–2010', in Paul Johnson and Roderick Floud (eds), *Cambridge Economic History of Modern Britain*, Volume 2 (Cambridge: Cambridge University Press, 2013).
15. On the impact of poverty on leisure see Davies, *Leisure, Gender and Poverty*.
16. Gorer, *Exploring English Character*, 74.
17. Ferdynand Zweig, *The Worker in an Affluent Society* (London: Heinemann, 1961), 155.
18. Carter, *Education, Employment and Leisure*, 167–8.

19. *Manchester Evening News*, 8 May 1930, 6.
20. MOA, DR 1093, June 1939, man born in 1912.
21. MOA, DR C2654, Summer 2001, woman born in 1992.
22. On twentieth-century student life see Carol Dyhouse, *Students: A Gendered History* (London: Taylor & Francis, 2006).
23. MOA, D 5111, November 1940.
24. Average earnings for adult men in 1960 stood at £14 6s 5d. The equivalent figure for adult women was £7 10s 7d. Gazeley, 'Income and Living Standards'.
25. Todd, *Young Women, Work, and Family in England*, 220.
26. *Woman's World*, 11 December 1948, 20.
27. Edwards and Beyfus, *Lady Behave*, 135.
28. Edwards and Beyfus, *Lady Behave*, 135.
29. On the complexities of the companionate marriage see Janet Finch and Penny Summerfield's seminal essay, 'Social Reconstruction and the Emergence of Companionate Marriage, 1945–59', in David Clark (ed.), *Marriage, Domestic Life and Social Change. Writings for Jacqueline Burgoyne (1944–88)* (London: Routledge, 1991), 7–32.
30. Barbara Cartland, *Etiquette Handbook* (London: Paul Hamlyn, 1962), 232–4.
31. Stanley, *Sex Surveyed 1949–1994*, 182–5.
32. *Woman*, 13 July 1963, 16.
33. *Woman's Own*, 27 April 1940, 50.
34. Jephcott, *Rising Twenty*, 74–5.
35. Elizabeth Alice Clement, *Love for Sale. Courting, Treating and Prostitution in New York City, 1900–1945* (Chapel Hill: University of North Carolina Press, 2006), 47.
36. Reynolds, *Rich Relations*, 264–9. See also McCormick, ' "One Yank and They're Off" '.
37. MOA, DR 3285, December 1942, man born in 1918.
38. Stanley, *Sex Surveyed*, for a full discussion, 58–64.
39. MOA, DR D2205, Summer 1990, woman born in 1929.
40. Cecil Bishop, *Women and Crime* (London: Chatto and Windus, 1931), 29.
41. By 1970 Mary Grant even provided a free leaflet to her readers entitled 'Petting'. *Woman's Own*, 28 February 1970, 69.
42. Gray, 'Preparation for Marriage', 304.

43. *Woman*, 4 July 1959, 57.
44. Woodside, 'Courtship and Mating in an Urban Community', 31.
45. Roberts, *Women and Families*, 64.
46. For an extensive discussion of the relationship between past and present in memories of sex see Kate Fisher, *Birth Control, Sex and Marriage in Britain, 1918–1960* (Oxford: Oxford University Press, 2006), 12–25, and Szreter and Fisher, *Sex Before the Sexual Revolution*, 1–60.
47. Fisher, *Birth Control, Sex and Marriage in Britain*, 24–5.
48. MOA, DR B1898, Summer 2001, woman born in 1931.
49. Szreter and Fisher refer to 'subtle combative gendered codes', in *Sex Before the Sexual Revolution*, 131.
50. Angela Woollacott, 'Khaki Fever and its control: gender, class, age and sexual morality on the British home front in the First World War', *Journal of Contemporary History*, 29:2 (1994), 325–47.
51. MOA, FR 64, *US 9*, 29 March 1940, 81.
52. Bailey, *From Front Porch to Back Seat.*
53. MOA, DR 2863, December 1942, woman born in 1914.
54. Fernando Henriques, *Love in Action. The Sociology of Sex* (London: Macgibbon, 1959), 176.
55. *Woman's Own*, 24 March 1944, 18.
56. *Woman's Own*, 18 December 1942, 22.
57. *Woman's Own*, 16 March 1945, 22.
58. *Woman's Own*, 8 January 1943, 22.
59. *Woman's Own*, 23 April 1943, 22.
60. E. R. Matthews, *Sex, Love and Society* (London: Victor Gollancz, 1959); Vincent Long, *Health Education Journal*, 18:3 (1960), 170.
61. Matthews, *Sex, Love and Society*, 78.
62. *Woman's Own*, 9 May 1936, 188.
63. Roberts, *Women and Families*, 64. The interviewee was born in 1947.
64. Mace, *Marriage Crisis*, 43.
65. Schofield, *The Sexual Behaviour of Young People*, 132.
66. *Marriage Today. An Excellent Mystery?* (BBC2, 14 October 1964).
67. Gorer, *Sex and Marriage in England Today*, 30.
68. Gorer, *Sex and Marriage in England Today*, 30.
69. Schofield, *The Sexual Behaviour of Young People*, 130.
70. *Woman*, 4 July 1959, 27, 47.

71. Willmott, *Adolescent Boys of East London*, 56.
72. *Woman's Own*, 25 September 1942, 18.
73. *Woman's Own*, 17 December 1943, 22.
74. On the press campaign see Adrian Bingham, 'The British Popular Press and Venereal Disease during the Second World War', *Historical Journal*, 48:4 (2005), 1055–76. See also MOA, FR 1633, 'V.D. Publicity in the Press', 20 March 1943.
75. MOA, DR R1418, Summer 1990, man born in 1922.
76. MOA, DR C1624, Summer 1990, woman born in 1928.
77. *Woman's Own*, 1 June 1940, 30.
78. For more on attitudes towards unmarried mothers see Pat Thane and Tanya Evans, *Sinners? Scroungers? Saints? Unmarried Motherhood in Twentieth-Century England* (Oxford: Oxford University Press, 2012).
79. Madeline Kerr, *The People of Ship Street* (London: Routledge & Kegan Paul, 1958).
80. Virginia Wimperis, *The Unmarried Mother and Her Child* (London: George Allen and Unwin Ltd, 1960), 113.
81. MOA, DR B2086, Summer 1990, woman born in 1908.
82. Based on the 1960 Stan Barstow novel.
83. *Woman's Own*, 23 February 1950, 38.
84. Jephcott, *Some Young People*, 67.

Chapter 7

1. *Boyfriend*, 16 May 1959.
2. *Boyfriend*, 6 June 1959, 17.
3. *Boyfriend*, 16 May 1959, 14, 16.
4. Hoggart, *The Uses of Literacy*, 51.
5. Pierce, 'Marriage in the Fifties', 215.
6. Pierce, 'Marriage in the Fifties', 217.
7. For a rich history of post-war lesbian life see Rebecca Jennings, *Tomboys and Bachelor Girls. A Lesbian History of Post-war Britain, 1945–71* (Manchester: Manchester University Press, 2007); for an important revisionist history of mid-century homosexuality see Houlbrook, *Queer London*.
8. MOA, D 5383, June 1940.
9. Slater and Woodside, *Patterns of Marriage*, 16.
10. MOA, DR C1624, Summer 1990, woman born in 1928.

11. Gorer, *Exploring English Character*, 85.
12. Margot Lawrence, *The Complete Guide to Wedding Etiquette* (London: Ward, Lock & Co, 1963), 19.
13. *Modern Marriage*, July 1931, 23.
14. *Woman's Own*, 2 May 1936, 148.
15. Gallup, *The Gallup International Public Opinion Polls: Great Britain, 1937–1975*, 266.
16. Leonora Eyles, *Sex for the Engaged* (London: Robert Hale, 1952), 71.
17. Zweig, *Women's Life and Labour*, 59.
18. *Woman's Own*, 12 January 1950, 34.
19. Anon, *Every Woman's Book of Love and Marriage and Family Life*, 6.
20. Eyles, *Sex for the Engaged*, 40.
21. *Modern Marriage*, May 1931, 96.
22. Anon, *Every Woman's Book of Love and Marriage and Family Life*, 5.
23. *Brighton Evening Argus*, 24 October 1957, 3.
24. David R. Mace, *Marriage: The Art of Lasting Happiness* (London: Hodder & Stoughton Ltd, 1952), 23–4.
25. Matthews, *Sex, Love and Society*, 152; Eyles, *Sex for the Engaged*, 53–66.
26. *Woman's Own*, 26 January 1950, 34.
27. *Woman's Own*, 14 July 1955, 57.
28. *Woman's Own*, 2 March 1950, 45.
29. *Woman's Own*, 24 January 1970, 69.
30. *Woman's Own*, 12 May 1944, 22.
31. *Woman's Own*, 5 January 1950, 30.
32. Macandrew, *Friendship, Love Affairs and Marriage*, 119.
33. National Marriage Guidance Council, *Sex in Marriage* (London: National Marriage Guidance Council 1961), 4.
34. Anon., *Every Woman's Book of Love and Marriage and Family Life*, 6.
35. Eustace Chesser, *Women. A Popular Edition to the Chesser Report* (London: Jarrolds, 1958), 99.
36. Willmott, *Adolescent Boys in East London*, 57.
37. Pierce, 'Marriage in the Fifties', 221–2.
38. Lawrence, *The Complete Guide to Wedding Etiquette*, 9.
39. Mace, *Marriage*, 21–2.
40. Frost, *Promises Broken*, provides a succinct history of the action, 13–24.
41. Frost, *Promises Broken*, 1–8.
42. Macandrew, *Friendship, Love Affairs and Marriage*, 122.

43. *Woman's Own*, 20 August, 22.
44. Sutton, *We Didn't Know Aught*, 40.
45. On the 'disappointed fiancées' of the interwar post office see Helen Glew, 'Women's employment in the General Post Office, *c.*1914–*c.*1939', Ph.D. thesis, London, 2010.
46. *Daily Mirror*, 8 July 1958, 3.
47. *Daily Mirror*, 7 March 1958, 13.
48. *Daily Mirror*, 25 March 1958, 1.
49. *Daily Mirror*, 26 March 1930, 4.
50. *Daily Mirror*, 4 December 1931, 5.
51. *Daily Mirror*, 11 February 1932, 7.
52. *Daily Mirror*, 13 November 1958, 9.
53. *Daily Mirror*, 4 December 1931, 5.
54. *Daily Mirror*, 7 December 1934, 2.
55. *Daily Mirror*, 18 June 1937, 4.
56. *Daily Mirror*, 27 February 1936, 10; 28 February 1936, 14.
57. *Daily Mirror*, 24 February 1936, 10; 25 February 1936, 10.
58. *Woman's Own*, 6 April 1945, 22.
59. *Daily Mirror*, 23 July 1951, 4.
60. *Daily Mirror*, 8 June 1960, 15.
61. *Daily Mirror*, 7 April 1970, 3.
62. MOA, TC 32, 32/3/E, 'Morality at Digby—a first impression', 31 July 1941, 7.
63. MOA, DR 2979, December 1942, man born in 1921.
64. J. S. Pudney, *Collected Poems* (London: Putnam, 1957), 35. The poem was first published by the *News Chronicle* and famously featured in the 1945 film *The Way to the Stars*, directed by Anthony Asquith.
65. Office for National Statistics, *Marriage in England and Wales, 2010* (London: ONS, 2012), 4.
66. MOA, FR 499, 21 November 1940, 'The Hope of Youth', 3.
67. Mass-Observation, *Britain and Her Birth-rate* (London: John Murray, 1945), 63.
68. Mass-Observation, *Britain and Her Birth-rate*, 63.
69. Mass-Observation, *Britain and Her Birth-rate*, 63
70. MOA, Directive, December 1942.
71. MOA, DR 3338, December 1942, man born in 1912.

72. MOA, DR 1393, December 1942, man born in 1909.
73. MOA, DR C1878, Summer 1990, woman born in 1920.
74. Jephcott, *Rising Twenty*, 80.
75. MOA, DR 2670, December 1942, man born in 1920.
76. MOA, DR 2863, December 1942, woman born in 1914.
77. Coleman and Salt, *The British Population*, 194.
78. Coleman, 'Population and Family', 27–93, 70.
79. *Parade*, 20 October 1962, 10–11.
80. Todd, *Young Women*, 222.
81. Grebenik and Rowntree, 'Factors Associated with the Age at Marriage in Britain', 194.
82. Zweig, *The Worker in an Affluent Society*, p. 11.
83. Selina Todd, 'Breadwinners and Dependants: Working-Class Young People in England, 1918–1955', *International Review of Social History*, 52:1 (2007), 57–87.
84. *Woman*, 1 June 1963, 55.
85. *Manchester Evening News*, 29 January 1960, 4.
86. *Manchester Evening News*, 2 January 1960, 3.
87. Royal Commission on Marriage and Divorce, *Report 1951–1955* (London: HMSO, 1956), 9.
88. Griselda Rowntree, 'More Facts on Teenage Marriage', *New Society*, 1:4 (1962), 12–15, 12.
89. Dyhouse, *Students*, 92.
90. *The Times*, 20 April 1960, 8.
91. Leonard, *Sex and Generation*, 114.
92. *Daily Mirror*, 15 February 1956, 1.
93. Leonard, *Sex and Generation*, 101.
94. The Marriage (Scotland) Act of 1939 put an end to the so-called 'Blacksmith Priests' by insisting that legal wedding ceremonies could only conducted by a minister or registrar. Before this 'irregular' marriages based upon mutual consent were recognized in law.
95. Only one person needed to demonstrate residence.
96. *Daily Mirror*, 30 June 1930, 1.
97. *Daily Mirror*, 24 February 1931, 20.
98. *Daily Mirror*, 10 May 1950, 4.
99. *Daily Mirror*, 6 April 1939, 18.

100. *Daily Mirror,* 25 August 1950, 9.
101. *Daily Mirror,* 2 December 1939, 11.
102. *Daily Mirror,* 5 May 1955, 1.
103. *Daily Mirror,* 23 August 1954, 3; 23 September 1954; and 6 and 18 October 1954, 5.
104. *Daily Mirror,* 18 April 1957, 1, 3.
105. *Daily Mirror,* 2 April 1938, 3.
106. *Daily Mirror,* 11 October 1958, 5; 13 October 1958, 1; and 14 October 1958, 3.
107. *Evening Standard,* 24 May 1943, 1.
108. *Report of the Committee on the Age of Majority* (London: HMSO, 1967), Cmnd. 3342, 42–3.
109. *Report of the Committee on the Age of Majority,* 53–5.
110. *Report of the Committee on the Age of Majority,* 51.
111. On the passage of this 'permissive' legislation see Brooke, *Sexual Politics.*
112. Willmott, *Adolescent Boys of East London,* 52.

Chapter 8

1. Royal Commission on Marriage and Divorce, *Report 1951–1955* (London: HMSO, 1956).
2. Royal Commission on Marriage and Divorce, *Report 1951–1955,* 1–2.
3. *Daily Mirror,* 22 March 1956, 2.
4. Royal Commission on Marriage and Divorce, *Report 1951–1955,* 7.
5. Liz Stanley, *Sex Surveyed,* 114, 117.
6. *Picture Post,* 30 October 1954, 21.
7. On the pressures of demobilization see Alan Allport, *Demobbed. Coming Home After the Second World War* (New Haven: Yale, 2009).
8. Mace, *Marriage Crisis,* 31.
9. Royal Commission on Marriage and Divorce, *Report 1951–1955,* 9.
10. Slater and Woodside, *Patterns of Marriage,* 126.
11. White, *The Worst Street in North London,* 214.
12. Mass-Observation, *Britain and Her Birth Rate,* 63.
13. Mass-Observation, *An Enquiry into People's Homes* (London: Murray, 1943), 159.
14. Hoggart, *The Uses of Literacy,* 34.
15. Judy Giles, 'A Home of One's Own. Women and Domesticity in England, 1918–1950,' *Women's Studies International Forum,* 16:3 (1993), 239–53, 240.

16. John Burnett, *A Social History of Housing 1815–1985* (London: Methuen, 1986), 249, 286. For an excellent recent history of working-class experiences of home see Ben Jones, *The Working Class in Mid Twentieth-Century England. Community, Identity and Social Memory* (Manchester: Manchester University Press, 2012), 155–96.
17. Slater and Woodside, *Patterns of Marriage*, 119.
18. Slater and Woodside, *Patterns of Marriage*, 140.
19. *Woman's Own*, 23 May 1936, 225.
20. *Evening Standard*, 24 May 1943, 5.
21. *Manchester Evening News*, 28 January 1935, 3.
22. MOA, FR 1616, 'Some Psychological Factors in Home-Building', 3 March 1943, 9, 10.
23. *Woman's Own*, 18 December 1942, 22.
24. MOA, DR 3075, December 1942, man born in 1913.
25. MOA, FR 2495, 'The State of Matrimony', 20 June 1947, 15.
26. Slater and Woodside, *Patterns of Marriage*, 117.
27. Jephcott, *Rising Twenty*, 37–8.
28. Rowntree and Lavers, *English Life and Leisure*, 78–9.
29. Pierce, 'Marriage in the Fifties', 233.
30. Young and Willmott, *Family and Kinship in East London*, 31.
31. Young and Willmott, *Family and Kinship in East London*, 33.
32. National Marriage Guidance Council, *A Home of Your Own* (London: National Marriage Guidance Council, 1962), 3.
33. *Modern Marriage*, July 1931, 30.
34. Stopes, *Mother England*, 156.
35. For a revisionist account of the revolution in contraceptive behaviour see Fisher, *Birth Control, Sex and Marriage in Britain 1918–1960*. For an account with longer chronological reach and a different interpretative stance see Cook, *The Long Sexual Revolution*.
36. Gorer, *Sex and Marriage in England Today*, 74.
37. Gorer, *Sex and Marriage in England Today*, 74.
38. Gorer, *Sex and Marriage in England Today*, 63.
39. Gorer, *Sex and Marriage in England Today*, 63.
40. Gorer, *Sex and Marriage in England Today*, 71.
41. MOA, DR H260, Summer 1990, woman born in 1930.
42. Stopes, *Married Love*, 71.

43. Hilary Hinds, 'Together and Apart. Twin Beds, Domestic Hygiene and Modern Marriage, 1890–1945', *Journal of Design History*, 23:3 (2010), 275–304, 301.
44. *Daily Mirror*, 15 May 1933, 10.
45. *Daily Mirror*, 15 May 1933, 10.
46. Griffith, *Modern Marriage and Birth Control*, 73.
47. Macandrew, *Friendship, Love Affairs and Marriage*, 140.
48. Lewis, 'Public Institution and Private Relationship', 258.
49. National Marriage Guidance Council, *Sex Difficulties in the Wife*, 1.
50. Ibid. 10.
51. Lewis, 'Public Institution and Private Relationship', 252.
52. In her oral history of marriage, Natalie Higgins found that people who married in the 1950s had higher expectations than those who married in the 1930s. They were also more likely to express dissatisfaction. Higgins, 'The Changing Expectations and Realities of Marriage in the English Working Class, 1920–1960', 271.
53. Hansard, *House of Lords Debates*, 20 May 1953, vol. 182, cc 659–60, Bishop of Sheffield.
54. Royal Commission on Marriage and Divorce, *Report 1951–1955*, 9.
55. The National Archives (hereafter TNA), LCO 2/6124, Royal Commission on Marriage and Divorce, *Minutes of Evidence: days 1–19*, Monday 21st July 1952, memorandum submitted by Mrs Moya Woodside, 437:17.
56. *Marriage Today. A Social Institution*, BBC2, 16 September 1964.
57. *Marriage Today. Intimate Lives*, BBC2, 30 September 1964.
58. An edited version of the diary was published in 2005 by Robert W. Malcolmson (ed.), *Love and War in London. A Woman's Diary 1939–1942* (Waterloo: Wilfrid Laurier University Press, 2005).
59. Malcolmson, *Love and War in London*, 129.
60. Malcolmson, *Love and War in London*, 111.
61. Malcolmson, *Love and War in London*, 159.
62. Malcolmson, *Love and War in London*, 168.
63. The details of Cockett's life after 1942 are assembled by Malcolmson in *Love and War in London*, 193–8.
64. Gallup, *Gallup International Public Opinion Polls: Great Britain, 1937–1975*, 1.
65. MOA, DR 2031.1, July 1939, woman born in 1901.

66. Stanley, *Sex Surveyed*, 127.
67. Stanley, *Sex Surveyed*, 127.
68. Gallup, *The Gallup International Public Opinion Polls. Great Britain 1937–1975*, 245.
69. Gallup, *The Gallup International Public Opinion Polls. Great Britain 1937–1975*, 374.
70. Archbishop of Canterbury's Group on the Divorce Law, *Putting Asunder: A Divorce Law for Contemporary Society* (London: S.P.C.K, 1966); The Law Commission, *Reform of the Grounds of Divorce. The Field of Choice* (London: HMSO, 1966). On the relationship between Church and state in formulating the reform of 1969 see Jane Lewis and Patrick Wallis, 'Fault, Breakdown, and the Church of England's involvement in the 1969 Divorce Reform', *Twentieth Century British History*, 11:3 (2000), 308–32.
71. Gallup, *The Gallup International Public Opinion Polls. Great Britain 1937–1975*, 965–6.
72. *Panorama. Divorce*, BBC, 1 March 1963.
73. *Panorama. Divorce*, BBC, 1 March 1963.
74. *Man Alive. Living in Sin?*, BBC2, 2 March 1966.
75. *Daily Mirror*, 22 March 1956, 2.
76. Mass-Observation, *Britain and Her Birth Rate*, 67.
77. Mass-Observation, *Britain and Her Birth Rate*, 68.
78. Stanley, *Sex Surveyed*, 122.
79. *The Times*, 3 May 1954, 2.
80. *The Times*, 23 December 1959, 8.
81. *Brief Encounter* (David Lean, 1945).
82. *Woman in a Dressing Gown* (J. Lee-Thompson, 1957).
83. *Woman's Own*, 27 October 1944, 22.
84. *The Tribune*, 11 April 1941, 8.
85. *Modern Marriage*, May 1931, 96.
86. *Woman's Own*, 3 March 1944, 18.
87. *Woman's Own*, 9 July 1943, 22.
88. *Woman's Own*, 30 March 1940, 2.
89. *Woman's Own*, 23 May 1936, 264.
90. *Woman's Own*, 14 July 1934, 444.
91. Smith, *The Single Woman of Today*, 45.
92. *Woman's Own*, 9 March 1950, 45.

93. *Woman's Own*, 25 February 1944, 18.
94. MOA, DR 3238, December 1942, man, date of birth unknown.
95. Slater and Woodside, *Patterns of Marriage*, 219.
96. Slater and Woodside, *Patterns of Marriage*, 156
97. Slater and Woodside, *Patterns of Marriage*, 156.
98. MOA, TC 12, 'Sexual Behaviour', box 11, file A, no. 564.
99. MOA, TC 12, 'Sexual Behaviour', box 11, file A, no. 352.
100. Stanley, *Sex Surveyed*, 122.
101. Gorer, *Exploring English Character*, 154.
102. Gorer, *Exploring English Character*, 145.
103. *The Times*, 30 January 1969, 3.
104. Gorer, *Sex and Marriage in England Today*, 85.
105. Gorer, *Sex and Marriage in England Today*, 159.
106. Martin P. M. Richards and B. Jane Elliott, 'Sex and Marriage in the 1960s and 1970s', in David Clark (ed.), *Marriage, Domestic Life and Social Change*, 44.
107. *Picture Post*, 9 July 1949, 7.
108. Frost, *Living in Sin*.
109. Joanne Klein, 'Irregular Marriages: Unorthodox Working-Class Domestic Life in Liverpool, Birmingham, and Manchester, 1900–1939', *Journal of Family History*, 30:2 (2005), 210–29, 224.
110. MOA, FR 2206, 'Sex Morality and the Birthrate', February 1945, 2.
111. Rowntree and Lavers, *English Life and Leisure*, 205.
112. *Marriage Today. An Excellent Mystery?* BBC2, 14 October 1964.
113. *Man Alive. Living in Sin?* BBC2, 2 March 1966.
114. Hansard, *House of Commons Debates*, 2 February 1939, vol. 343 c383. Surnames changed by deed poll: written question from Major Stourton.
115. TNA, LCO 2/5639, 'Deed poll', June 1947. Letter from Lambeth Palace to Viscount Jowitt, Lord Chancellor, 12 December 1947 enclosing the Report of Church of England Moral Welfare Council for the upper House of Convocation entitled 'Illegal 'wives'.
116. TNA, LCO 2/5639, 'Deed poll', June 1947. Letter from the Lord Chancellor to A. S. Robertson, 24 June 1947.
117. TNA, LCO 2/5639, 'Deed poll', June 1947. Letter from Lambeth Palace to Viscount Jowitt, Lord Chancellor, 12th December 1947 enclosing the Report of Church of England Moral Welfare Council for the upper House of Convocation entitled 'Illegal 'wives'; TNA, LCO

2/5639, 'Deed poll', Letter from the Housewives' Association for the Protection of Family Life to the Attorney-General, 20 January 1955.

118. NA, LCO 2/5639, 'Deed poll', June 1947. Letter from the Home Secretary to the Lord Chancellor, 22 January 1948; TNA, LCO 2/5639, 'Deed poll', Letter from S. H. E. Burley to Mrs Carrington Wood, 22 March 1955.
119. *Woman's Own*, 2 January 1965, 51.
120. Frost, *Living in Sin*, 72.
121. Frost, *Living in Sin*, 73.
122. Frost, *Living in Sin*, 73.
123. *Criminal Statistics for England and Wales, 1928* (London: HMSO, 1930), Table A, 3.
124. *Criminal Statistics for England and Wales, 1939–1945* (London: HMSO, 1947), Table A, 26.
125. *The Yorkshire Post and Leeds Mercury*, 25 November 1942, 5.
126. *Criminal Statistics for England and Wales, 1968* (London: HMSO, 1969), Table B, 8.
127. *Criminal Statistics for England and Wales, 1968* (London: HMSO, 1969), Table B, 8.
128. *Daily Mirror*, 26 May 1937, 5.
129. *Yorkshire Post and Leeds Mercury*, 10 March 1942, 1.
130. *Yorkshire Post and Leeds Mercury*, 7 May 1943, 3.
131. *Yorkshire Post and Leeds Mercury*, 7 May 1943, 3.
132. *Daily Mirror*, 28 April 1937, 4.
133. *Daily Mirror*, 31 January 1945, 7.
134. *Picture Post*, 5 September 1942, 3.

Epilogue

1. *Daily Mirror*, 14 February 1938, 22.
2. Joseph Bradshaw, 'The Stability of Marriage', *The Eugenics Review*, 44:2 (1952), 88–9.
3. *Daily Mirror*, 20 September 1956, 11.
4. *Picture Post*, 21 May 1955, 53, 70.
5. Mass-Observation, *First Year's Work*, 32.
6. MOA, DR C2570, Summer 2001, woman born in 1921.
7. MOA, DR 1039, July 1939, woman born in 1905.

8. MOA, DR C1713, Summer 2001, woman born in 1948; MOA, DR E743, Summer 2001, woman born in 1951.
9. The statistics on marriage presented here are all taken from Office of National Statistics, *Statistical Bulletin: Marriages in England and Wales, 2010* (London: ONS, 2012) at http://www.ons.gov.uk/ons/dcp171778_258307.pdf
10. Office of National Statistics, *Statistical Bulletin: Marriages in England and Wales, 2010*, at http://www.ons.gov.uk/ons/dcp171778_258307.pdf, 10.
11. Griffith, *Modern Marriage and Birth Control*, 21.
12. MOA, D 5165, December 1940.
13. MOA, D 5165, March 1942.

Bibliography

A. Unpublished Primary Sources

Mass-Observation Archive, University of Sussex

The National Archives, London

B. Published Sources

Journals and Newspapers

American Mercury Magazine

Boyfriend

Brighton Evening Argus

Daily Express

Daily Mail

Daily Mirror

Evening Standard

Guardian

Manchester Evening News

Miss Modern

Modern Marriage

News of the World

Picture Post

The Matrimonial Post and Fashionable Marriage Advertiser

The New Statesman and Nation

The Observer

The Times

The Tribune

Woman

Woman's Friend and Glamour

Woman's Own

Woman's Weekly
Woman's World
Yorkshire Post and Leeds Mercury

Television Programmes

The Brain's Trust (BBC, 1945) at http://www.britishpathe.com/record.php?id=75152
Man Alive. Living in Sin? (BBC2, 2 March 1966).
Marriage Today. An Excellent Mystery? (BBC2, 14 October 1964).
Marriage Today: A Social Institution (BBC2, 16 September 1964).
Marriage Today: Intimate Lives (BBC2, 30 September 1964).
Panorama. Divorce (BBC, 11 March 1963).

Films

Brief Encounter (David Lean, 1945).
Flame in the Streets (Roy Ward Baker, 1961).
How to Marry a Millionaire (Jean Negulesco, 1953).
'I Know Where I'm Going!' (Michael Powell and Emeric Pressburger, 1945).
Millions Like Us (Sidney Gilliat and Frank Launder, 1943).
Sapphire (Basil Dearden, 1959).
The Way to the Stars (Anthony Asquith, 1945).
Woman in a Dressing Gown (J. Lee Thompson, 1957).

Books and Articles

Abrams, Mark Alexander, *Social Surveys and Social Action* (London: Heinemann, 1951).

Abrams, Mark Alexander, *Teenage Consumer Spending in 1959 (Part II): Middle Class and Working Class Boys and Girls* (London: London Press Exchange, 1961).

Adair, Richard, *Courtship, Illegitimacy and Marriage in Early Modern England* (Manchester: Manchester University Press, 1996).

Age Concern Manchester, *Life in Manchester* (Manchester: Age Concern Manchester, 1986).

Alexander, Sally, *Becoming a Woman and Other Essays in Nineteenth and Twentieth Century Feminist History* (London: Virago, 1994).

Allport, Alan, *Demobbed. Coming Home After the Second World War* (New Haven and London: Yale University Press, 2009).

Anderson, Michael, 'The Emergence of the Modern Life Cycle in Britain', *Social History*, 10:1 (1985), 69–87.

Anderson, Michael, 'The Social Implications of Demographic Change', in F. M. L. Thompson (ed.), *The Cambridge Social History of Britain 1750–1950*: Vol. 2, *People and their Environment* (Cambridge: Cambridge University Press, 1990), 1–70.

Anderson, Robert, *British Universities. Past and Present* (London: Hambleton Continuum, 2006), 131.

Anon., *Every Woman's Luck Book* (London: Amalgamated Press, 1935).

Anon., *Every Woman's Book of Love and Marriage and Family Life* (London: Amalgamated Press, 1937).

Appignanesi, Lisa, *All About Love. Anatomy of an Unruly Emotion* (London: Virago, 2011).

Archbishop of Canterbury's Group on the Divorce Law, *Putting Asunder: A Divorce Law for Contemporary Society* (London: S.P.C.K., 1966).

Aston, T. H., and Harrison, Brian Howard (eds), *The History of the University of Oxford*: Vol. 8, *The Twentieth Century* (Oxford: Clarendon Press, 1994).

Bailey, Beth L., *Front Porch to Back Seat. Courtship in Twentieth-Century America* (Baltimore: Johns Hopkins University Press, 1988).

Bailey, Peter, 'Jazz at the Spirella: Coming of Age in Coventry in the 1950s', in Becky Conekin, Frank Mort, and Chris Waters (eds), *Moments of Modernity: Reconstructing Britain, 1945–1964* (London: River Oram Press, 1999), 22–40.

Baldwin, M. Page, 'Subject to Empire: Married Women and the British Nationality and Status of Aliens Act', *Journal of British Studies*, 40:4 (2001), 522–56.

Ballinger, Annette, 'The Guilt of the Innocent and the Innocence of the Guilty: The Cases of Marie Fahmy and Ruth Ellis', in Alice Myers and Sarah Wight (eds), *No Angels. Women who Commit Violence* (London: Pandora, 1996), 1–28.

Bamford, Samuel, *Early Days* (London: Simpkin, Marshall & Co., 1849).

Barry, Iris, *Let's Go to the Movies* (New York: Payson & Clarke, 1926).

Barthes, Roland, *A Lover's Discourse. Fragments* (London: Vintage, 2002).

Bauman, Zygmunt, *Liquid Love. On the Fragility of Human Bonds* (Cambridge: Polity, 2003).

Beck, Ulrich, and Beck-Gersheim, Elizabeth, *The Normal Chaos of Love* (Cambridge: Polity, 1995).

Bertaux, Daniel, and Thompson, Paul (eds), *Pathways to Social Class. A Qualitative Approach to Social Mobility* (Oxford: Oxford University Press, 1997).

Bessel, Richard, 'Hatred after War. Emotion and the Postwar History of East Germany', *History and Memory*, 17:1/2 (2005), 195–216.

Bessel, Richard, and Schumann, Dirk (eds), *Life after Death. Approaches to a Cultural and Social History of Europe during the 1940s and 1950s* (Cambridge: Cambridge University Press, 2003).

Bingham, Adrian, 'The British Popular Press and Venereal Disease during the Second World War', *Historical Journal*, 48:4 (2005), 1055–76.

Bingham, Adrian, *Family Newspapers? Sex, Private Life and the British Popular Press 1918–1978* (Oxford: Oxford University Press, 2009).

Bingham, Adrian, 'The "K-Bomb": Social Surveys, the Popular Press and British Sexual Culture in the 1940s and 1950s', *Journal of British Studies*, 50:1 (2011), 156–79.

Bingham, Adrian, 'Newspaper Problem Pages and British Sexual Culture since 1918', *Media History*, 18:1 (2012), 51–63.

Bishop, Cecil, *Women and Crime* (London: Chatto and Windus, 1931).

Bland, Lucy, 'White Women and Men of Colour: Miscegenation Fears in Britain after the Great War', *Gender and History*, 17:1 (2005), 29–61.

Bland, Lucy, 'The Trials and Tribulations of Edith Thompson: the Capital Crime of Sexual Incitement in 1920s England', *Journal of British Studies*, 47:3 (2008), 624–48.

Bland, Lucy, and Mort, Frank, 'Look out for the "Good Time" Girl: Dangerous Sexualities as a Threat to National Health', in Formations Editorial Collective (eds), *Formations of Nation and People* (London: Routledge & Kegan Paul, 1984), 131–51.

Bott, Elizabeth, *Family and Social Network: Roles, Norms, and External Relationships in Ordinary Urban Families* (London: Tavistock Publications, 1957).

Bourdieu, Pierre, *Distinction. A Social Critique of the Judgement of Taste* (London: Routledge, 2000).

Bourke, Joanna, 'Fear and Anxiety: Writing about Emotion in Modern History', *History Workshop Journal*, 55 (2003), 111–33.

Bourke, Joanna, *Fear: a Cultural History* (London: Virago, 2006).

Bradshaw, Joseph, 'The Stability of Marriage', *The Eugenics Review*, 44:2 (1952), 88–9.

Braine, John, *Room at the Top* (London: Eyre & Spottiswoode, 1957).

Broad, Richard, and Fleming, Suzie (eds), *Nella Last's War: The Second World War Diaries of 'Housewife 49'* (London: Profile, 2006).

Brooke, Stephen, *Sexual Politics. Sexuality, Family Planning and the British Left, from the 1880s to the Present Day* (Oxford: Oxford University Press, 2011).

Brown, Callum G., *Religion and Society in Twentieth-Century Britain* (Harlow: Longman, 2006).

Burnett, John, *Destiny Obscure. Autobiographies of Childhood, Education and Family from the 1820s to the 1920s* (London: Allen Lane, 1982).

Burnett, John, *A Social History of Housing 1815–1985* (London: Methuen 1986).

Burnett, John, Vincent, David, and Mayall, David (eds), *The Autobiography of the Working Class: An Annotated Critical Bibliography*: Vol. 1, *1790–1900* (Brighton: Harvester Press, 1984).

Carter, M. P., *Education, Employment and Leisure. A Study of 'Ordinary' Young People* (London: Pergamon Press, 1963).

Carter, Thomas, *Memoirs of a Working Man* (London, 1845).

Cartland, Barbara, *Etiquette Handbook* (London: Paul Hamlyn, 1962).

Chesser, Eustace, *Women. A Popular Edition to the Chesser Report* (London: Jarrolds, 1958).

Chinn, Carl, *They Worked all their Lives: Women of the Urban Poor in England, 1880–1939* (Manchester: Manchester University Press, 1984).

Clark, David (ed.), *Marriage, Domestic Life and Social Change. Writings for Jacqueline Burgoyne (1944–88)* (London: Routledge, 1991).

Clement, Elizabeth Alice, *Love for Sale. Courting, Treating and Prostitution in New York City 1900–1945* (Chapel Hill: University of North Carolina Press, 2006).

Cocks, Harry G., '"Sporty" Girls and "Artistic" Boys: Friendship, Illicit Sex and the British "Companionship" Advertisement, 1913–1928', *Journal of the History of Sexuality*, 11:3 (2002), 457–82.

Coleman, David, 'Population and Family', in A. H. Halsey and Josephine Webb (eds), *Twentieth-Century British Social Trends* (Basingstoke: Macmillan, 2000), 27–93.

Coleman, David, and Salt, John, *The British Population: Patterns, Trends, and Processes* (Oxford: Oxford University Press, 1992).

Collins, Marcus, 'Pride and Prejudice: West Indian Men in Mid-twentieth Century Britain', *Journal of British Studies*, 40:3 (2001), 391–418.

Collins, Marcus, *Modern Love. An Intimate History of Men and Women in Twentieth-century Britain* (London: Atlantic, 2003).

Collins, Sydney F., 'The Social Position of White and "Half Caste" Women in Coloured Groupings in Britain', *American Sociological Review*, 16:6 (1951), 796–802.

Comer, Lee, *Wedlocked Women* (Leeds: Feminist Books, 1974).

Conekin, Becky, Mort, Frank, and Waters, Chris (eds), *Moments of Modernity. Reconstructing Britain 1945–1964* (London: River Oram Press, 1999).

Cook, Helen, and Cook, Bill, *Khaki Parish. Our War. Our Love 1940–1946* (London: Hodder & Stoughton, 1988).

Cook, Hera, *The Long Sexual Revolution. English Women, Sex, and Contraception 1800–1975* (Oxford: Oxford University Press, 2004).

Cross, Gary S. (ed.), *Worktowners at Blackpool. Mass-Observation and Popular Leisure in the 1930s* (London: Routledge, 1990).

Cubitt, Catherine, 'The History of Emotions: A Debate', *Early Medieval Europe*, 10:2 (2001), 225–7.

Daunton, M. J., and Rieger, Bernhard (eds), *Meanings of Modernity: Britain from the Late-Victorian Era to World War II* (Oxford: Berg, 2001).

Davies, Andrew, *Leisure, Gender and Poverty. Working-Class Culture in Salford and Manchester, 1900–1939* (Buckingham: Open University Press, 1992).

Davey, Charles, *Teenage Morals* (London: Councils and Education Press, 1961).

Day-Lewis, Tamasin (ed.), *Last Letters Home* (London: Pan, 1995).

Dayus, Kathleen, *Omnibus* (London: Virago, 1994).

de Beauvoir, Simone, *The Second Sex* (Harmondsworth: Penguin, 1983).

Delap, Lucy, Griffin, Ben, and Wills, Abigail (eds), *The Politics of Domestic Authority in Britain since 1800* (London: Palgrave Macmillan, 2009).

Denning, Alfred Thompson, *The Equality of Women: A lecture delivered at the Annual Conference of the National Marriage Guidance Council* (London: National Marriage Guidance Council, 1950).

Dennis, Norman, Henriques, Fernando, and Slaughter, Clifford, *Coal is our Life* (London: Eyre & Spottiswoode, 1956).

Department of Employment and Productivity, *British Labour Statistics. Historical Abstracts 1886–1968* (London: HMSO, 1971).

Dyhouse, Carol, 'Graduates, Mothers and Graduate Mothers: Family Investment in Higher Education in Twentieth Century England', *Gender and Education*, 14:4 (2002), 325–36.

Dyhouse, Carol, *Students: A Gendered History* (London: Taylor and Francis, 2006).

Dyhouse, Carol, *Glamour. Women, History, Feminism* (London: Zed, 2010).

Edwards, Anne, and Drusilla Beyfus, *Lady Behave. A Guide to Modern Manners* (London: Cassell and Company, 1956).

Edynbry, R., *Real Life Problems and Their Solution* (London: Odhams, 1938).

Elton, G. R., *Return to Essentials: Some Reflections on the Present State of Historical Study* (Cambridge: Cambridge University Press, 1991).

Erickson, Amy Louise, *Women and Property in Early Modern England* (London: Routledge, 1993).

Evans, Martin, and Lunn, Ken (eds), *War and Memory in the Twentieth Century* (Oxford: Berg, 1997).

Evans, Mary, *Love. An Unromantic Discussion* (Cambridge: Polity, 2003).

Eyles, Leonora, *Sex for the Engaged* (London: Robert Hale, 1952).

Feldman, Gene, and Gartenberg, Max (eds), *Protest. The Beat Generation and the Angry Young Men* (London: Souvenir Press, 1959).

Field, Deborah A., *Private Life and Communist Morality in Khrushchev's Russia* (London: Peter Lang, 2007).

Field, Geoffrey G., *Blood, Sweat and Toil. Remaking the Working Class 1939–1945* (Oxford: Oxford University Press, 2011).

Finch, Janet, and Summerfield, Penny, 'Social Reconstruction and the Emergence of Companionate Marriage, 1945–59' in David Clark (ed.), *Marriage, Domestic Life and Social Change. Writings for Jacqueline Burgoyne (1944–88)* (London: Routledge, 1991) 7–32.

Firestone, Shulamith, *The Dialectic of Sex* (London: Women's Press, 1979).

Fisher, Kate, *Birth Control, Sex and Marriage in Britain, 1918–1960* (Oxford: Oxford University Press, 2006).

Francis, Martin, 'Tears, Tantrums, and Bared Teeth: The Emotional Economy of Three Conservative Prime Ministers, 1951–1963', *Journal of British Studies*, 41:3 (2002), 354–87.

Francis, Martin, *The Flyer. British Culture and the Royal Air Force 1939–1945* (Oxford: Oxford University Press, 2008).

Frost, Ginger S., *Broken Promises: Courtship, Class and Gender in Victorian England* (Charlottesville: University Press of Virginia, 1995).

Frost, Ginger S., *Living in Sin: Cohabiting as Husband and Wife in Nineteenth-Century England* (Manchester: Manchester University Press, 2008).

Gallie, Duncan, 'The Labour Force' in A. H. Halsey and Josephine Webb (eds), *Twentieth-Century British Social Trends* (Basingstoke: Macmillan, 2000), 281–323.

Gallup, George Horace, *Gallup International Public Opinion Polls: Great Britain, 1937–1975*. 2 vols. (London: Random House, 1976).

Gazeley, Ian, 'Income and Living Standards, 1870–2010' in Paul Johnson and Roderick Floud (eds), *Cambridge Economic History of Modern Britain, Volume 2* (Cambridge: Cambridge University Press, 2013).

Giddens, Anthony, *The Transformation of Intimacy: Sexuality, Love and Eroticism in Modern Societies* (Cambridge: Cambridge University Press, 1992).

Giles, Judy, 'A Home of One's Own. Women and Domesticity in England 1918–1950', *Women's Studies International Forum*, 16:3 (1993), 239–53.

Giles, Judy, '"You Meet 'em and that's it": Working Class Women's Refusal of Romance Between the Wars in Britain', in Lynne Pearce and Jackie Stacey (eds), *Romance Revisited* (London: Lawrence & Wishart, 1995), 279–92.

Gillis, John R., *For Better, For Worse. British Marriages 1600 to the Present* (New York: Oxford University Press, 1985).

Gorer, Geoffrey, *Exploring English Character* (London: Cresset Press, 1955).

Gorer, Geoffrey, 'The Perils of Hypergamy' in Gene Feldman and Max Gartenberg (eds), *Protest. The Beat Generation and the Angry Young Men* (London: Souvenir Press, 1959), 373–8.

Gorer, Geoffrey, *Sex and Marriage in England Today. A Study of the Views and Experiences of the Under 45s* (London: Nelson, 1971).

Grandy, Christine, 'Paying for Love: Women's Work and Love in Popular Film in Interwar Britain', *Journal of the History of Sexuality*, 19:3 (2010), 483–507.

Gray, Revd. Herbert, 'Preparation for Marriage', in Sybil Neville-Rolfe (ed.), *Sex in Social Life* (London: George Allen & Unwin, 1949), 288–319.

Grebenik, E., and Rowntree, Griselda, 'Factors Associated with the Age at Marriage in Britain', *Proceedings of the Royal Society of London, Series B, Biological Sciences*, 159:974 (1963), 178–202.

Griffith, Edward F., *Modern Marriage and Birth Control* (London: Victor Gollancz, 1937).

Gurney, Peter, '"Intersex" and "Dirty Girls": Mass-Observation and Working-class Sexuality in England in the 1930s', *Journal of the History of Sexuality*, 8:2 (1997), 256–90.

Hall, Gladys Mary, *Prostitution: a Survey and a Challenge* (London: Williams & Norgate, 1933).

Hall, Lesley A., *Hidden Anxieties: Male Sexuality, 1900–1950* (Cambridge: Polity, 1991).

Hall, Stuart, 'Reconstruction Work: Images of Postwar Black Settlement', in James Proctor (ed.), *Writing Black Britain 1948–1998* (Manchester: Manchester University Press, 2000).

Halsey, A. H., and Webb, Josephine (eds), *Twentieth-century British Social Trends* (Basingstoke: Macmillan, 2000).

Hamilton, Patrick, *The Gorse Trilogy* (London: Black Spring Press, 2007).

Hansard. Publications and Records of the UK Parliament.

Harper, Sue, and Porter, Vincent, 'Weeping in the Cinema in 1950. A Reassessment of Mass-Observation material', *Mass-Observation Archive Occasional Paper No. 3* (Sussex: Mass Observation Archive, 1995).

Hemming, James, *Problems of Adolescent Girls* (London: Heinemann, 1960).

Henriques, Fernando, *Love in Action. The Sociology of Sex* (London: Macgibbon, 1959).

Heron, Liz (ed.), *Truth, Dare, Promise. Girls Growing Up in the Fifties* (London: Virago, 1985).

Herzog, Dagmar, *Sexuality in Europe. A Twentieth-Century History* (Cambridge: Cambridge University Press, 2011).

Hill, Clifford S., *How Colour Prejudiced is Britain?* (London: Victor Gollancz, 1965).

Hinds, Hilary, 'Together and Apart. Twin Beds, Domestic Hygiene and Modern Marriage, 1890–1945', *Journal of Design History*, 23:3 (2010), 275–304.

Hinton, James, '"The 'Class' Complex": Mass-Observation and Cultural Distinction in Pre-war Britain', *Past and Present*, 199:1 (2008), 207–36.

Hoggart, Richard, *The Uses of Literacy: Aspects of Working-class Life with Special Reference to Publications and Entertainments* (London: Chatto, 1957).

Hoggart, Richard, *A Sort of Clowning. Life and Times 1940–1959* (Oxford: Oxford University Press, 1990).

Holtzman, Ellen, 'The Pursuit of Married Love: Women's Attitudes toward Sexuality and Marriage in Great Britain, 1918–1939', *Journal of Social History*, 16:2 (1982), 39–51.

Hopkins, Harry, *The New Look. A Social History of the Forties and Fifties in Britain* (London: Secker and Warburg, 1963), 424.

Houlbrook, Matt, *Queer London. Perils and Pleasures in the Sexual Metropolis, 1918–1957* (Chicago: University of Chicago Press, 2005).

Houlbrook, Matt, '"A Pin to See the Peepshow": Culture, Fiction, and Selfhood in Edith Thompson's Letters, 1921–1922', *Past and Present*, 207:1 (2010), 215–49.

Howarth, Janet, 'Women', in T. H. Aston and Brian Howard Harrison (eds), *The History of the University of Oxford*: Vol. 8, *The Twentieth Century* (Oxford: Clarendon Press, 1994).

Hubback, Judith, *Wives Who Went to College* (London: Heinemann, 1957).

Hubble, Nick, *Mass-Observation and Everyday Life: Culture, History, Theory*, (Basingstoke: Palgrave Macmillan, 2005).

Illouz, Eva, *Consuming the Romantic Utopia* (Berkeley: University of California Press, 1997).

Jackson, Louise, '"The Coffee Club Menace": Policing Youth, Leisure and Sexuality in post-War Manchester', *Cultural and Social History*, 5:3 (2008), 289–308.

Jennings, Rebecca, *Tomboys and Bachelor Girls. A Lesbian History of Post-War Britain, 1945–71* (Manchester: Manchester University Press, 2007).

Jephcott, (Agnes) Pearl, *Girls Growing Up* (London: Faber & Faber, 1942).

Jephcott, Pearl, *Rising Twenty. Notes on Some Ordinary Girls* (London: Faber & Faber, 1948).

Jephcott, Pearl, *Some Young People* (London: George Allen & Unwin, 1954).

Joannou, Maroula, *'Ladies, Please Don't Smash These Windows'. Women's Writing, Feminist Consciousness and Social Change 1918–38* (Oxford: Berg, 1995).

Johnson, Paul, and Lawler, Steph, 'Coming Home to Love and Class', *Sociological Research Online*, 10:3 (2005).

Jolly, Margaretta, 'Love Letters Versus Letters Carved in Stone: Gender, Memory and the "Forces Sweethearts" Exhibition', in Martin Evans and Ken Lunn (eds), *War and Memory in the Twentieth Century* (Oxford: Berg, 1997), 279–92.

Jones, Ben, *The Working Class in Mid Twentieth-Century England. Community, Identity and Social Memory* (Manchester: Manchester University Press, 2012).

Kent, Robin, *Aunt Agony Advises. Problem Pages through the Ages* (London: W. H. Allen, 1979).

Kerr, Madeline, *The People of Ship Street* (London: Routledge & Kegan Paul, 1958).

Klein, Joanne, 'Irregular Marriages: Unorthodox Working-Class Domestic Life in Liverpool, Birmingham, and Manchester, 1900–1939', *Journal of Family History*, 30:2 (2005), 210–29.

Kristeva, Julia, *Tales of Love* (New York: Columbia University Press, 1987).

Kuhn, Annette, *Family Secrets: Acts of Memory and Imagination* (London: Verso, 1995).

Kuhn, Annette, *Dreaming of Fred and Ginger: Cinema and Cultural Memory* (New York: New York University Press, 2002).

Kushner, Tony, *We Europeans? Mass-Observation, 'Race', and British Identity in Twentieth-century Britain* (London: Ashgate, 2004).

Lake, Marilyn, 'The Desire for a Yank: Sexual Relations between Australian Women and American Servicemen during World War II', *Journal of the History of Sexuality*, 2:4 (1991), 621–33.

Lampard, Richard, 'Couples' Places of Meeting in Late 20th Century Britain: Class, Continuity and Change', *European Sociological Review*, 23:2 (2007), 357–72.

Langford, Wendy, *Revolutions of the Heart: Gender, Power and the Delusions of Love* (London: Routledge, 1999).

Langhamer, Claire, *Women's Leisure in England, 1920–1960* (Manchester: Manchester University Press, 2000).

Law Commission, *Reform of the Grounds of Divorce. The Field of Choice* (London: HMSO, 1966).

Lawrence, Margot, *The Complete Guide to Wedding Etiquette* (London: Ward, Lock & Co, 1963).

Leonard, Diana, *Sex and Generation. A Study of Courtship and Weddings* (London: Tavistock, 1980).

Lewis, Jane, 'Public Institution and Private Relationship. Marriage and Marriage Guidance, 1920–1968', *Twentieth Century British History*, 1:3 (1990), 233–63.

Lewis, Jane, *The End of Marriage? Individualism and Intimate Relations* (Cheltenham: Edward Elgar, 2001).

Lewis, Jane, Clark, David, and Morgan, David, *Whom God Hath Joined Together. The Work of Marriage Guidance* (London: Routledge, 1992).

Lewis, Jane, and Wallis, Patrick, 'Fault, Breakdown, and the Church of England's Involvement in the 1969 Divorce Reform', *Twentieth Century British History*, 11:3 (2000), 308–32.

Long, Vincent [review], *Health Education Journal*, 18:3 (1960), 170.

Lyon, Percy Hugh Beverley, *Happy Ever After?* (London: National Marriage Guidance Council, 1949).

Lystra, Karen, *Searching the Heart. Women, Men, and Romantic Love in Nineteenth-Century America* (Oxford: Oxford University Press, 1989).

Macandrew, Rennie, *Friendship, Love Affairs and Marriage. An Explanation of Men to Women and Women to Men* (London: Wales Publishing Co., 1939).

MacCarthy, Fiona, *Last Curtsey. The End of the Debutantes* (London: Faber & Faber, 2006).

Mace, David R., *Marriage Crisis* (London: Delisle, 1948).

Mace, David R., 'What Britain is Doing', *Marriage and Family Living*, 10:1 (Winter 1948), 6.

Mace, David R., 'An English Advice Column', *Marriage and Family Living*, 12:3 (August 1950), 100–12.

Mace, David R., *Marriage: The Art of Lasting Happiness* (London: Hodder & Stoughton Ltd, 1952).

Machin, G. I. T., *Churches and Social Issues in Twentieth-Century Britain* (New York: Clarendon Press, 1998).

Madge, Charles, and Harrisson, Tom, *Mass-Observation* (London: Frederick Muller, 1937).

Makins, Peggy, *The Evelyn Home Story* (Glasgow: Fontana, 1975).

Malcolmson, Patricia, and Malcolmson, Robert (eds), *Nella Last's Peace: the Post-War Diaries of Housewife 49* (London: Profile, 2008).

Malcolmson, Patricia, and Malcolmson, Robert (eds), *Nella Last in the 1950s: Further Diaries of Housewife 49* (London: Profile, 2010).

Malcolmson, Robert W. (ed.), *Love and War in London. A Woman's Diary 1939–1942* (Waterloo: Wilfrid Laurier University Press, 2005).

Marx, Karl, and Engels, Frederick, *Collected Works*: Vol. 11, *1851–53* (London: Lawrence and Wishart, 1979).

Mass-Observation, *First Year's Work, 1937–38* (London: Lindsay Drummond, 1938).

Mass-Observation, *An Enquiry into People's Homes* (London: John Murray, 1943).

Mass-Observation, *Britain and Her Birth-rate* (London: John Murray, 1945).

Mass-Observation, *The Press and Its Readers. A Mass-Observation Survey* (London: Art & Technics, 1949).

Matt, Susan J., 'Current Emotion Research in History: Or, Doing History from the Inside Out', *Emotion Review*, 3:1 (2011), 117–24.

Matthews, E. R., *Sex, Love and Society* (London: Victor Gollancz, 1959).

May, Simon, *Love. A History* (New Haven and London: Yale University Press, 2011).

McCormick, Leanne, '"One Yank and They're Off": Interaction between US Troops and Northern Irish Women, 1942–1945', *Journal of the History of Sexuality*, 15:2 (2006), 228–57.

McLellan, Josie, *Love in the Time of Communism. Intimacy and Sexuality in the GDR* (Cambridge: Cambridge University Press, 2011).

Mikes, George, *How to Be An Alien: A Handbook for Beginners and More Advanced Pupils* (London: Allan Wingate, 1946).

Mitchell, B. R., *British Historical Statistics* (Cambridge: Cambridge University Press, 1987).

Morris, Penny, 'From Private to Public: Alba de Céspedes' Agony Column in 1950s Italy', *Modern Italy*, 9:1 (2004), 11–20.

Mort, Frank, *Capital Affairs. London and the Making of the Permissive Society* (New Haven and London: Yale University Press, 2010).

Moyse, Cordelia, *A History of the Mothers' Union: Women, Anglicanism and Globalisation, 1876–2008* (Woodbridge: Boydell & Brewer, 2009).

Mullan, Bob, *The Mating Trade* (London: Routledge, 1984).

Myers, Alice, and Wight, Sarah (eds), *No Angels. Women who Commit Violence* (London: Pandora, 1996).

National Marriage Guidance Council, *Sex Difficulties in the Wife* (London: National Marriage Guidance Council, 1953).

National Marriage Guidance Council, *Sex in Marriage* (London: National Marriage Guidance Council, 1961).

National Marriage Guidance Council, *A Home of Your Own* (London: National Marriage Guidance Council, 1962).

National Marriage Guidance Council, *16. For All Young Adults* (London: National Marriage Guidance Council, 1964).

Nava, Mica, and O'Shea, Alun (eds), *Modern Times: Reflections on a Century of English Modernity* (London: Routledge, 1996).

Neville-Rolfe, Sybil (ed.), *Sex in Social Life* (London: George Allen & Unwin, 1949).

Nott, James J., *Music for the People. Popular Music and Dance in Interwar Britain* (Oxford: Oxford University Press, 2002).

O'Connell, Sean, *The Car in British Society. Class, Gender and Motoring, 1896–1939* (Manchester: Manchester University Press, 1998).

O'Hara, Diana, *Courtship and Constraint: Rethinking the Making of Marriage in Tudor England* (Manchester: Manchester University Press, 2002).

Offer, Avner, *The Challenge of Affluence. Self-Control and Well-Being in the United States and Britain since 1950* (Oxford: Oxford University Press, 2006).

Office for National Statistics, *Marriage in England and Wales, 2010* (London: ONS, 2012).

Office of National Statistics, *Statistical Bulletin: Marriages in England and Wales, 2010* (London: ONS, 2012).

Ortolano, Guy, *The Two Cultures Controversy. Science, Literature and Cultural Politics in Postwar Britain* (Cambridge: Cambridge University Press, 2008).

Osborne, John, *Look Back in Anger: A Play in Three Acts* (London: Faber & Faber, 1956).

Osgerby, Bill, *Youth in Britain Since 1945* (Oxford: Blackwell, 1998).

Passerini, Luisa, *Europe in Love. Love in Europe. Imagination and Politics in Britain between the Wars* (London: I.B. Tauris, 1999).

Pearce, Lynne, and Stacey, Jackie (eds), *Romance Revisited* (London: Lawrence & Wishart, 1995).

Perkin, Harold, *The Rise of Professional Society: England since 1880* (London: Routledge, 1989).

Pierce, Rachel M., 'Marriage in the Fifties', *The Sociological Review*, NS 11:2 (March 1963), 215–40.

Pixner, Stef, 'The Oyster and the Shadow', in Liz Heron (ed.), *Truth, Dare or Promise. Girls Growing Up in the Fifties* (London: Virago, 1985), 79–102.

Plummer, Kenneth, *Telling Sexual Stories: Power, Change, and Social Worlds* (London: Routledge, 1995).

Pollock, Linda A., 'Anger and the Negotiation of Relationships in Early Modern England', *Historical Journal*, 47:3 (2004), 567–90.

Popenoe, Paul, 'Mate Selection', *American Sociological Review*, 2:5 (1937), 735–43.

Pudney, J. S., *Collected Poems* (London: Putnam, 1957).

Purbrick, Louise, *The Wedding Present. Domestic Life Beyond Consumption* (Aldershot: Ashgate, 2007).

Reddy, William M., *The Navigation of Feeling. A Framework for the History of Emotions* (Cambridge: Cambridge University Press, 2001).

Report of the Committee on the Age of Majority (London: HMSO, 1967), Cmnd. 3342.

Reynolds, David, *Rich Relations. The American Occupation of Britain, 1942–1945* (London: Phoenix, 2000).

Richards, Martin P. M., and Elliott, B. Jane, 'Sex and Marriage in the 1960s and 1970s', in David Clark (ed.), *Marriage, Domestic Life and Social Change. Writings for Jacqueline Burgoyne (1944–88)* (London: Routledge, 1991), 33–54.

Roberts, Elizabeth, *A Woman's Place: An Oral History of Working-Class Women, 1890–1940* (Oxford: Wiley, 1984).

Roberts, Elizabeth, *Women and Families: An Oral History, 1940–1970* (Oxford: Wiley, 1995).

Roberts, Robert, *The Classic Slum. Salford Life in the First Quarter of the Century* (Manchester, 1971; London: Penguin, 1990).

Roper, Michael, 'Between Manliness and Masculinity: The "War Generation" and the Psychology of Fear in Britain, 1914–1950', *Journal of British Studies*, 44:2 (2005), 343–62.

Roper, Michael, 'Slipping out of view: Subjectivity and Emotion in Gender History', *History Workshop Journal*, 59 (2005), 57–72.

Rose, Sonya O., *Which People's War? National Identity and Citizenship in Wartime Britain 1939–1945* (Oxford: Oxford University Press, 2003).

Rosenwein, Barbara H. (ed.), *Anger's Past. The Social Uses of an Emotion in the Middle Ages* (New York: Cornell University Press, 1998).

Rosenwein, Barbara H., 'Writing Without Fear about Early Medieval Emotions', *Early Medieval Europe*, 10:2 (2001), 229–34.

Rosenwein, Barbara H., *Emotional Communities in the Early Middle Ages* (London: Cornell University Press 2006).

Ross, Helen, Gask, Karen, and Berrington, Ann, *Civil Partnerships Five Years On* (London: ONS, 2011).

Rosser, Colin, and Harris, Christopher, *The Family and Social Change. A Study of Family and Kinship in a South Wales Town* (London: Routledge & Kegan Paul, 1965).

Rowntree, B. Seebohm, and Lavers, G. R., *English Life and Leisure. A Social Study* (London: Longmans, 1951).

Rowntree, Griselda, 'More Facts on Teenage Marriage', *New Society*, 1:4 (1962), 12–15.

Royal Commission on Marriage and Divorce, *Report 1951–1955* (London: HMSO, 1956).

Royal Commission on Population, *Report* (London: HMSO, 1949).

Savage, Mike, 'Working-Class Identities in the 1960s. Revisiting the Affluent Worker Study', *Sociology*, 39:5 (2005), 929–46.

Savage, Mike, *Identities and Social Change in Britain since 1940* (Oxford: Oxford University Press, 2010).

Schofield, Michael, *The Sexual Behaviour of Young People* (London: Longmans, 1965).

Schwarz, Bill, 'Black Metropolis, White England', in Mica Nava and Alun O'Shea (eds), *Modern Times: Reflections on a Century of English Modernity* (London: Routledge, 1996), 176–207.

Sheridan, Dorothy (ed.), *Wartime Women. A Mass-Observation Anthology, 1937–45* (London: Heinemann, 1990).

Sheridan, Dorothy, Street, Brian, and Bloome, David, *Writing Ourselves. Mass-Observation and Literary Practices* (Cresskill: Hampton Press, 2000).

Shorter, Edward, *The Making of the Modern Family* (London: Collins, 1976).

Sinfield, Alan, *Literature, Politics and Culture in Postwar Britain* (Oxford: Blackwell, 1989).

Slater, Eliott, and Woodside, Moya, *Patterns of Marriage. A Study of Marriage Relationships in the Urban Working Classes* (London: Cassell, 1951).

Smart, Carol, *Personal Life* (Cambridge: Polity, 2007).

Smith, Cyril S., *Young People at Leisure. A Report on Bury* (Manchester: University of Manchester Press, 1966).

Smith, M. B., *The Single Woman of Today. Her Problems and Adjustment* (London: Watts & Co., 1951).

Spinley, B. M., *The Deprived and the Privileged. Personality and Development in English Society* (London: Routledge, 1953).

Stacey, Margaret, *Tradition and Change: A Study of Banbury* (Oxford: Oxford University Press, 1960).

Stanley, Liz (ed.), *The Diaries of Hannah Cullwick, Victorian Maidservant* (London: Virago, 1984).

Stanley, Liz, *Sex Surveyed, 1949–1994. From Mass-Observation's 'Little Kinsey' to the National Survey and the Hite Reports* (London: Taylor & Francis, 1995).

Stone, Lawrence, *The Family, Sex and Marriage in England, 1500–1800* (London: Weidenfeld & Nicolson, 1977).

Stopes, Marie C., *Mother England. A Contemporary History Self-Written by those who have had no Historian* (London: J. Bale & Co., 1929).

Stopes, Marie C., *Married Love. A New Contribution to the Solution of Sex Difficulties* (1918, Oxford: Oxford University Press, 2004).

Summerfield, Penny, *Reconstructing Women's Wartime Lives. Discourse and Subjectivity in Oral Histories of the Second World War* (Manchester: Manchester University Press, 1998).

Summerfield, Penny, 'Culture and Composure: Creating Narratives of the Gendered Self in Oral History Interviews', *Cultural and Social History*, 1:1 (2004), 65–93.

Summerfield, Penny and Crockett, Nicole. '"You weren't taught that with the welding": Lessons in Sexuality in the Second World War', *Women's History Review*, 1:3 (1992), 435–54.

Sutton, Maureen, *We Didn't Know Aught. A Study of Sexuality, Superstition and Death in Women's Lives in Lincolnshire during the 1930s, '40s and '50s* (Lincolnshire: Paul Watkins, 1992).

Swanson, Gillian, *Drunk with the Glitter. Space, Consumption and Sexual Instability in Modern Urban Culture* (Abingdon: Routledge, 2007).

Szreter, Simon, and Fisher, Kate, 'Love and Authority in Mid-Twentieth-Century Marriages: Sharing and Caring', in Delap, Lucy, Griffin, Ben, and Wills, Abigail (eds), *The Politics of Domestic Authority in Britain since 1800* (London: Palgrave Macmillan, 2009), 132–54.

Szreter, Simon, and Fisher, Kate, *Sex Before the Sexual Revolution. Intimate Life in England 1918–1963* (Cambridge: Cambridge University Press, 2010).

Szreter, Simon, and Kate Fisher, '"We weren't the sort that wanted intimacy every night": Birth control and abstinence in England, c. 1930–60', *The History of the Family*, 15 (2010), 139–60.

Tabili, Laura, 'Women "of a Very Low Type": Crossing Racial Boundaries in Imperial Britain', in Laura L. Frader and Sonya O. Rose (eds), *Gender and Class in Modern Europe* (New York: Cornell University Press, 1996), 165–90.

Thane, Pat, 'Family Life and "Normality" in Post-War British Culture', in Richard Bessel and Dirk Schumann (eds), *Life after Death. Approaches to a Cultural and Social History of Europe during the 1940s and 1950s* (Cambridge: Cambridge University Press, 2003).

Thane, Pat, and Evans, Tanya, *Sinners? Scroungers? Saints?: Unmarried Motherhood in Twentieth-Century England* (Oxford: Oxford University Press, 2012).

Thompson, Derek, 'Courtship and Marriage in Preston', *Oral History*, 3:2 (1975), 39–44.

Thompson, F. M. L. (ed.), *The Cambridge Social History of Britain 1750–1950*: Vol. 2, *People and their Environment* (Cambridge: Cambridge University Press, 1990).

Thompson, Paul, 'Women, Men and Transgenerational Family Influences in Social Mobility', in Daniel Bertaux and Paul Thompson (eds), *Pathways to Social Class. A Qualitative Approach to Social Mobility* (Oxford: Oxford University, 1997), 32–61.

Thomson, Matthew, 'Psychology and the "Consciousness of Modernity" in Early Twentieth Century Britain', in M. J. Daunton and Bernhard Rieger (eds), *Meanings of Modernity: Britain from the Late-Victorian Era to World War II* (Oxford: Berg, 2001).

Thomson, Matthew, *Psychological Subjects: Identity, Culture and Health in Twentieth-Century Britain* (Oxford: Blackwell, 2006).

Tinkler, Penny, *Constructing Girlhood. Popular Magazines for Girls Growing Up in England 1920–1950* (London: Taylor & Francis, 1995).

Todd, Selina, *Young Women, Work, and Family in England, 1918–1950* (Oxford: Oxford University Press, 2005).

Todd, Selina, 'Breadwinners and Dependants: Working-Class Young People in England, 1918–1955', *International Review of Social History*, 52:1 (2007), 57–87.

Todd, Selina, 'Domestic Service and Class Relations in Britain, 1900–1959', *Past and Present*, 203:1 (2009), 181–204.

Todd, Selina, and Young, Hilary, 'Baby-boomers to "Beanstalkers": Making the Modern Teenager in Post-War Britain', *Cultural and Social History*, 9:3 (2012), 451–67.

Veness, Thelma, *School Leavers. Their Aspirations and Expectations* (London, Methuen & Co, 1962).

Vincent, David, *Bread, Knowledge and Freedom. A Study of Nineteenth-Century Working Class Autobiography* (London: Europa, 1981).

Walkerdine, Valerie, 'Dreams of an Ordinary Childhood', in Liz Heron (ed.), *Truth, Dare, Promise. Girls Growing Up in the Fifties* (London: Virago, 1985), 63–77.

Waller, Willard, 'The Rating and Dating Complex', *American Sociological Review*, 2:5 (1937), 727–34.

Walton, John K., *The British Seaside. Holidays and Resorts in the Twentieth Century* (Manchester: Manchester University Press, 2000).

Waters, Chris, '"Dark Strangers in our Midst": Discourses of Race and Nation in Britain, 1947–1963', *Journal of British Studies*, 36:2 (1997), 207–38.

Weeks, Jeffrey, *The World We Have Won. The Remaking of Erotic and Intimate Life* (London: Routledge, 2007).

White, Jerry, *The Worst Street in North London. Campbell Bunk, Islington, Between the Wars* (London: Routledge & Kegan Paul, 1986).

Whitehorn, Katharine, *Selective Memory* (London: Virago, 2007).

Willcock, Bob, 'Mass-Observation', *American Journal of Sociology*, 48:4 (1943), 445–56.

Willmott, Peter, *Adolescent Boys of East London* (1966; London: Pelican 1969).

Wilson, Amrit, *Finding a Voice. Asian Women in Britain* (London: Virago, 1978).

Wimperis, Virginia, *The Unmarried Mother and Her Child* (London: George Allen and Unwin Ltd, 1960).

Wood, Andy, 'Fear, Hatred and the Hidden Injuries of Class in Early Modern England', *Journal of Social History*, 39:3 (2006), 803–26.

Woodside, Moya, 'Courtship and Mating in an Urban Community', *Eugenics Review*, 38 (1946), 29–30.

Woollacott, Angela, 'Khaki Fever and its Control: Gender, Class, Age and Sexual Morality on the British Home Front in the First World War', *Journal of Contemporary History*, 29:2 (1994), 325–47.

Wouters, Cas, *Sex and Manners. Female Emancipation in the West, 1890–2000* (London: Sage, 2004).

Young, Michael, and Willmott, Peter, *Family and Kinship in East London* (1957; London: Penguin, 1962).

Zubrzycki, Jerzy, *Polish Immigrants in Britain. A Study of Adjustment* (The Hague: Martinus Nijhoft, 1956).

Zweig, Ferdynand, *Women's Life and Labour* (London: Gollancz, 1952).

Zweig, Ferdynand, *The Worker in an Affluent Society* (London: Heinemann, 1961).

Zweig, Ferdynand, *The Student in the Age of Anxiety. A Survey of Oxford and Manchester Students* (London: Heinemann, 1963).

Unpublished papers

Sheridan, Dorothy, 'Anticipating History: Historical Consciousness and the "Documentary Impulse"', paper presented at *The Second World War: Popular Culture and Cultural Memory Conference*, July 2011.

Unpublished theses

Glew, Helen, 'Women's Employment in the General Post Office, c.1914–c.1939', unpublished Ph.D. thesis, London, 2010.

Higgins, Natalie, 'The Changing Expectations and Realities of Marriage in the English Working Class, 1920–1960', unpublished D.Phil. thesis, Cambridge, 2002.

Milcoy, Kathy, 'Image and Reality: Working-Class Teenage Girls' Leisure in Bermondsey during the Interwar Years', unpublished D.Phil. thesis, Sussex, 2000.

Picture Acknowledgements

Bert Hardy/Picture Post/IPC Magazines/Getty Images: **11**; C. Arthur Pearson Ltd: **8**; Caley's of Norwich Ltd: **4**; City Magazines Ltd: **15**; Reproduced with permission of Curtis Brown Group Ltd, London, on behalf of The Trustees of the Mass Observation Archive © The Trustees of the Mass Observation Archive: **1**; Francis Marshall images © Victoria and Albert Museum, London: **13**; Francis Marshall/V&A Images: **17**; Icon Books Ltd: **6, 9, 14**; © IPC+ Syndication: **2, 5, 7, 10, 12, 16**; © Mirrorpix: **3**

Index

abortion 47, 143
Abrams, Mark 122–3
adultery 189–91, 194–8
The Adventures of Don Quick 108
advertising 27, 173, 189, 221 n. 2
affairs, *see* adultery
affection 36
age 61–2, 64–6, 87, 100
  of majority 116
    see also under marriage
agony aunts 15–17, 131, 138, 158
air-raid shelters 117–18
Aldrington, Rector of 156
Allen, Clifford 15
Americans 70, 101, 103–4, 217 n. 34
  servicemen 72–3, 97, 118, 135, 137–8, 197
Anderson, Michael 66
Angry Young Men 56, 144
Anne, Princess 108
Appignanesi, Lisa 8
Appleton, Helen 119
Armstrong, Edward 164
Army, the 120, 147
  NAAFI Clubs 102
  Royal Army Service Corps 205
  Royal Engineers 120
  6th Armoured Division 119
Asante, Nadine 75
Asquith, Anthony 243 n. 64
Attlee, Clement 183
attraction 36–7, 44–6
  as 'chemistry' 29, 221 n. 19–222 n. 19
Ayrshire 167

baby-boom, the 183
Bacall, Lauren 52
background 62, 86, 137
Bailey, Beth 18, 137
Bailey, Peter 47
Bamford, Samuel 12
Banfield, Beryl 174
Barclay's Bank 4
Barry, Iris 99
Bates, Alan 144
BBC 61, 140
  The Brains Trust 14–15
  Marriage Today 140, 189, 201
  Panorama 192
  The Six-Five Special 30

Beckett, John 172
Bertram, Dr 74
Best, George 165
bigamy 202–5
Bingham, Adrian 10
Birkett, Mr Justice 204
Black, Marie 70
black-outs 102–3, 117
Blackpool xviii, 94–5
'Blacksmith Priests' 244 n. 94
Bland, Lucy 71
Bolton, Lancashire xvii–xix, 98, 214 n. 10
  Aspin Hall 95
Bourdieu, Pierre 77
Boyfriend 34, 105, 149–51
  'Café Congo' 149–51
Bradshaw, Joseph 208
Braine, John 57
  Room at the Top 57
Brighton 92, 106
  Royal Albion Hotel 94
Bristol 174
Britain and Her Birth Rate 193
Britannic Insurance 55
British Union of Fascists 172
Brooke, Stephen 8, 28
Brown, Callum 68
Brown, Mary 43
Burchill, Mr Under-Sheriff 163

Calais 10
Calvert, Ellen 13
Cambridge 137
  University:
    St John's College 74
Canadians 70, 75, 103, 135, 165
Canterbury, Archbishop of 194
Cardiff 33
Caribbean, the 71
  Crown Colonies, Dominions and Allied Powers 72
Carlisle 174
Carter, M.P. 98, 129
Carter, Thomas 13
Cartland, Barbara 131
Cassels, Mr Justice 161
Chesser, Eustace 189
Chesser Report, the (1956) 159
childbirth 142–3
children 76, 82, 143, 180, 183–4, 190, 192, 195, 202
  gaining independence from parents, *see* independence
  'mixed race' 71–2, 74
  unplanned 49
Church, the 18, 58, 68
  Catholic 49; *see also* religion, Catholicism
  of England 49, 67, 191, 248 n. 70
    Moral Welfare Council 202
    Putting Asunder 191
  going to 104
  teachings on contraception 67
  teachings on marriage 1
Cinderella (story of) 56–7
Clarks commercial college 69
class xvii, 23, 48, 75–80, 83–7, 214 n. 10
  and marriage, *see under* marriage

middle 5, 35, 37, 75, 104–5, 111, 123, 180, 217 n. 34
couples of the 129
upper 75
social 93, 111, 129
social class I 6
social class V 6
working 5–6, 11–13, 78, 84, 87, 93, 105, 123, 143, 171, 246 n. 16
couples of the 48, 115, 129
women of the 26, 37, 83, 131, 151, 180
see also status
Clement, Elizabeth Alice 134
coffee bars 105
Colchester 136
Collins, Marcus 8
Modern Love 8
Collins, Sydney 75
Comer, Lee 35
commitment 136, 152, 154, 160, 168–9, 175–6, 179, 188, 200, 206, 208, 210–11
Committee on the Age of Majority 175
community:
influence of 13, 122
networks 92
surveillance 103, 112
Commonwealth, the 73
contraception 47–9, 67, 125, 133, 142, 185, 210, 246 n. 35
Cook, Bill 119
Cooper, Gary 63
Cornwall 25
Costello, Sir Leonard 98
Courtney, Mr de 174
courtship 89, 91, 99, 102–3, 124–5, 142, 144–5, 209
money and 125–132, 134–5, 139, 155
patterns of 101, 138–9, 152, 154, 170, 236 n. 14
practices 109, 111–17, 119, 123, 132–4
success in 97
wartime 116–19, 122
Coventry 47
Cricklewood xvi
Crockett, Olivia xviii, 189, 192–3, 201
Croon-Johnson, Mr Justice 204
Crowther Report, the 171
Cubitt, Catherine 36
Cullwick, Hannah 12
culture 62, 83, 138, 217 n. 31
popular 214 n. 14
teen 149

Daily Express 2
Daily Herald 231 n. 112
Daily Mail 57
Daily Mirror 1–2, 30, 43, 108, 163, 174, 178, 186, 193, 201, 204, 207–8
dance xix, 101–2; *see also* leisure, dance halls
Davy, Reverend Charles 25
Dawson, Jane 118
Day Lewis, Cecil
'Newsreel' 113
Day-Lewis, Tamasin 120

Dayus, Kathleen 92
Dearden, Basil 74
De Beauvoir, Simone 50
Denning, Lord 194
Digby, Lincolnshire 165
Dight, Reuben 203
disease (sexually transmitted) 142, 195
dishonesty 195
Disney, Walt 56
divorce xviii, 190–3, 195, 209
  difficulty obtaining 5, 42
  law 177–8, 187, 191–3, 199
  rates 178
  statistics 169
divorcees 23, 67
Dix, Dorothy, 207
domestic
  security 54, 178, 180
  skills 13
  sphere 24
Dorset 190
Dorseys, the 97
Dunton, John 15
Dyhouse, Carol 82

Eakers, Shirley 97–8
economic:
  affluence 3, 59, 79, 83, 130, 145, 152; *see also* income
  circumstances 111, 165, 168, 171
  security 35, 56, 155, 170, 210
economics 130
Eddy, Nelson 209
Eden, Anthony 190
Edgebaston 167
education 5–6, 58, 61–2, 79–81, 83–7
  secondary 105
  university 104, 130
Edward VIII 1–2
Edwards and Beyfus 123, 131
Edynbry, R. 25, 34, 76
Egypt 75
Elizabeth II 3
Ellis, Havelock 48
Ellis, Ruth 50
elopement 172
Elton, G. R. 9
emotional authenticity 32, 39–42, 52, 60, 68, 78, 187, 196, 198
emotional intimacy 14, 17, 38, 44, 110, 211, 215 n. 14
emotional libertarianism 35
emotional matters 79, 185–6, 188, 199
emotions 9, 165, 171, 174, 194, 196, 208–9, 217 n. 31
  autonomy of 79, 82
  as causal factor 3, 19, 34, 45, 55, 200, 202
  disturbed xvi
  importance of 13, 24, 44, 59
  as plastic 7
  suspicion of 169
  use of 8
employment, *see under* work
engagement 152–7, 159–61, 164–5, 167–8, 173, 209
  age of 147
  broken 160–5
ethnicity 62, 66

Eugenics Society 74
European Volunteer Worker Scheme 73
Every Night at Eight 98
Every Woman's Book of Love and Marriage and Family Life 41, 44, 155, 159
Every Woman's Luck Book 62–3
Eyles, Leonora 15–16, 35, 43, 46 7, 55, 64, 72–3, 102, 106, 119, 122, 134, 138–9, 141–2, 154–5, 158–9, 181, 195–6
'Life and You' 35

Fabian Society 177
family 68, 104, 130, 182–3, 185, 188
endorsement of partnerships 115–16, 123–4, 152
influence of 13, 86, 122
life 10, 178, 181
nuclear 28
fathers 143, 181
femininity 63
feminism 215 n. 14
Firestone, Shulamith 50
Fisher, Kate 8, 49, 136
Flame in the Street 73 4
Fleet Air Arm 175
Fletcher, Peter 189
flirting 98
Forbes, Rosita 45–6
Foreign Office 4
foreigners 69–70, 228 n. 30
Fortescue, E. Russel 127
Francis, Martin 8, 10, 116, 128
freedom 39, 154, 209
Frenchmen 70
Freud, Sigmund 28, 48
friends 44, 47, 78
Frost, Ginger 160, 200, 202
Living in Sin 13
Fury, Billy 149

Garbo, Greta 52
Gallup 2, 74, 154, 191
gender:
inequality 163
relations 9, 132
roles 4, 23, 39, 54, 99, 125–7, 155, 180–1, 183, 188, 199, 214 n. 10
see also sexes
generational change 183, 210
Germany 10
gifts 127–8, 136
Giles, Judy 54, 180
Gill, Arthur 13
Gillingham 175
Glamour 15
Gloucester 181
Glover, Gordon 164
Goddard, Mr Justice 204
Gorer, Geoffrey 34–5, 56, 101, 128, 140, 154, 185, 198–9
Exploring English Character 198
Sex and Marriage in England Today 34, 140
Grable, Betty 52
Grandy, Christine 52
Grant, Mary 7, 43, 45, 51, 85, 144, 154, 156, 158–9, 164

Gray, Herbert 25, 44, 50, 64, 66–7, 72, 136
Greece (Ancient) 111
Gregory, Edward 204
Gretna Green 172, 174–5
Griffith, Edward F. 76, 186, 211
The Guardian 75

Hall, Gladys Mary 126
Hall, Stuart 71
Hallett, Mr Justice 203
Hamilton, Patrick:
The West Pier 92
Haraldsted, Eva 165
Harrowgate 208
Harry, Pearl 70
Hawk, Mr Justice 163
Henriques, Fernando 137
Hepburn, Audrey 52
heterosexuality 6, 10, 30, 94, 126, 145, 151, 209–10
Hickey, William 2
Higgins, Natalie 48, 247 n. 52
Hill, Clifford 74
Hiller, Wendy 52
Hoggart, Richard 9, 63, 105, 151, 180
Hole, Bill 189, 192, 201
holidays 94
Hollywood 26, 52, 70
Holton, Ivy May 163
home 115, 152, 180–4, 188, 210, 246 n. 16; *see also* housing
Home, Evelyn 126, 136, 202
Home Service 201
homosexuality 17, 94, 210–11, 221 n. 2
honesty 141, 199; *see also* dishonesty
Hope, Ted 175
Hopkins, Harry 122–3
Houghton, Stanley:
Hindle Wakes 58
Houlbrook, Matt 121
housing 82, 183, 188; *see also* home
Howard, Trevor:
Brief Encounter 194
How to Marry a Millionaire 52
Hubback, Judith 104
Wives Who Went to College 104
Hull 78
Huxley, Aldous xx

I Know Where I'm Going 52–3
I'm in the Mood for Love 98–9
illegitimacy 143
income 127–8, 130–1
disposable 122
see also economic: affluence
independence 89, 112, 122–4, 169, 171, 174, 180, 183, 185–6
Indians 74
individual, the 33, 188, 200, 214 n. 14
interests 83–4
Illouz, Eva 93, 112
Ipswich 119

Jackson, Louise 105
Jamaica 70
James, Harry 97
Jenner, Heather 106–7
Jephcott, Pearl 6, 26, 69, 96, 100,

121, 124, 127, 134, 144, 168, 182
Rising Twenty 69
Johnson, Paul 77, 81
Jolly, Margaretta 119
Jones, Alec 199
Jones, Paul 96

Kent 102
Kerr, Madeline 143
Kettering, Alice 15
A Kind of Loving 144
Klein, Joanna 200
Knight, Mavis 179
Knowles, Willie 180
Kuhn, Annette 76, 113
Kushner, Tony 71

Labour Government 180, 183
Langhamer, Zdzislaw 70
Laski, Marghanita 189
Last, Nella xviii
Latey, Mr Justice 175
law, the 160–1, 164–5, 178, 181, 191, 200, 206, 210, 244 n. 94
Law Commission, the 164
The Field of Choice 191
Lawler, Steph 77, 81
Lawrence, D. H.
Lady Chatterley's Lover 49
Lawrence, Margot 154, 160
The Complete Guide to Wedding Etiquette 154
Laws:
British Nationality Act 73
Civil Partnership Act 210
Divorce Reform Act (1969) 5, 42, 193, 199, 202–3, 248 n. 70
Family Law Reform Act 176
Hardwicke's Marriage Act (1753) 12
Herbert Act (1937) 5, 191
Marriage (Scotland) Act (1939) 172, 244 n. 94
Matrimonial Causes Act (1857) 5
Offences Against the Person's Act (1828) 202
Lean, David:
Brief Encounter 24
leisure 93, 104–5, 114, 131, 155
cinema 93, 98–102, 104, 109, 113–14, 128, 152
commodification of 125, 128
dance halls 93–8, 104, 108, 152; *see also* dance
evening walkabout 102, 109
nightclubs 105
London Palladium 109
Putney Phoenix 107
Richmond Renaissance 107
parks 114
public houses 103–5
Leonard, Diana 57, 123, 171
letters/letter-writing 118–22
Levey, Phyllis 203
Lewis, Jane 30
Lincoln 43, 92, 103
Lincolnshire 120, 161, 165
Liverpool 78, 143
University 161
Lockwood, Margaret 63

London 81, 94, 96, 106, 109, 113, 116, 130, 161, 181, 189
  Bethnal Green 183
  East End 141
  East Ham 77
  Enfield 97
  Islington 180
  Lambeth Walk 96
  Ludgate Hill 107
  Whitechapel 163
  Wimbledon Common 110
  Woolwich 197
London Housewives' Association 202
Lonely hearts 106
Lord Chancellor 202
Love:
  as basis for partnership 53–60, 203–4
  and class, *see* class
  factors determining 80
  falling in 36, 51, 187, 205
    at first sight 30–4
  idea of 27–30, 134, 145, 179, 194, 206, 208, 210
  let down by 39
  looking for 25
  and marriage, *see under* marriage
  mistaking something for 46, 194, 208
  nature of 37, 40, 42–4, 108, 209–11
  and personal development 38, 52, 200
  power of 28, 82
  primacy of 11, 176
  repeatability of 34–5
  romantic 18, 24, 60, 82, 86, 182, 184, 186, 189, 191, 198, 206
  and sex, *see* sex, love and
  tokens of 12
  training in 26
Luton 135
Lyon, Hugh 45
Lyons Corner House 105
Lyttelton, Edith 186

McDonald, Malcolm 57
McKay, Jeff 70–1
Macandrew, Rennie 17, 30, 36, 63, 158–9, 161, 186
  Courtship by Post 119
  Friendship, Love Affairs and Marriage 17
Macdonald, Jeanette 209
Mace, David 15, 44, 140, 156, 160, 177
Madge, Charles 190
Makins, Peggy 15
Malaya 75
Man Alive 192, 201
Manchester 14, 84, 102
  Bury 105
  University 86, 231 n. 112
Manchester Evening News 84, 113–14, 118, 171, 181
Manley, Edith 163
manners books 14
Mansfield, Nigel 15
Margaret, Princess 1–3
marriage 4, 107, 145, 160, 166,

176–7, 181–8, 194, 201–6, 219 n. 62, 228 n. 30, 247 n. 52
and age 116, 147, 152, 167–8, 170–1, 173, 175, 188, 211
and age difference 5, 61–2, 64–6
arranged 108
ceremonies 244 n. 94
clandestine 12
and class 61, 78–80
conventions of 165
in crisis 178–9, 188
cross-class 24, 77, 86
elopement, *see* elopement
factors determining 61–2, 64–8, 86–7, 143, 166, 179–80
forms of 13, 210
idea of 27, 151, 193, 200
imminence of 6
length of 39
life-long 178, 188
 decline of 7
love and 10, 13, 29, 48–9, 55, 79, 86, 170, 179, 187, 194, 198, 204, 210
parental permission and 116, 171, 174
pragmatic approach to 7, 19, 34, 53–6, 60, 68, 156, 168, 170, 182, 200
preparation for 156
and race, *see under* race
rate 210, 216 n. 19
same sex 211
sex and 13, 48–9, 135, 137, 152, 156, 158, 161, 187, 196–8, 211
stability of 29, 178, 188
unhappy 39, 144, 179, 187, 207
unofficial 200–201, 210, 244 n. 94
wartime 55, 166–9
Married Woman's Association 164
Marx, Karl 19
masculinity 3, 127, 217 n. 31
Mason, James 63
Mass Observation Archive xv–xix, 2, 17, 40, 77, 102, 167, 189, 193–4, 198, 208
 'Little Kinsey' xviii, 15, 49, 110, 132, 191
 see also under Sussex University
Mass-Observers 28, 38, 42, 61, 63, 68–9, 71, 79, 81, 85, 87, 94, 97–8, 103, 106, 113, 115, 123, 130, 135–7, 144, 152, 165, 169, 178, 180–1, 209, 211
material considerations 13, 19, 185
The Mating Machine 108
The Matrimonial Post and Fashionable Marriage Advertiser 23–4, 82, 97, 106
Matthews, Alice Constance 163
Matthews, E.R. 139
 Sex, Love and Society 139
Maunder, Jimmy 97
May, Simon 8
meeting (potential partners):
 clubs for 106–8
  The Catholic Introduction Bureau 107
  The Golden Circle Club 106
  Happy Circle 106
  The Inter-Varsity Club 107
  Two-ways Contact Club 106

meeting (potential partners) (*cont.*)
Victory Correspondence Club 106
correspondence agencies 108, 221 n. 2
Dateline 107
places for 105
ways of 94
see also 'picking up'
men 127, 239 n. 24
and love 36–7, 39
older 100
sex and 140, 144
young 51, 100, 129, 135, 169, 237 n. 62, 238 n. 14
Middle East 121
Middlesborough 132
military service 83, 120, 135
Miller, Glenn 97
Millions Like Us 75–6
Ministry of Health 142
Mitchison, Naomi 28
mobility 103
Modern Marriage 25–6. 154–5, 184
'Heart-to-Heart Bureau' 36, 69, 195
money, *see under* courtship; income
monogamy 196, 198
Monroe, Marilyn 52
morality 139, 201
Morrison, Gladys 204
Mother's Union 3, 26
mothers 4, 181, 183
Munby, Arthur 12
music 102
love songs 95
National Council for the Unmarried Mother and Her Child 143
National Marriage Guidance Council xv, 3, 10, 14, 25, 44, 50–1, 64, 76, 158–9, 177, 184, 187, 208
National Service 123, 145, 147, 170, 174
National Union of Women Teachers 171
nationality 62, 70, 73, 83, 228 n. 30
Nazis 118
New Statesman xv
Newport 77
News Chronicle 243 n. 64
Norfolk 119
'normality' 24
Northern Ireland 205
Nott, James J. 95
Nottingham 144–5
Notting Hill 74
Novello, Ivor 14

The Observer 105
outlook (on life) 61, 81–2, 84
Oxford 149
University 86, 104, 231 n. 112

Page, Larry 30
Paget, Horace 174
Pakistan 75
Parade 170
parents 58, 78, 82, 112, 123–4, 145, 183–4, 192

gaining independence from, *see* independence
involvement in the lives of their children 116, 143, 154, 171, 174–6, 209
see also motherhood
Parson, Sheenagh 174
Passerini, Luisa 8
passion 28, 47, 59
control of 45
patriotism 139
Patterson, John 107
Paul VI (Pope)
Humanae Vitae 67
Penguin (publishing house) 49
personality 24, 63
flaws with 156–7
Peters, Ronald William 175
Phillips, Eva 163
Philpott, Trevor 73–4
'picking up' 93, 96, 98
Picture Post 15, 73, 118, 178, 199, 205, 208
Pierce, Rachel 151, 160, 183
Poles 70
Population Investigation Committee Marriage Survey 57
Powell and Pressburger 52
power dynamics (of relationship) 131, 145
pragmatism 37, 44, 168, 182, 200
and love 53, 55–60, 108, 209
and marriage, *see* marriage, pragmatic approach to
pregnancy 47, 142–4, 160, 171, 197, 205
Presley, Elvis 63
press, the 172
Preston 102, 165
private
assertions xx–xxi
courting in 111–13, 117–19, 122, 124, 236 n. 14
life 24, 28, 160
sense of the 4, 211
space 18, 113, 117–19, 124
private-public boundary 8, 109, 116, 163, 211
Proops, Marjorie 164, 201
prostitutes 216 n. 24
public:
assertions xxi, 160
attitudes 191; *see also* social, expectation
displays of affection 110–11, 113–4
policy 28
sense of the 4, 211
space 18, 113–14, 236 n. 14
Pudney, John
'For Johnny' 166
Purbrick, Louise 128

Queen Christina 52

race 71–2, 74–5, 87, 138
interracial relationships 71–5
Raft, George 98
rationality 34
Rebecca 114
relationship as exchange 126–7, 129, 134–7, 140–2, 145

religion 62, 66–8, 87, 137
  Christianity 72; *see also* Church, the
    Anglicanism 67
    Catholicism 66–9, 107; *see also under* Church, the
    Methodism 67
    Protestantism 69
    Unitarianism 81
  Judaism 66, 69
Rennison, Richard 172, 174
Rentoul, Gervais 175
The Report of the Royal Commission on Population 73
respect 28
Richard, Cliff 149
Richards and Elliott 199
Robbins Report 85
Roberts, Elizabeth 48, 136, 139–40
Roberts, Robert 96
  The Classic Slum 93
Rolls, Ursula Winifred 163
Roman Holiday 52
romance 42, 58, 68, 76, 94, 102, 145, 164, 168
  computerisation of 107–8
  idea of 27, 100, 189
Rosenwein, Barbara 7
Rowntree, Griselda 171
Rowntree and Lavers 68, 183, 200
  English Life and Leisure 67, 100
Royal Air Force 61–2, 103, 116, 118, 142, 178
Royal Commission on Marriage and Divorce 171, 177–8, 188, 192
Royal Ordnance Factory 197
Rugby School 45
Russell, Dora 28

Salford 93–4
Sapphire 73
satisfaction 38
Savage, Mike 84
Schofield, Michael 105, 140
  The Sexual Behaviour of Young People 51
Scotland 172
Scott of the Antarctic 114
secularization 3
Sekka, Johnny 74
self (sense of) 176
self-determination 180
self-development 38, 124
self-fulfilment 3, 24, 200, 207
self-improvement xvi, 97
self-restraint 4
self-sacrifice 200, 207
separation 5
sex 30, 125–6, 168, 176, 187–8, 209
  avoidance of, *see* sexual, abstinence and moderation
  attitudes towards xviii, 110, 136, 211
  extra-marital 50, 198, 211
  initiation of 103
  love and 47, 49–51, 133–4, 136, 211
  and marriage, *see* marriage, sex and
  pre-marital 50–1, 125, 141–2, 158, 210

avoidance of 46, 136–7
theorists 48
sexes:
differences between 30, 39, 127
sexual:
abstinence and moderation 49, 136
compatibility 182, 184–5, 199
desire 13, 134–5, 194
double standards 140, 145, 194–5, 211
equality 129
intercourse 50–1, 125, 144, 160
intimacy 110, 139, 156, 161
libertarianism 11, 32, 35
misconduct 203
pleasure 49, 97, 135, 152, 158–60, 184–5, 187–8, 224 n. 25
reputation 126, 161
satisfaction 7
Sheffield 94, 98, 129
Bishop of 188
Sheridan, Dorothy xvii
Shrewsbury 116
Sicilians 69
Slater, Eliot 177
Slater, Valerie 161
Slater and Woodside 30, 33, 37, 56, 93, 121, 151, 178, 180, 182, 197
Smith, John 204
Smith, M.B. 196
Smith, William 11
sociability 94
social:
cement 28
change 28, 176
circles 3, 58
class, *see under* class
differences 62, 76, 85
expectation 111, 125, 132, 143, 188, 193, 199–200, 204–5, 209
identity 33, 77, 84
institutions 188, 210
mobility 56–7, 80–1, 144
organization 81, 210
relations 9
values 82, 200–201
Socialists 81
Somalia 75
South Africa 77
Soviet Union 217 n. 34
Spinley, B. M.
The Deprived and the Privileged 37
standard of living 24
status 57, 59, 79, 171
professional 83
The Star 15
Stewart, James 70
Stoke on Trent 102
Stopes, Marie 47–8, 158, 177, 184–5
Married Love 48, 184
Sunday Pictorial 72
The Sunday Times 222 n. 38
Sussex University 201
Mass Observation Archive xvi
Sutton, Maureen 92, 120, 161
Swansea 57, 102, 123

Sweet Georgia Brown 95
Sylvester, Victor 97
Syms, Sylvia 74
Szreter, Simon 8, 49

Talbot, Jeannie 149
Talbot, Johnny 149
Taylor, Elizabeth 101
teenagers 25, 51, 103, 122–3, 141, 145, 149, 151, 160, 176, 237 n. 62, 238 n. 14
The Times 49
Todd, Selina 82, 131, 170
Townsend, Captain Peter 1–2
The Tribune 16, 195
Turner, Florence 94

Upton, Dr Francis 184

Valentine 105
Valentino, Rudolph 63, 228 n. 30
values:
  false 100
  see also social, values
Vaughan, Frankie 149
Veness, Thelma 91
violence 50, 203
virginity 50, 135, 137, 139–40

Wales 123, 197
Waller, Willard 93
War:
  effort 218 n. 40
  experience of 9, 28, 117, 167–9
  impact of 3, 118, 152, 168, 178, 196
  People's 76
  wartime 46, 55, 63, 70, 130, 137, 181, 196–7, 206, 208
    couples 71, 116–18, 122, 133, 166–9, 200
Wars:
  First World War 4
    post 71, 93
  Interwar Period 167, 180
  Second World War:
    eve of 77
    period of 16, 133, 135, 142, 189, 193, 201, 210
    post 6, 23–4, 84, 97, 116, 122, 124, 163, 179, 183, 198–9
    pre 48, 54, 115, 154
    as watershed 9–10, 28, 101–2, 145, 203, 218 n. 40
Watford 103
The Way to Happy Marriage 159
The Way to Healthy Womanhood 159
The Way to the Stars 243 n. 64
wealth, *see* economic, affluence
Weavers, Janet 172
welfare state, the 38, 56, 201
Weston-Super-Mare 164
Wheel of Fortune 108
Whitcomb, Noel 204
White, Eirene 191
Whitehorn, Katherine 10, 175
Wilde, Marty 149
Wilkinson, Florence 175
Williams, Angela 15
Williams, Shirley 57
Wilmott, Peter 176
  Adolescent Boys of East London 160
Wilson, Amrit 74
Wimperis, Virginia 143

Wimpy Bars 105
Windsor 115
Woman 15, 26, 141
Woman in a Dressing Gown 194
Woman's Land Army 102
Woman's Own 7, 15–16, 43, 45–6, 51, 54, 58–9, 85, 127, 138, 143–4, 159, 161, 181, 196, 202
Woman's World 131
women 44, 113, 127, 160, 162–3, 218 n. 40, 222 n. 19
  changing status of 188
  employment of 145, 216 n. 17, 238 n. 14, 239 n. 24
    bars to 4
    wages of 130–1
  and love 36–7
  roles of, *see* gender, roles
  and sex 103, 135–6, 139–40
  successful 52
  young 51, 134, 151, 167, 216 n. 24, 237 n. 62, 238 n. 14
Women's Auxiliary Air Force xix, 15, 46, 63, 71, 83, 103, 165–6
Women's Cooperative Guild 177
Woodside, Moya 57, 136, 177, 188
Worcester 130
work:
  careers 52
  changes in the nature of 210
  earnings 237 n. 62, 238 n. 14, 239 n. 24
  employment levels 170
  segregation of sexes in the workplace 105
  women at, *see* women, employment of
Worle (Somerset) 72
Worth, Helen 36–7, 69, 154, 195

Yemen 75
Yorkshire 102, 204
  West Riding Assizes 204
Young and Willmott 116, 141, 183

Zweig, Ferdynand 56, 84, 86, 128, 154, 170, 231 n. 112
  The Student in the Age of Anxiety 86
  Women's Life and Labour 84